Trommer's analysis imparts theoretical and empirical insight into free trade policies and the limits to social justice in African countries in a thoughtful, rigorous and measured manner. This study should be read by anyone interested in learning more about the relationship between trade and citizen participation in the global South.

Susanne Soederberg, Professor and Canada Research Chair in Global Political Economy, Queen's University, Canada

Silke Trommer's meticulous analysis shows how and why civil society actors are able to influence trade policymaking. In so doing, Transformations in Trade Politics provides an important corrective to an existing body of work that tends to cast civil society influence in the field of trade as weak. This prize winning work—which draws insights from extensive fieldwork in West Africa together with theoretical innovation—is compelling and incisive throughout. A must read work for all interested in civil society engagement in processes of global policymaking, this book makes a genuinely new contribution to scholarship in the field.

Rorden Wilkinson, Professor of International Political Economy, University of Manchester, UK, and Research Director, Brooks World Poverty Institute

Trommer's theoretically sophisticated book is written with exceptional clarity. Based on solid fieldwork, she not only tells a fascinating story about the West African trade model. She also provides a persuasive analysis of the increasingly political nature of transnational trade. Most importantly, she helps open the field of global political economy to concerns of democratic participation. Now is a good time to learn from this insightful book.

Teivo Teivainen, Professor of World Politics, University of Helsinki, Finland

Conventional wisdom on trade and grassroots civil society movements is either that the latter are an irrelevant nuisance or locally segmented and unable to influence the agenda of transnationally mobile elites. Trommer finds surprising results in ECOWAS and West Africa that challenge these assumptions and affirm that transformations to a more democratic world order might be possible. Drawing on impressive fieldwork and knowledge of international trade law as well as international political economy, this book delivers as a piece of critical scholarship that is very   ⁻ᵗʰ reading.

*Magnι   ' Political Economy,
               ιllege London, UK.*

Transformations in Trade Politics

This book examines the evolution and application of participatory trade politics in West Africa and discusses the theoretical implications for political economy and global governance approaches to trade policy-making.

The author traces the involvement of a network of West African global justice nongovernmental organizations (NGOs), local NGOs and movement platforms, and trade unions in the negotiations for an Economic Partnership Agreement with the European Union (EU). Building on this empirical analysis, she develops a theoretical framework of trade policy formation that is not limited to conceptualizing trade as a policy field aimed exclusively at regulating exporting and importing activities in the global economy. Instead, she analyzes how material and ideational spheres interact in the way in which communities set the rules that enable them to trade across long distances. Attempting to reconcile demands for inclusivity with current economic policy-making, the author reframes the way in which we theoretically pose questions of who makes trade policy decisions, through which mechanisms and why trade policy-making practices change, or resist change.

Transformations in Trade Politics will be of interest to students and scholars of International Political Economy, Global Governance, Social Movement Studies, International Economic Relations, International Trade Relations, African Politics, the Politics of African/International Development, EU Politics and EU-African Relations.

Silke Trommer is a post-doctoral researcher at the Asia Research Centre at Murdoch University in Perth, Australia, and an affiliated researcher with the Erik Castrén Institute of International Law and Human Rights in Helsinki, Finland, and the African Centre for Trade, Integration and Development in Dakar, Senegal.

Routledge Global Institutions Series

Edited by Thomas G. Weiss
The CUNY Graduate Center, New York, USA
and Rorden Wilkinson
University of Manchester, UK

About the series

The Global Institutions Series has two "streams." Those with blue covers offer comprehensive, accessible, and informative guides to the history, structure, and activities of key international organizations, and introductions to topics of key importance in contemporary global governance. Recognized experts use a similar structure to address the general purpose and rationale for specific organizations along with historical developments, membership, structure, decision-making procedures, key functions, and an annotated bibliography and guide to electronic sources. Those with red covers consist of research monographs and edited collections that advance knowledge about one aspect of global governance; they reflect a wide variety of intellectual orientations, theoretical persuasions, and methodological approaches. Together the two streams provide a coherent and complementary portrait of the problems, prospects, and possibilities confronting global institutions today.

Related titles in the series include:

Integrating Africa (2012)
by Martin Welz

Trade, Poverty, Development (2012)
edited by Rorden Wilkinson and James Scott

The International Trade Centre (2011)
by Stephen Browne and Sam Laird

African Economic Institutions (2010)
by Kwame Akonor

The World Trade Organization (2007)
by Bernard M. Hoekman and Petros C. Mavroidis

Transformations in Trade Politics

Participatory trade politics in West Africa

Silke Trommer

LONDON AND NEW YORK

First published 2014
by Routledge
2 Park Square, Milton Park, Abingdon, Oxfordshire OX14 4RN

and by Routledge
711 Third Avenue, New York, NY 10017

First issued in paperback 2016

Routledge is an imprint of the Taylor & Francis Group, an informa business

© 2014 Silke Trommer

The right of Silke Trommer to be identified as author of this work has been asserted in accordance with sections 77 and 78 of the Copyright, Designs and Patents Act 1988.

All rights reserved. No part of this book may be reprinted or reproduced or utilised in any form or by any electronic, mechanical, or other means, now known or hereafter invented, including photocopying and recording, or in any information storage or retrieval system, without permission in writing from the publishers.

Trademark notice: Product or corporate names may be trademarks or registered trademarks, and are used only for identification and explanation without intent to infringe.

British Library Cataloguing in Publication Data
A catalogue record for this book is available from the British Library

Library of Congress Cataloging in Publication Data
Trommer, Silke.
   Transformations in trade politics : participatory trade politics in West Africa / Silke Trommer. 1 Edition.
      pages cm. – (Routledge global institutions series ; 77)
   Includes bibliographical references and index.
   1. Africa, West–Commercial policy. 2. International trade. I. Title.
   HF1615.5.T76 2013
   382'.30966–dc23
             2013007388

ISBN 13: 978-0-415-79117-5 (pbk)
ISBN 13: 978-0-415-81973-2 (hbk)

Typeset in Times New Roman
by Taylor & Francis Books

Contents

List of illustrations	ix
Foreword	x
Acknowledgments	xii
List of abbreviations	xiv

PART I
West African participatory trade politics   1

Introduction   3

1   Transformative agency in EPA negotiations   32

2   Beyond trade economism   60

PART II
Transformations in trade politics   85

3   The historical evolution of West African participatory
trade politics   87

4   Actors' assessments of West African participatory
trade politics   114

5   The social dimensions of trade policy formation   143

6   Conclusion   176

viii *Contents*

Appendix I: EPA regional groups in 2003	194
Appendix II: West Africa-EU trade statistics	195
Appendix III: EPA state of play	196
Appendix IV: List of interviewees (affiliations as at time of interview)	201
Appendix V: Harmonized system lists of products in informal West African trade	203
Index	223

Illustrations

Figures

I.1	West Africa's negotiation structure	12
A.1	West Africa: main exports to the EU (2008)	195
A.2	West Africa: main imports from the EU (2008)	195

Tables

I.1	West African EPA group and regional integration configuration	9
I.2	Interviewees	16
I.3	West Africa on development indices	20
1.1	Platform membership in 2009	33
5.1	West African dates of independence	154
5.2	GATT de facto application and accession	156
A.1	EPA regional groups in 2003	194
A.3	EPA state of play: 1 January 2008	196
A.4	EPA state of play: 14 November 2008	198
A.5	Harmonized system lists of products in West African trade: HS4 list of unprocessed products in informal West African trade	203
A.6	Harmonized system lists of products in West African trade: The major artisanal products in West African informal trade	205
A.7	Harmonized system lists of products in West African trade: Non-exhaustive HS4 list of major products for re-export in West Africa	207
A.8	Harmonized system lists of products in West African trade: List of pharmaceutical products traded in the informal sector	211

Foreword

Silke Trommer's book—*Transformations in Trade Politics: Participatory Trade Politics in West Africa*—is the twelfth in a growing number of research volumes in our "global institutions" series examining crucial global problems and the policies and strategies aimed at their solution. These volumes—written by some of the very best scholars in the field and representing cutting-edge scholarship in their respective areas—serve as lengthier and more specialized treatments of given topics than is possible in the general series. As such, they are essential components in advancing the overarching aim that motivated us to launch the series in 2005: to render more visible the often complex and poorly understood world of "global governance."

In addition to these longer research volumes, the series strives to provide readers with user-friendly and short (usually 50,000 words) but definitive guides to the most visible aspects and institutions of contemporary global governance as well as authoritative accounts of the issues and debates in which they are embroiled. We have over 80 books in print that act as key points of departure for the most significant global organizations and the evolution of the issues that they confront. Our intention has always been to provide one-stop guides for all readers—students (both undergraduate and postgraduate), interested negotiators, diplomats, practitioners from nongovernmental and intergovernmental organizations, and interested parties alike—seeking information about the most prominent institutional aspects of global governance.

Silke Trommer's book offers a genuinely new contribution to thinking about the way that non-state actors participate in global policy-making. In exploring the capacity of nongovernmental organizations (NGOs) to affect change in trade policy-making in the Economic Partnership Agreement (EPA) negotiations between the Economic Community of West African States (ECOWAS) and the European Union, she finds that—contrary to much received wisdom—a discrete sub-set of civil

Foreword xi

society actors were able to gain access and influence policy. Previously, scholars have highlighted the inability of civil society to penetrate core trade policy-making constituencies. What Trommer shows, however, is that this isolation is breaking down in key areas, a development with considerable theoretical and practical importance. It reflects a new stage in the representation of non-state interests in the global governance of trade; and the increasing involvement of civil society groups has the capacity to overcome a measure of the knowledge deficit from which many developing and in particular least developed countries suffer in global trade negotiations. Moreover, the involvement of civil society actors in global policy-making—though it is itself not unproblematic—helps address the profound democratic deficit that exists in global economic governance generally and global trade governance more specifically.

This insightful book draws on prize-winning research and offers the reader a compelling and incisive analysis of civil society participation in trade policymaking. It cements Trommer's growing reputation as a rising academic star, and we are proud to count her book among our finest works. Ideally, this and other volumes in the research stream will be used as complementary readings in courses in which other specific titles in this series are pertinent—a selection of which can be found in the "About the Series" section at the front of this book, and a complete list at the back. Our aim is to provide enough room for specialized topics of importance to be dealt with exhaustively but also to complement them with shorter, authoritative treatments.

As always, we look forward to comments from our readers.

Thomas G. Weiss, The CUNY Graduate Center, New York, USA
Rorden Wilkinson, University of Manchester, UK
March 2013

Acknowledgments

The research community at the University of Helsinki, Finland, was the intellectual home outside of which my doctoral dissertation on which this book is based would never have been written. The Centre of Excellence in Global Governance Research in Helsinki provided indispensible material and moral support between 2008 and 2011. When the Centre closed its doors, the Erik Castrén Institute of International Law and Human Rights in Helsinki and the Asia Research Centre at Murdoch University in Perth, Australia, allowed me to finish my project in its own good time and I would like to acknowledge their support. In Dakar, Senegal, I would like to thank the Council for the Development of Social Science Research in Africa for granting me access to their facilities and the non-governmental organization Environment and Development of the Third World for letting me research and partake in its important work.

My supervisor Teivo Teivainen never tired of discussing my ideas with me and has commented on uncountable draft versions as this piece evolved over time. His approach to supervision has been empowering and liberating and I am glad to see this validated by the fact that my thesis received the 2013 Best Dissertation Award from the International Political Economy Section of the International Studies Association. Tim DiMuzio and Milja Kurki have equally contributed through uncountable conversations as well as detailed commentary on parts of the book. Andreas Bieler, Martin Björklund, Kirsten Fisher, Jamie Morgan, Heikki Patomäki, Ryan Shram and Rene Urueña gave important feedback at various stages. I would also like to thank Erin Hannah, Magnus Ryner and Susanne Soederberg for the insights and challenges that they have brought to my arguments. Emma Dakin and Kelly Gerard helped with editorial work. Giuseppe Caruso and Reetta Toivanen are colleagues and friends without whom I would not have crossed the finishing line. Cheikh Tidiane Dièye and El Hadji Diouf are a source of inspiration.

Acknowledgments xiii

Parts of this book appear in "Activists Beyond Brussels: Transnational NGO Strategies on EU–West African Trade Negotiations," *Globalizations* 8, no. 1 (2011): 113–26, and "Legal Opportunity in Trade Negotiations: International Law, Opportunity Structures and the Political Economy of Trade Agreements," *New Political Economy*, DOI: 10.1080/13563467.2012.753520 (2013).

I would like to dedicate this book to Ingrid and Jürgen and thank them for everything.

Silke Trommer
Perth
8 February 2013

Abbreviations

ACP	African, Caribbean, Pacific
ATN	Africa Trade Network
CECIDE	Centre du Commerce International pour le Développement
DG	Directorate-General
DSB	Dispute Settlement Body
EBA	Everything but Arms
ECOWAS	Economic Community of West African States
EDF	European Development Fund
ENDA	Environment and Development of the Third World
EPA	Economic Partnership Agreement
EU	European Union
GATS	General Agreement on Trade in Services
GATT	General Agreement on Tariffs and Trade
GAWU	General Agricultural Workers' Union
GDP	Gross Domestic Product
GRAPAD	Groupe de Recherche et d'Action pour la Promotion de l'Agriculture et du Développement
GSP	Generalized System of Preferences
ICTSD	International Centre for Trade and Sustainable Development
IMF	International Monetary Fund
LDC	Least Developed Country
MFN	Most Favored Nation
MMC	Ministerial Monitoring Committee
NANTS	National Association of Nigerian Traders
NGO	Non-Governmental Organization
OECD	Organization for Economic Co-operation and Development
PASCIB	Plate-forme des Acteurs de la Société Civile au Bénin
PTA	Preferential Trade Agreement
RNC	Regional Negotiating Committee

Abbreviations xv

ROPPA	Réseau des Paysans et des Producteurs Agricoles de l'Afrique de l'Ouest
SAP	Structural Adjustment Program
SDT	Special and Differential Treatment
TWN	Third World Network
UN	United Nations
UNCTAD	United Nations Conference on Trade and Development
UNECA	United Nations Economic Commission for Africa
WAEMU	West African Economic and Monetary Union
WTO	World Trade Organization

Part I

West African participatory trade politics

Introduction

- **EPA negotiations**
- **Participatory rights in West Africa**
- **Theorizing transformation in trade policy formation**

In 1999, the Seattle protests became a global symbol for trade policy's potential to spark social and political conflict. Starting as a legitimacy crisis in the 1990s, the controversy around the World Trade Organization (WTO) today finds further expression in the Doha Development Agenda's deadlock and a growing web of bilateral and plurilateral trade agreements regulating goods and services flows across world markets. Confronted with challenges such as climate change, energy crises, as well as increasing distributional imbalances and social unrest across the globe, the mechanisms of economic policy-making and their perceived legitimacy remain essential fields of political contestation in and around the world economy today.

Post-Seattle, public policy-makers and trade scholars reflected on the relationship between trade institutions and non-state, non-corporate actors. It is widely recognized that trade rules affect public policy beyond import-export activities. The view that trade policy, first and foremost, serves economic goals nonetheless suggests a seemingly natural order of who should have a say in trade politics. Observers that doubt the desirability of open trade policy processes assert: "The 'democratic deficit' in trade politics is there for a good reason; the trick is to ensure that the forces of protectionism are not unleashed in the quest for a democratic nirvana."[1] In practice, trade institutions rarely engage profoundly with their critics. Consultative mechanisms, in which civil society groups voice broader societal concerns in public meetings are, by and large, accepted as the outer limits of democratic forms of trade governance today.

4   *Introduction*

Trade officials and a network of West African global justice non-governmental organizations (NGOs), local NGOs and social movement platforms, and trade unions challenge this consensus in the negotiations towards an Economic Partnership Agreement (EPA) between the Economic Community of West African States (ECOWAS) and the European Union (EU). Despite not sharing public officials' trade political views, the "Platform of West African Civil Society Organizations on the Cotonou Agreement" (herein: the Platform) began participating both in West African trade institutions' internal decision-making processes and in negotiating sessions with the EU. Going substantially beyond increasingly common consultative mechanisms and exceeding the standard for participation anchored in the Cotonou Agreement, ECOWAS and EU officials not only negotiated with Platform members present in the room, but civil society representatives also actively contributed to policy deliberations in these traditionally closed-door settings. Full access to the negotiating process and a voice at the table thus characterized West African trade politics and made the mechanism participatory rather than consultative.

Trade officials had initially been skeptical about the inclusion of critical actors in trade policy-making for reasons that echo familiar concerns from other trade institutions and the literature. Nonetheless, these perceptions and the Platform's role in the negotiating set-up gradually changed. During the course of negotiations, the legal and procedural rights that West African trade ministers had initially provided came to be put into practice in ways that enabled the Platform to make substantive contributions to the entire policy-making process, rather than limiting interaction to consultation on select EPA issues. European Commission officials accepted ECOWAS' decision to include civil society representatives at the West African side of the negotiating table, despite the fact that the Cotonou Agreement, which set the framework for EPA talks, had not specifically spelled out such a high level of inclusion. Although public officials retained final decision-making power over trade policy choices, the high quality of inclusion put Platform organizations in a position to influence EPA negotiations in, at times, decisive ways. Although policy debates were sometimes confrontational, public officials and civil society representatives agreed that participatory trade politics was in principle a positive achievement.

In this book, I examine the evolution and application of participatory trade politics in West Africa and discuss its theoretical implications. I contend that the evidence from ECOWAS-EU EPA negotiations prompts an unduly neglected research question for theories on trade policy formation: Under what conditions do critics of the global trade

Introduction 5

agenda succeed in influencing trade institutions? Two observations from West African participatory trade politics question the validity of common assumptions in the political economy and global governance literatures. The evidence suggests that trade policy-making can weather more political contestation and transparency than is typically expected. Claims that "a democratic nirvana" would throw economic policy-making into disorder are overstated. More importantly perhaps, my data shows that perceptions of legitimacy in trade decision-making are not static, but can change over time. Through continued interaction, the actors engaged in West African EPA negotiations not only revised their views on what types of social and political agents legitimately participated in trade policy-making. Their assessment of possible forms of cooperation among previously antagonistic trade political groups equally changed. The relevance of West African participatory trade politics for more general debates on cooperation in the global economy and in economic policy lies here.

My book draws on and contributes to several academic traditions. By mapping out an advocacy campaign on trade and development issues, my study adds insights to the transnational studies and development studies literatures. I further collect evidence from concrete efforts to democratize trade policy-making beyond consultative arrangements. In this way, I speak to the trade and global governance literatures in two distinct ways. I add empirical and theoretical considerations to the ongoing search for conceptualizing the relationship between trade officials and civil society's critical branches. I further tease out the practical lessons that the West African experience holds for possible, if today rarely tested, mechanisms for opening trade politics to broader societal interests. Struggling with issues such as representation and legitimacy in participatory politics and post-national governance, West African EPA actors tackled some of the most longstanding and unresolved problems in political theory. They gradually developed practical responses that found acceptance within their policy context. Representing and analyzing their various debates, I thus deliver empirical data on theoretical discussions that, though passionately held, are seldom charged with real world experiences.

On the theoretical level, I argue that we must make room in our conceptual frameworks for the social dimensions of the trading activity in order to be able to integrate all political forces that shape trade policy formation in our analyses. I identify economism, that is to say "an exaggeration of the economic sphere's importance in the determination of social and political relations, and as a result, an underestimation of the autonomy and integrity of the political sphere,"[2] as a

6 *Introduction*

key stumbling block for resolving the efficiency/legitimacy deadlock in current trade governance practice. While it is futile to deny that material considerations guide economic policy choices, I trace how trading has gradually come to be conceptualized as an activity that is void of intrinsic social and political content throughout the historical evolution of political economy as a field of inquiry. I show that this disputed premise has found its way into trade policy formation theories during the era of neoclassical economics' intellectual hegemony, in tandem with the general desocialization and dehistoricization of political economy and the reduction of economics to a science predominantly concerned with maximizing marginal utility under conditions of scarcity.

Conceptualizing trade as a human activity in which only desocialized, dehistoricized economic exchanges occur naturalizes the perspective and privileged position of utility-maximizing agents in trade policy-making, whether scholars perceive this as normal, or as a reflection of dominant ideologies. Trade is, however, not specific to any historical era and its socio-political orders, but a widespread tool for providing the material basis of society throughout recorded history. Because trade involves interaction between geographically distant social formations, historical scholarship reminds us that it transforms and shapes not only the economic, but also the social realities of the groups that engage in mutual trading. Phillip Curtin thus explains: "trade and exchange across cultural lines have played a crucial role in human history, being perhaps the most important external stimuli to change."[3]

Asking why the level of civil society involvement in West Africa went substantially beyond what we usually witness in trade politics today, I develop a theoretical framework for trade decision-making that recognizes that trade is deeply influenced and constituted by the social and that considers how economic and social spheres shape each other over time. Building on Marisa von Bülow's theoretical framework that empha-sizes the social embeddedness of trade political practice,[4] I respond to the longstanding search in the political economy literature for ways of capturing the interests-ideas nexus in trade politics.[5]

Material factors, political purposes, frameworks of norms and rules, values, collective experiences, and perceptions all play a role in trade politics. Matthew Eagleton-Pierce, for example, shows how the construction of knowledge claims and the material struggle for international trade are intertwined in global trade governance.[6] Rejecting the idea of a spe-cific, potentially universal hierarchy among structural and agency-based elements conceptualized in isolation from each other, I argue that their interrelations and co-constitutions in specific historical and geographical contexts are what theory needs to account for in order to

Introduction 7

deliver a complete explanation of trade political phenomena. Tracing how ideas and interests interact in trade politics, rather than observing that they interact, frees intellectual space for devising novel approaches to global governance dilemmas related to international trade.

Seen through the lens of my framework, transformation in West African trade political practice occurred in the following way: actors who are typically sidelined in trade talks started to make political claims against EPA negotiations because they perceived the region's past trade policy choices as producing negative socio-economic results. When these trade critics met skepticism from public officials, they began to create pathways to influence through a combination of tactics. They recognized the political opportunity to which rights to participation enshrined in domestic and international legal texts gave rise. Socio-economic asymmetries between the negotiating parties provided them with further opportunities for inserting themselves into the policy-making process. Over time, public officials started to recognize trade critics as beneficial allies in trade talks, because the groups added trade political expertise and helped to alter the balance of negotiating power between ECOWAS and the EU. Both sides also forged a sense of unity among West Africans against the negotiating partner, which enabled them to cooperate in trade policy-making despite their diverging perspectives on and preferences for trade policy. Crucially, the explanatory factors were only partly present in the political environment of EPA negotiations at the outset. To a degree, political actors created these elements through framing the ideas and discourses that shaped the perceptions of their structuring conditions and, possibly, their very nature in the long run. At the time of writing, both sides continued to engage in trade policy-making through an ongoing process of legitimization marked by both cooperation and conflict.

Setting the stage for a detailed analysis in the ensuing chapters, the Introduction unfolds in three steps. I first give background information on EPA negotiations. I then present the institutional setting through which West African participatory trade politics operated in practice. Finally, I provide a detailed outline of my theoretical approach and discuss the benefits and risks of theoretical generalizations made on the basis of African politics.

EPA negotiations

The course of EPA negotiations over the past 10 years does not support the common expectation that global trade powers have less difficulty in pursuing their preferences with small countries outside of the WTO's

8 Introduction

multilateral framework. In 1997, the WTO's Dispute Settlement Body (DSB) sanctioned African, Caribbean and Pacific (ACP) countries' unilateral preferential access to EU markets in the so-called *EC— Bananas* case on account of discriminating against other developing country members.[7] The ACP group and the EU subsequently signed a cooperation agreement on 23 June 2000 in Cotonou. The Cotonou Agreement replaced the Lomé Conventions which had provided the legal framework for development and trade cooperation between Europe and its former dependent territories since the 1970s. While the Cotonou Agreement secured the continuity of the European Development Fund (EDF) established under Lomé, it effectively decoupled trade and development cooperation in Europe's relationship with the ACP as new trade regimes were to be negotiated under EPAs. The decision reflected the separation of trade and development policy instruments in the EU's external relations with the ACP.[8] Overall, the Cotonou Agreement presents a substantial shift towards the domination of deregulatory and market-opening ideas in the EU-ACP relationship.[9] It explicitly highlights the importance of integrating ACP countries into the global economy and stresses the role of competitive markets and the private sector in bringing about economic development.[10]

It is interesting to note in this regard that, unlike Europe, West African countries carry out most of their trade with the outside world. According to the Nigeria Import/Export Bank, about 90 percent of ECOWAS' trade is external. In 2008, a Nigerian newspaper reported: "the total ECOWAS intra-regional trade was valued at $6.9 billion, while total ECOWAS trade with the world was valued at $64.4 billion."[11] The Common External Tariff of the predominantly francophone West African Economic and Monetary Union (WAEMU) is low compared to other regional integration organizations in the world.[12] As I discuss in more detail below, the idea that African countries are protectionist generally prevails in trade discourse, although it may be more the pattern, rather than level of integration in the global economy that deserves rectification.

The EPA process was launched at an all EU-ACP level in 2002 and was ongoing, though fragmented, at the time of writing. From October 2003, the EU negotiated EPAs with six ACP regions, namely with the Caribbean, Central Africa, Eastern and Southern Africa, the Pacific, the South African Development Community and West Africa (for a detailed list see Appendix I). At the start of EPA talks in West Africa, the two regional integration organizations ECOWAS and WAEMU presented a feasible negotiating framework. After some debate, the region decided in 2003 to negotiate under the auspices of ECOWAS with support from the WAEMU Secretariat.

Membership of both organizations overlaps. Table I.1 displays the West African EPA group according to regional integration configurations.

Extreme economic and political asymmetries as well as West African dependence on Europe mark ECOWAS-EU EPA negotiations. West Africa accumulated a gross domestic product (GDP) of US$271.091 billion in 2009. With roughly twice the population number of West Africa, the EU's GDP exceeded the amount over 60 times and stood at $16.525 trillion in 2009.[13] The EU accounted for 39 percent of world exports and 37 percent of world imports in 2007.[14] ECOWAS held 6 percent of world exports and world imports respectively. Bilateral relations are equally unbalanced. West Africa was the EU's biggest trading partner among ACP regions, accounting for 40 percent of trade, in 2010. Overall, however, all of ACP trade taken together constituted 4.3 percent of EU imports from the world and 5.1 percent of EU exports to the world.[15] The EU was, in turn, West Africa's biggest trading partner, accounting for 32 percent of trade. Eighty percent of exports were from three countries alone, namely Côte d'Ivoire, Ghana and Nigeria.[16] The main exports from West Africa to the EU were oil, gas, cocoa and iron. The main imports were oil, mechanical machinery, electrical machinery and vehicles.[17] As shown in the Appendices, the West African EPA region had a net trade deficit with the EU between 2002 and 2009,

Table I.1 West African EPA group and regional integration configurations

EPA group members only	*ECOWAS only*	*ECOWAS and WAEMU*
Mauritania*	Cape Verde**	Benin*
	The Gambia*	Burkina-Faso*
	Ghana	Côte d'Ivoire
	Guinea*	Guinea-Bissau*
	Liberia*	Mali*
	Nigeria	Niger*
	Sierra Leone*	Senegal*
		Togo*

Notes: All countries except Liberia are WTO members; * LDCs; ** Cape Verde lost LDC status in 2007. However, for the purpose of trade policy, the EU continued to treat Cape Verde as an LDC under its GSP until 31 December 2011. In December 2011, Cape Verde became the first African country to be granted GSP+ status, which is less preferential than LDC but more preferential than GSP treatment (DG Trade 2011, *Cape Verde Secures Access to EU Markets and Boosts Its Development*, trade.ec.europa.eu/doclib/press/index.cfm?id=763). GSP+ is a special market access scheme under the EU's ordinary GSP and is granted under the condition that beneficiary countries adhere to a number of international human rights, labor rights, environmental and good governance conventions.

10 *Introduction*

indicating dependence on European imports and net capital flows from West Africa to the EU. West African public resources further rely disproportionately on trade compared to Europe. According to the European trade commissioner, in 2005 customs revenues made up 15 percent of West African public budgets on average, half of which was taxed on EU imports.[18] At the same time, since the start of negotiations the fiscal balance was consistently negative in the region.[19] In addition, Europe is West Africa's primary donor of overseas development aid with €9.5 billion donated in 2009 from EU institutions alone.[20]

Reflecting a general tendency to shape global trade rules in ways that facilitate foreign direct investment and the establishment of transnational production chains, the EU not only envisaged negotiating trade-in-goods agreements under Article XXIV of the General Agreement on Tariffs and Trade (GATT) with the ACP. Based on the European Commission's *Global Europe Strategy*, the new EU-ACP trade regimes were supposed to cover service trade, trade-related intellectual property, trade-related investment matters, competition, public procurement, and topics such as trade-related aspects of environmental and social policies, and personal data protection. A deadline to accomplish EPA negotiations in all ACP regions had been set for 31 December 2007. Since the derogation that the EU had negotiated at the WTO for Lomé preferences ran out on this day, the European Commission insisted that ACP countries would be treated according to Europe's ordinary Generalized System of Preferences (GSP) from 1 January 2008 unless they signed EPAs.

The fragmentation of the EPA process became evident during the build-up to the first negotiating deadline. On the one hand, the negotiating agenda did not significantly advance past the trade-in-goods stage in any region except the Caribbean. Instead, the substantial coverage of agreements varied between the six regions from early on in the process. In addition, while the Caribbean signed an extensive EPA in 2008, no other region moved towards conclusion at that time. For many ACP countries, failure to meet the deadline implied few changes to their trade regime. The countries on the United Nations (UN) list of least developed countries (LDCs) are eligible for unilateral duty-free, quota-free access to European markets under the EU's so-called Everything but Arms (EBA) initiative. Most West African countries fall within this category. However, Côte d'Ivoire, Ghana and Nigeria only qualify for the GSP applicable to all developing countries. Threatened with the loss of European market access in 2007, Côte d'Ivoire and Ghana signed on to interim goods-only agreements with the EU. Because the move jeopardized West African ambitions for creating a customs union under

Introduction 11

the definition of Article XXIV of the GATT, it factually pressured the entire region into continuing EPA negotiations with the EU.

On 31 December 2007, 35 out of 78 ACP countries had signed on to initial EPA deals, with a view to continuing negotiations on further topics, or, in the case of the Caribbean, on implementation. The geographical application has since failed to expand significantly beyond the original EPA signatories in 2007.[21] The list of EPA defectors is only partly congruent with the list of ACP members that are LDCs. Seeing that the non-LDCs Botswana, Cameroon, Côte d'Ivoire, Fiji, Ghana, Namibia, Kenya, and Swaziland have failed to move to ratification of existing agreements, the EU has recently given the countries until 2016 to ratify, before it will withdraw duty-free, quota-free market access.[22] In addition, EPA negotiations on topical issues have made slow progress since 2008. Across the regions, talks are focusing on trade-in-goods, rules of origin, services and development cooperation, leaving the fate of the EU's other requests uncertain.

Participatory rights in West Africa

West African trade ministers adopted the ECOWAS Roadmap for Negotiations in August 2004.[23] Formal rights of participation included in the Roadmap go beyond more informal decision-making standards or best practices and eventually guaranteed a high standard of inclusion in the policy processes. According to the wording of the Roadmap, West Africa takes a "participatory approach" to EPA negotiations and gives an "appropriate role" to "non-state actors." It explicitly establishes that "civil society and private sector representatives … participate in the West African Regional Negotiation Committee."[24] While views on how the provision should apply in political practice varied at the start of negotiations, as I show in Chapter 3, the Roadmap over time became the accepted legal basis for participatory, rather than consultative, trade policy-making. The negotiating structure summed up in Figure I.1 shows how participation works in practice.

In line with the Roadmap, ECOWAS' EPA negotiating structure includes one private-sector and one civil society representative at every level of technical and political negotiations, both internally and at the negotiating table. The ECOWAS Council of Ministers, which is responsible for the implementation of the EPA mandate that West African heads of states and governments had given in January 2003, presents the only exception to this rule.

The Roadmap establishes several political organs through which negotiations proceed and defines their roles. The Ministerial Monitoring

12 *Introduction*

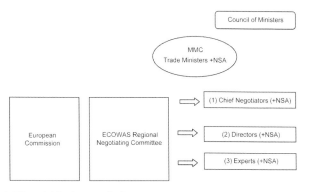

Figure I.1 West Africa's negotiation structure

Committee (MMC) facilitates the internal cooperation between ECOWAS members on EPA. It consists of the national trade and finance ministers of the 16 countries, as well as one representative of the West African private sector and one representative of West African civil society. The Committee's task is to report to the Council of Ministers on the evolution of negotiations. It meets twice a year and controls the work of the Regional Negotiating Committee (RNC).

The RNC meets with the European negotiating teams to negotiate the substance of the agreement. It convenes in three constellations, namely chief negotiators level, directors level and experts level. At chief negotiators level (1), it consists of the presidents of ECOWAS and WAEMU, up to three technical experts nominated by each country, as well as one private-sector and one civil society representative. In this configuration, the RNC meets with the European Commission negotiating team headed by the EU trade commissioner at the start and the conclusion of every negotiation phase. Chief negotiators make the broad political decisions underlying the EPA process. They conclude on preliminary negotiating outcomes, establish priorities and give direction for consecutive phases. At directors level (2), the ECOWAS vice-president, the WAEMU trade commissioner, technical experts as well as one private-sector and one civil society representative constitute the RNC. It meets twice a year with a European Commission delegation headed by the director responsible for West African EPA negotiations in the Directorate-General (DG) for Trade. Directors take stock of the negotiating progress, adopt provisional conclusions, and decide the timetable and the agenda of future negotiating meetings at experts level. The experts level (3) is the technical negotiating level. In principle, experts meet every two months to negotiate individual EPA chapters and

Introduction 13

clauses. At this level, the trade directors of ECOWAS and WAEMU, technical experts from ECOWAS and WAEMU Secretariats, as well as one private-sector and one civil society representative sit on the RNC. The EU team at experts level comprises technical experts from DG Trade, DG Development and related DGs such as Agriculture, Taxation and Customs Union, Fish, or any DG relevant to the agenda.[25]

Civil society actors further cooperate with select national ministries on the elaboration of the national EPA positions. In my interviews, Platform members from Benin, Ghana, Nigeria, and Senegal reported their participation in domestic trade policy-making in more or less institutionalized forms (Platform representatives 3, 4, 5, 6, 7). In Senegal, for example, civil society representatives are routinely invited to ministry meetings where EPA policies and negotiation strategies are discussed and formulated.

Two practices fill the provisions of the Negotiating Roadmap with life. On the one hand, civil society actors are allowed to access both information and the meeting rooms in which EPA discussion are ongoing. The EDF supports the participation in negotiating rounds, as discussed in Chapter 3. One West African public official qualified this set-up in my interview as providing "unprecedented access to all levels of negotiation" for civil society actors. This makes a qualitative difference to their insights into the negotiating process, the official argued, because "they have the information first hand. It's not hearsay or reports, they have primary knowledge of exactly what happened" (West African public official 2).

On the other hand, non-state actors hold the same status as ECOWAS and WAEMU technical experts in the RNC. Internally, civil society actors contribute to preparatory works in the crafting of ECOWAS' official negotiating positions and during preparations of negotiating sessions with the EU where strategies are elaborated (Platform representative 4). Externally, the practice includes the right to make oral submissions for the West African side in negotiations (Platform representative 4, West African public officials 2, 3). It is only at the chief negotiators level that the civil society and private-sector representatives are not entitled to make oral statements. Like ECOWAS and WAEMU technical staff, they participate as silent observers, who can submit written statements to their commissioners during negotiations. The commissioners subsequently raise the points with the European Commission at their discretion (Platform representative 1).

West African and European public officials reported during my interviews that despite not being connected to any public institution, the civil society representative behaves like any other technical expert

14   *Introduction*

on the West African delegation during negotiations. This includes advising decision-makers, providing technical input, and defending the ECOWAS official position (West African public official 2, European public officials 1, 2). Despite the high level of involvement, non-state actor participation of both the private sector and civil society in West Africa stops short of co-decision (West African public official 4). Many public officials see their role as mediating between various perspectives and interests. One official explained that civil society actors "have as much influence or as much voice [as state officials and private-sector representatives] in the general debate ... But we should recall that civil society have a certain perspective ... [State officials] have the job ... to take on their concerns and take on the concerns of other stakeholders to ensure that it is a comprehensive approach that we have adopted" (West African public official 2).

The statement shows that West African officials were under the impression that civil society organizations approached trade policy with a specific agenda, but one that they felt needed to be taken into consideration. Most trade institutions today aim to cater to these concerns in public hearings or consultations that occur outside of the trade policy process. In West Africa, over time, the concerns found a way into the trade policy-making process itself, both within ECOWAS and the region's negotiations with the EU. The transformation towards participatory forms of trade policy-making presents puzzles for standard approaches to trade policy formation.

Theorizing transformation in trade policy formation

The contemporary compartmentalization of trade political theory presents obstacles to theorizing transformations in trade politics. The state-centric tradition is ill-equipped to account for the transnational phenomenon that is West African participatory trade politics, notably because participation evolved against initial resistance from (some) state actors, thus highlighting the non-unified nature of public institutions and the state. Structuralist approaches routinely stress consumers' limited individual costs and benefits from trade policy adjustments as an obstacle to collective citizen action on trade. The view is based on the idea that economic operators importing and exporting in large quantities bear the brunt of the cost when trade barriers are imposed or maintained, while the margin of loss on end products is perceived as negligible for consumers. As I explore in Chapter 2, this strand of the literature cannot conceptualize trade political actors like the Platform, because it cannot explain why a group like the Platform becomes active

Introduction   15

on trade issues in the first place. Institutionalist theories view trade policy outcomes as a function of formal structures and procedures of government. While the Cotonou Agreement announced participation as a principle of the EU-ACP partnership, it made no prescription on the exact policy mechanisms that would fulfill this criterion. Furthermore, there was initial controversy over how to apply the ECOWAS Roadmap. Thus, institutionalist approaches assume as given what needs to be explained in this case, namely that trade policy-making became participatory in ECOWAS, while remaining consultative in the other EPA regions. While constructivist accounts stress the role of ideas, norms and values in shaping interests and thus trade policy preferences, I am not aware of a comprehensive theoretical framework for trade policy formation that systematically incorporates this insight. This brings us full circle to my starting hypothesis that the interactions between and co-constitutions of the ideational and the material world in trade policy-making are the missing pieces in the puzzle.

With this recognized, I trace how perceptions of trade political interests, relevant legal frameworks, and appropriate trade political strategies, as well as ideas, purposes, values, and collective experiences mutually shaped each other in a way that transformed ECOWAS-EU EPA talks from an exclusive into an inclusive policy-making mechanism between the launch of negotiations in 2002 and 2009, when I carried out my main field research. Below, I set out my methodology and theoretical framework to accomplish this task.

Methodology

I rely on empirical data that I collected from interviews, official documents and media sources during research in Dakar, Geneva, Brussels and Helsinki. I conducted my main field work in Geneva between February and April 2009 at the International Trade Centre, in Dakar between June and August 2009 at the NGO Environment and Development of the Third World (ENDA), and between November 2010 and February 2011 at ENDA and the Council for the Development of Social Science Research in Africa. My main sources are 48 interviews that I held with 35 African and European EPA actors between March 2009 and February 2011 (with all but six interviews taking place in 2009, see Appendix IV). I focused predominantly on the West African side of the negotiating table since West African participatory trade politics is essentially a West African political phenomenon, although one that unfolded in the context of international trade negotiations. My interviews with European public officials mainly served the purpose of assessing

16 *Introduction*

how participatory trade politics affected the negotiating partner. Table I.2 shows how interviews were divided among the various types of actors involved in the EPA negotiating process.

In Appendix IV, I provide a list of interviewees indicating the date, location, and language of interviews. All translations from French and German in this book are my own. Although I categorize actors as West African and European, the limits of such a classification in studies on transnational policy-making are clear. Some interviewees represented European or West African organizations, while holding citizenship from a country on the other continent. In cases where the fact that an interviewee had a different nationality than the organization for which the person worked became relevant for the evidence provided, I signal this in the text.

The fact that both Platform events and an official EU-ECOWAS negotiating session took place in Dakar during my stays there meant that I was not required to raise additional research funding to travel to the other countries. Despite remaining predominantly in Dakar, I covered most of the key Platform member organizations and balanced out the number of interviewees from the West African regional integration organizations ECOWAS and WAEMU in this way. To address potential imbalances in my data further, I considered primary and secondary sources from the entire region as far as they were available.

Since negotiations were ongoing during my empirical research, I highlighted in interviews that my study concerned West Africa's policy-making mechanism rather than EPA substance. For some interviewees, not being quizzed on content was an important condition for being interviewed on an ongoing negotiating process and it is also the reason why direct citations from interviews are anonymous throughout the book. I also attempted to create distance from the perspective of my interviewees between my own identity as a European researcher and the ongoing trade negotiations involving the EU as a negotiating party in this way.

Table I.2 Interviewees

Types of actors	Number of interviewees
Platform	8
West African civil society*	6
Central African civil society	1
European civil society	5
West African public officials	11
International public official	1
European public officials	3

Note: * Journalist, singer, peasants' movement representative, private-sector representative, social movement representative, trade unionist.

Introduction 17

Two specific research questions guided my semi-structured, open-ended interviews. They were: "How did the high level of civil society inclusion come about?"; and "What are your experiences with it?" Sub-questions evolved as I gained more detailed insights on West African participatory trade politics. Although the methodology prevented strict comparison between interviews, the approach allowed me to incorporate insights resulting from my own learning. In addition, it enabled me to confront interviewees with statements that others had previously made. Since my interview strategy was based on my own interaction with the subjects of my research, the challenge in my approach lay in continuously securing analytical distance from my interviewees. As I experienced while in the field, assessing the West African policy process from an office desk in the global North carried the almost inevitable risk of adopting the wrong underlying assumptions about West African politics, which could lead to the wrong research questions and produce doubtful results. Of the two risks, I chose the former.

My method generated evidence that created a basis for the assessment of the political process through which participatory trade politics was established and maintained in West Africa. I discuss the explanations that European and West African trade political actors advanced during my interviews in Chapters 3 and 4. Individual interviewees typically preferred certain explanations over others and neglected, or at times explicitly denied some explanatory factors that others had stressed. In Chapters 3 and 4, I treat all elements that interviewees raised at face value and as equally important. I understand interviewees' statements as personal interpretations of a social reality in which they all participated. To the extent that interviewees' accounts are contradictory, or to the extent that the reader might doubt the reliability of certain statements, these dynamics between the actors, the reader, and me are testament to the complex and contested nature of participatory trade politics. I consider the heterogeneity of the collected accounts, therefore, not as a weakness in my data, but as particularly enriching evidence for tracing the politics in trade politics.

Theoretical framework

As mentioned above, von Bülow's relational approach to studying trade politics inspires my theoretical framework. In her book *Building Transnational Networks: Civil Society and the Politics of Trade in the Americas*, she argues that transnational collective action on trade must be understood as a *"dynamic process of configuration and reconfiguration of interactions."*[26] The strength in von Bülow's approach lies in the

18 *Introduction*

emphasis that she puts on actors' perceptions of the various elements that structure collective action on trade. She explicitly refers to trade political actors' political environment, their relationship to other actors in that environment, or social embeddedness, and their real and potential opportunities for pursuing their agendas. Traditional considerations such as material interests or broader public policy aspirations come into this framework because they are part and parcel of the political environment of trade negotiations. Structural factors such as a given legal framework or asymmetrical power relations are other elements that may characterize political environments.

It is, however, important to consider the way in which social agents perceive this environment, how they attempt to mould it and what the consequences of their actions are, across all policy levels and national divides. None of the elements are predictable nor are interpretations unified among actors. Instead, these views are a result of actors' social embeddedness and partly arise from and influence their relations with each other. The framework thus accepts the possibility that certain structural features of the social world can appear fixed from the perspective of agency in a specific temporal and geographical context, while not being immutable in the long run. Crucially, the attitudes of trade political actors under this perspective are not static, but evolve within political context over time.

Von Bülow further argues that "in order to explain collaborative ties among actors, it is not enough simply to reveal their common interests, but it is also necessary to identify the mechanisms by which they are able (or unable) to overcome their differences and construct common purpose."[27] In West African EPA politics, trade policy-making was initially exclusive, reflecting the widespread consensus that critics of the global trade agenda are ill-equipped to make positive contributions to trade policy formation. What occurred among West African EPA actors was a transformation in policy-makers' appreciation of what types of social groups were legitimate actors in trade policy-making, which evolved through a series of repeated and sustained political contestations. In other words, the example confirms von Bülow's view that common purpose is not a fact of life that results mechanically from the structural conditions of the global political economy, but can also be actively created among groups of actors that are so inclined.

In sum, von Bülow's relational approach provides a dynamic framework that makes visible the interactions between agency and structure in shaping the ways in which society governs itself. It respects the fact that economic interests are rooted in the ideas and values that emanate from and resonate in a specific social and political context. I apply her

Introduction 19

approach for studying the interactions between civil society actors to my analysis of the interactions between all types of trade political actors, across state and non-state, and corporate and non-corporate divides. To this end, I build on my empirical observations, the arguments of others in the literature,[28] and the assumption that perceptions, political environments and social embeddedness not only affect civil society actors, but all social agents.

On terminology

In Chapter 2 I argue that economistic trade policy formation theories fail to conceptualize adequately non-state, non-corporate actors in trade politics, in part because economistic conceptual frameworks cannot incorporate variations in meanings of economic concepts due to their rationalistic underpinnings. Since language is a crude tool for describing and debating reality, however, competing interpretations of terms always characterize social interaction. Frank Trentmann's analysis of the interface between political culture and political economy shows "how groups understand economic concepts may be complex, ambiguous, indeed contradictory compared to high theory."[29]

The West African EPA process similarly reveals that certain taken-for-granted terminologies in our current debates are subject to considerable variations of meaning in day-to-day political practice. As will become apparent throughout the book, controversies over trade policy substance were intermingled with contestations around the very meaning and practical implications of some of the most common terms in the political economy and global governance vocabularies today. Below, I discuss "development," "free trade," and "civil society."

Throughout the book, I understand the term "development" as shorthand for the desire to better people's lives. Reflecting the standing of West African countries on three development indices, Table I.3 points to the equivocal nature of the term.[30]

No universally accepted method of measuring development levels exists. The World Bank ranks countries according to per capita income. The UN Human Development Index considers income, life expectancy, and literacy rates. While 12 ECOWAS members show low human development according to the Human Development Index, four had reached medium human development in 2007, although the four countries do not coincide entirely with the World Bank's income classifications. The NGO Save the Children uses under five-year-old mortality rates, under five-year-old malnutrition rates, and primary school enrolment. Save the Children finds considerable variations with

20   *Introduction*

Table I.3 West Africa on development indices

Country	World Bank income classification*	United Nations Human Development Index**	Child Development Index***
Benin	Low income	Low Human Development (161)	107
Burkina-Faso	Low income	Low Human Development (177)	134
Cape Verde	Lower middle income	Medium Human Development (121)	–
Côte d'Ivoire	Lower middle income	Low Human Development (163)	121
The Gambia	Low income	Low Human Development (168)	113
Ghana	Low income	Medium Human Development (152)	109
Guinea	Low income	Low Human Development (170)	120
Guinea-Bissau	Low income	Low Human Development (173)	128
Liberia	Low income	Low Human Development (169)	–
Mali	Low income	Low Human Development (178)	130
Mauritania	Low income	Medium Human Development (154)	108
Niger	Low income	Low Human Development (182)	137
Nigeria	Lower middle income	Medium Human Development (158)	126
Senegal	Lower middle income	Low Human Development (166)	103
Sierra Leone	Low income	Low Human Development (180)	136
Togo	Low income	Low Human Development (159)	96

Notes: * According to four categories in respect of data for 2009: high income, upper middle income, lower middle income, and low income; ** According to four categories in respect of data for 2007: Very High Human Development, High Human Development, Medium Human Development, Low Human Development, of 182 countries (individual ranking in brackets); *** Ranking countries in respect of data for 2000–06.

the UN Human Development Index. In the case of West Africa, for example, Nigeria features three ranks above Benin on the Human Development Index, while scoring 19 ranks below Benin on the Child Development Index. Similarly, both countries do better on the Human Development Index when compared to Senegal, but the relationship is the inverse on the Child Development Index. This is compatible with Save the Children's hypothesis that the income component of the Human Development Index boosts the ranking of countries that are rich in resources, although this does not necessarily raise living standards for all members of society.

Across the global economy, development policy initiatives further show mixed performances in leading to development. The question of what brings development about has produced much disagreement in the literature and in international policy circles ever since US President Harry S. Truman introduced the concept in his 1949 Inaugural Address.[31] Development scholarship has subsequently pointed to the political functions of the term in the real world. Wolfgang Sachs, for example, argues that "development is much more than just a socio-economic endeavour; it is a perception which models reality, a myth which comforts societies, and a fantasy which unleashes passions."[32] Gilbert Rist understands development as "refer[ring] to a set of beliefs and assumptions about the nature of social progress, rather than anything more precise."[33]

Mirroring the unresolved state of the broader debates, references to development in West African participatory trade politics typically made allusion to a long-term policy goal, but left several concrete questions unanswered. For example, what specific policy decisions development required and what developed West African societies would look like was subject to much discussion. While participants to the West African EPA debate further fought over the question of what type of trade reform would bring development, the historical connections between trade and socio-economic decline in West Africa that I outline in Chapter 5 were rarely directly discussed. As I show in the next chapter, the questions "What is development?" and "How can it be achieved?" were far from clear, but constituted key fields of political contestation among the various participants in the West African EPA process.

Similarly, I treat the terms "trade liberalization" and "free trade" as shorthand for a specific trade political outlook, including resulting policy recommendations for trade reform, at a given historical moment. The *WTO Dictionary of Trade Policy Terms* defines the term free trade "in principle, [as] the free movement across borders of goods, services, capital and people," but clarifies: "in practice, national policy and regulatory objectives put greater or lesser constraints on the movement

22   Introduction

of each."[34] Trade liberalization, on the other hand, is "a general term for the gradual or complete removal of existing impediments to trade in goods and services." However, the dictionary highlights that "free trade may be its ultimate aim, but more likely it is freer trade."[35] The point that free trade is not the ultimate aim of trade policy is most clearly stressed in the trade law literature. Legal scholars regularly confront questions of how trade interests and other public policies are to be balanced in the application of international trade law and recognize that it is impossible to separate the regulation of trade flows from the regulation of many other things in society.[36]

In view of the balancing exercise required, it is unsurprising that the term free trade has shifted meaning historically several times. While scholars such as John Hobson and Trentmann go back to the Victorian and Edwardian eras to demonstrate this point,[37] it is obvious from the history of the multilateral trade system that the terms have stayed in motion since. Under the GATT, "trade liberalization" referred to a specific set of policy lines, namely the lowering of high post-war tariffs among mainly industrialized countries in mainly industrial sectors of their economies. The Uruguay Round leading to the establishment of the WTO in 1995 made substantial additions including rules on trade in services and investment and harmonization of intellectual property and health and safety standards. With the Doha Round and the recent proliferation of Preferential Trade Agreements (PTAs), the trade agenda is further expanding to policy domains such as competition and government procurement, among many others. Thus, trade liberalization has shifted target and technique, from removing classical trade policy instruments that regulate trade flows at the border towards so-called "trade-related" rules that open markets through interference with domestic regulation in other policy areas.

In the realm of trade theory, the move produces several interconnected conceptual rifts. Many of the policies that are currently branded as liberalizing trade do not fall within the logic of the neoclassical argument that undergirds the hegemonic position of free trade discourse.[38] Rather than reducing opportunity costs for all, the policies create opportunities to establish dominant market positions for specific types of economic operators in the global economy through regulatory reform. In fact, many policies that are considered free trade today fit well with Karl Polanyi's observation that "the road to the free market [is] opened and kept open by an enormous increase in continuous, centrally organized and controlled interventionism."[39] Since trading is not only an economic, but also always a social activity, the idea that it can operate in a rules-free sphere nurtured since David Ricardo was

Introduction 23

and remains flawed. As economic operators' increasing regulatory and standard-setting activities testify, under free trade policies, the setting of the rules under which the trading system runs is gradually shifting from the visible hand of the state to the visible hand of corporate actors.[40]

More serious analytical problems arise from the fact that the terms do not respect the nuances and complexities at work in a global trading system that continuously expands the topical areas considered to be trade-related, as several scholars note.[41] If theory can only subsume calls for strong public health exemptions to intellectual property rules under the politically charged notion of protectionism, for example, this is not only conceptually unimaginative. As Rorden Wilkinson observes, participants to trade debates "become bound up in a language, and a realm of political possibility, from which they cannot escape."[42] The lack of nuanced approaches to trade political attitudes in theoretical frameworks for trade policy-making also reproduces the argumentative deadlock in current trade political debates, rather than helping to envision policy alternatives. In addition, perceptions attached to the terms are used as discursive tools in international trade policy-making. Jane Ford points out that global South countries are commonly perceived in trade negotiations as pursuing protectionist trade policy lines, while global North countries are often thought of as free traders. She argues that these perceptions are part of the global trading culture and, while factually misleading, impact on the dynamics of trade negotiations.[43]

To avoid the conceptual and analytical problems inherent in these considerations, I use the terminology "global trade agenda" to refer to the dominant trade political outlook. Based on the Doha Ministerial Declaration, I understand the contemporary global trade agenda to include the following policy lines: tariff reduction or elimination in trade in goods, market access in service sectors, universalization of intellectual property protection, technical assistance to global South countries to facilitate foreign direct investment, competition policy and institutional capacity for trade facilitation, access to government procurement procedures and e-commerce.[44]

Despite the lack of unified understanding, the expression "civil society" dominates practical and theoretical debates and I use it in my study to refer to those actors that engaged with the EPA process under this label. All actors involved with West African EPA negotiations used the term to refer to the Platform and other political actors that did not represent the state or the corporate sector. They reproduced the current habit in trade politics of taking the division between state, market and civil society for granted. At the same time, my interviewees often

24 Introduction

conflated the terms "civil society," "NGO," and "social movement" in interviews. As becomes clear in Chapter 4, civil society is less an analytical tool to explain reality. Rather, how we understand the term and who we count under its heading in a given political situation is itself part of the reality to be explained.

This is particularly obvious from theoretical debates on African civil society.[45] The Eurocentric nature of the concept presents limits for conceptualizing the African context. In this sense, Thomas Callaghy asks:

> Is civil society thus defined by a particular outcome or set of definitions of a public sphere in the European context? Or is it but one particular example of a larger, more universal process of thinking politically about conflict, how it is carried out, and who has the "right" to engage in it? If it is the latter, as it most certainly is, then African societies ... are producing their own versions of these definitions.[46]

In the West African EPA process, the Platform saw itself as an expression of West African civil society and qualified as a non-state actor under the West African Negotiating Roadmap and the Cotonou Agreement. At the same time, the meaning of the term varied in the West African EPA debate and parts of the political struggle over authority in trade policy-making centered on who or what civil society was, and if and how it could be represented.

Conceptually, I therefore reject the term. I broadly divide trade political actors into those groups that are supportive of the global trade agenda and those that resist or challenge it. This is consistent with Jan Aart Scholte's categorization of civil society actors in trade politics on the basis of their attitude towards the global trade agenda. He identifies three basic attitudes, which constitute broad orientations that can and do overlap in practice. Conformers "follow mainstream discourses of trade theory and broadly endorse the existing aims and activities of the WTO." Reformers "aim to change the thinking, rules and procedures of the WTO ... to redress alleged undesirable effects of the existing trading order." Rejectionists "regard the existing global trade regime as incorrigible" and advocate its contraction or complete abolition according to the slogan "shrink or sink."[47]

Scholte's approach allows transcending the typical categorization of trade political actors into corporate and non-corporate groups. Instead, conformers aim to influence but conserve the global trade agenda, while reformers and rejectionists strive for its transformation. Based on Scholte's categorization, I therefore refer to reformers and

Introduction 25

rejectionists as "transformative" actors or claims in trade politics. The approach avoids inherent assumptions of how the state does or should interact with these actors. It also opens space for interesting new research puzzles beyond my study. Erin Hannah, for example, finds that European Commission officials resist cooperation with transformers, be they business organizations or civil society groups, rather than resisting cooperation with particular sets of interests.[48]

On theoretical abstractions from localized contexts

In this book, I make theoretical generalizations on the basis of a case study of an African political process. Speaking of African studies in general, Amina Mama and Ayesha Imam identify "a false universalism, constructed from idealized European conditions, against which Africa is constantly compared, and which forces African scholars to waste time tilting at windmills to find out why we deviate from these patterns instead of finding out what our own patterns and realities are."[49] This not only creates problems for collective learning in an African context. It also creates unnecessary analytical obstacles for scholars that approach Africa with some of the most fundamental research questions of the social sciences. John Harbeson identifies two distinct questions that are relevant for my research, namely: "when, how, why, and in what form do norms about how society is to be governed emerge, function, and/or decay, and with what outcomes?" and "when, how, and why do particular forms of dissensus as well as consensus emerge over principles determining how society is to be governed, and what are the merits and shortcomings in particular circumstances?"[50] If we resist learning collectively from African politics because our analytical concepts do not sit comfortably with its contexts, we risk missing potentially important lessons.

As with any case study, adequately capturing the West African political context is a crucial empirical and conceptual exercise that I carry on throughout the book. In line with ongoing efforts to shake off the Eurocentric foundations of international political economy and international relations theory,[51] I consider the implications of an African political experience for theory-building, rather than marginalizing Africa through the application of theory. In West Africa, civil society organizations interacted with state institutions in order to negotiate part of the rules under which the region interacts with the world economy. Although the state-market-civil society triangle is typically taken for granted in trade political analysis, its theoretical imposition on (West) African realities does not provide adequate analytical tools

26 *Introduction*

to reflect on problems that partly arose from the concepts' practical imposition on the region since the nineteenth century. At the same time, a considerable number of actors, including the Platform, make political claims against economic policy under the self-selected label of civil society, while both the state and the market are dominant forms of political and economic organization in West Africa today.

This provokes important analytical challenges. On the one hand, a discussion of West African trade politics that does not problematize its reference to state, market and civil society risks pushing West Africa (again) to theoretical irregularity without recognizing the distinct struggles over establishing both legitimate political authority and responsible economic policy that are ongoing in the region today. On the other hand, overstretching the inadequacy of these concepts minimizes the extent to which state, market, and civil society have become factual realities that structure West African trade politics. It not only creates a false depiction of the region's political realities, but also prematurely dismisses any lessons we can draw about social, political, and economic organization from the experience. In this sense, Harbeson argues:

> A key question is the extent to which African peoples accept as universally valid Western ideas of democracy and market economies, as international proponents seem to assume and expect. Certainly, it would not be surprising to find politically active Africans seeking to define goals for economic and political reform that, although perhaps closely analogous to Western ideas, are nevertheless infused with African cultural content.[52]

Considering the conceptual tensions that trouble the literature on the democratization of trade politics today, I contend that the West African struggle to come to terms with these tensions is an important example for trade policy-making and contains empirical material for pushing our debates forward. In this regard, I do not take the mixed performance of West African countries on most governance indices to present an obstacle for studying the emergence of participatory trade politics as a process of opening trade policy-making for three principal reasons. First, from the perspective of trade policy-making, the initial exclusiveness of decision-making styles in ECOWAS mirrored the situation of other political systems, including countries typically classified as consolidated representative democracies. Second, the interconnections between trade policy, democracy, and civil society are subject to vast, controversial debates in the literature.[53] Third, West

Introduction 27

African EPA state and non-state actors justified civil society participation in trade policy-making on the basis of the democratic ideal. As I show in Part II, West African trade officials acknowledged that trade policy decisions impacted on the population at large and argued that citizens therefore needed to be included. The Platform saw its EPA campaign as part of a broader struggle for democratization in the region.

A Platform representative explained during my interview: "If democracy is not consolidated at state level [in West Africa], it is even less so at the regional level ... I think that the small advances we have made expand democratic spaces and they expand the vision, the conception of what democracy could be in institutions such as ECOWAS or certain countries, by introducing a new procedure in international relations. Thirty years ago, this would not have been possible" (Platform representative 2). In line with this statement, I do not argue that West Africa chose the optimal path towards more open and transparent trade politics or that this path was unproblematic in terms of the democratic ideal. I do, however, argue that West Africa chose a path that gives reason to re-open the debate about the relationship between trade and democracy. To this end, I give an account of the characteristics and mechanisms of participatory trade politics in West Africa to the highest possible degree of detail in order to provide perspectives on possible, if currently rare, forms of trade policy-making.

Broader trends in world politics stress the relevance of the lessons to be learnt. Analyzing "Africa in the Global Political Economy at the End of the Millennium" almost two decades ago, Timothy Shaw explains:

> ... notwithstanding contemporary claims about the successes of capitalism and democracy, the realities at the end of the millennium are more mixed ... the escalation of complex problems and the absence of effective responses are apparent in the diversity of actors and reactions: from the fragmentation of states to the proliferation of groups in "civil society" ... so despite its manifold dilemmas, the South, particularly various levels and types of civil society groups, might seize the current conjuncture—not a brave "new world order", more a grave disorder—for its own purpose: to recapture the global agenda for sustainable human development/ security.[54]

West African participatory trade politics is one expression of the ongoing trend. Shaw sees Africa at the end of the twentieth century to be characterized by waning state influence due to internationalization and impoverishment, by erosion of democracy and by the rise of new

28 Introduction

actors from civil society in response to the decline of the state. The West African experience with participatory trade politics, that is to say its practice of including a broader range of actors than what is commonly thought possible in trade policy formation, supports Shaw's argument that "rather than being peripheral, in terms of confronting the new range of global issues, Africa may be in the *avant garde*, in part because it is especially vulnerable."[55]

In order to substantiate the claims made in the Introduction, the next chapter takes a closer look at the Platform as a transformative trade political actor in EPA negotiations. In Chapter 2, I discuss the historical trajectory of trade theory and its shortcomings for theorizing transformations in trade politics.

Notes

1 Phil Evans, "Is Trade Policy Democratic? And Should it Be?" in *The New Economic Diplomacy: Decision-Making and Negotiation in International Economic Relations*, ed. Nicholas Bayne and Stephen Woolcock (Aldershot: Ashgate, 2003), 158.

2 Richard Ashley, "Three Modes of Economism," *International Studies Quarterly* 27, no. 3 (1983): 463.

3 Philip Curtin, *Cross-cultural Trade in World History* (Cambridge: Cambridge University Press, 1984), 1.

4 Marisa von Bülow, *Building Transnational Networks: Civil Society and the Politics of Trade in the Americas* (Cambridge: Cambridge University Press, 2010).

5 See Helen Milner, "The Political Economy of International Trade," *Annual Review of Political Science* 2 (1999): 91–114; Marc Williams, "Contesting Global Trade Rules: Social Movements and the World Trade Organization," in *Global Tensions: Challenges and Opportunities in the World Economy*, ed. Lourdes Benería and Savitri Bisnath (London: Routledge, 2004), 193-206; Ann Capling and Patrick Low, *Governments, Non-State Actors and Trade Policy-Making: Negotiating Preferentially or Multilaterally?* (Cambridge: Cambridge University Press and World Trade Organization, 2010).

6 Matthew Eagleton-Pierce, *Symbolic Power in the World Trade Organization* (Oxford: Oxford University Press, 2012).

7 Appellate Body Report on *European Communities—Regime for the Importation, Sale and Distribution of Bananas*, WT/DS27/AB/R, adopted 9 September 1997.

8 See Martin Holland, *The European Union and the Third World* (Basingstoke: Palgrave Macmillan, 2002).

9 Richard Gibb, "Post-Lomé: The European Union and the South," *Third World Quarterly* 2, no. 3 (2000): 457–81.

10 Stephen Hurt, "Co-operation and Coercion? The Cotonou Agreement between the European Union and ACP States and the End of the Lomé Convention," *Third World Quarterly* 24, no. 1 (2003): 161–76.

Introduction 29

11 Siaka Momoh, "Brainstorming on Breaking Trade Barriers in West Africa," *Business Day*, 23 May 2011.
12 Hamidou Ouédraogo, "Organisations paysannes et APE: 'Pas la charrue avant les boeufs!'," *L'Observateur Paalga*, 31 May 2007.
13 IMF 2010, *World Economic Outlook Database*, www.imf.org.
14 Olawale Ogunkola and Adeolu O. Adewuyi, *Avenir du commerce intrarégional en Afrique de l'Ouest dans le contexte des négociations APE. Rapport de recherche présenté à ENDA* (Dakar: ENDA, 2009).
15 DG Trade 2011, *Rank of ACP in European Union Trade (2010)*, trade.ec. europa.eu/doclib/docs/2006/september/tradoc_113340.%20South%20Africa. pdf.
16 DG Trade 2011, *West Africa*, ec.europa.eu/trade/wider-agenda/developmen t/economic-partnerships/negotiations-and-agreements/#west-africa.
17 See Appendix II.
18 Peter Mandelson 2005, *Statement by EU Commissioner Peter Mandelson*, trade.ec.europa.eu/doclib/docs/2005/november/tradoc_125868.pdf.
19 African Development Bank 2011, *Fiscal Balance by Regions*, dataportal. afdb.org/Dashboards.aspx?key = 26615.
20 Calculated on the basis of European Commission 2011, *EU Donor Atlas*, development.donoratlas.eu/query.aspx.
21 See Appendix III.
22 European Parliament, *Press Release: Don't Rush Least Developed Countries into Partnership Agreements, say MEPs*, Reference No: 20120907IPR50828, 2012.
23 ECOWAS, *Feuille de Route des Négociations de l'Accord de Partenariat Economique entre l'Afrique de l'Ouest et la Communauté Européenne*, Abidjan: ECOWAS, 2004.
24 ECOWAS, *Feuille de Route des Négociations*, 12–13.
25 ECOWAS, *Ministerial Monitoring Committee Meeting Conclusions and Recommendations*, Abidjan: ECOWAS, 2007.
26 Von Bülow, *Building Transnational Networks: Civil Society and the Politics of Trade in the Americas*, 5 (italics in original).
27 Von Bülow, *Building Transnational Networks*, 7–8.
28 Notably Frank Trentmann, "Political Culture and Political Economy: Interests, Ideology and Free Trade," *Review of International Political Economy* 5, no. 2 (1998): 217–51; Laura Macdonald, "Globalization and Social Movements: Comparing Women's Movements' Responses to NAFTA in Mexico, the USA and Canada," *International Feminist Journal of Politics* 4, no. 2 (2002): 151–72; Jane Ford, *A Social Theory of the WTO: Trading Cultures* (Basingstoke: Palgrave Macmillan, 2003); Williams, "Contesting Global Trade Rules: Social Movements and the World Trade Organization"; Rorden Wilkinson, "Language, Power and Multilateral Trade Negotiations," *Review of International Political Economy* 16, no. 4 (2009): 597–619; Erin Hannah, "NGOs and the European Union: Examining the Power of Epistemes in the EC's TRIPS and Access to Medicines Negotiations," *Journal of Civil Society* 7, no. 2 (2011): 179–206; John Hobson, "Part 1—Revealing the Euro-centric Foundations of IPE: A Critical Historiography of the Discipline from the Classical to the Modern Era," *Review of International Political Economy* (2012), dxdoi.org/10.1080/ 09692290.2012.704519; John Hobson, "Part 2—Reconstructing the non-Eurocentric Foundations of IPE: From Eurocentric 'Open Economy

30 *Introduction*

Politics' to Inter-Civilizational Political Economy," *Review of International Political Economy* (2012), dxdoi.org/10.1080/09692290.2012.733498; Eagleton-Pierce, *Symbolic Power in the World Trade Organization*.

29 Trentmann, "Political Culture and Political Economy: Interests, Ideology and Free Trade."

30 Save the Children, *The Child Development Index. Holding Governments to Account for Children's Wellbeing* (London: Save the Children, 2008); World Bank 2010, *Countries and Economies*, data.worldbank.org/country; UNDP 2010, *The Human Development Index 2009*, hdr.undp.org/en/statistics/hdi/.

31 Allegedly as "a public relations gimmick" to make proposals for the West's relations with the emerging Third World sound "a bit original" in the context of the emerging Cold War. See Louis Halle, "On Teaching International Relations," *The Virginia Quarterly Review* 40, no. 1 (1964), cited in Gilbert Rist, "Development as a Buzzword," *Development in Practice* 17, no. 4–5 (2007): 485.

32 Wolfgang Sachs, *The Development Dictionary: A Guide to Knowledge as Power* (London: Zed Books, 1992), 1.

33 Rist, "Development as a Buzzword."

34 Walther Goode, *Dictionary of Trade Policy Terms* (Cambridge: Cambridge University Press, 2007).

35 Goode, *Dictionary of Trade Policy Terms.*

36 See Gabrielle Marceau and Joel Trachtman, "The Technical Barriers to Trade Agreement, the Sanitary and Phytosanitary Measures Agreement, and the General Agreement on Tariff and Trade: A Map of the World Trade Organization Law of Domestic Regulation of Goods," *Journal of World Trade* 36, no. 5 (2002): 811–81; Catherine Button, *The Power to Protect: Trade, Health and Uncertainty in the WTO* (Oxford: Hart Publishing, 2004).

37 Trentmann, "Political Culture and Political Economy: Interests, Ideology and Free Trade"; Goode, *Dictionary of Trade Policy Terms*; Hobson, "Part 2—Reconstructing the non-Eurocentric Foundations of IPE: From Eurocentric 'Open Economy Politics' to Inter-Civilizational Political Economy."

38 Carsten Fink and Patrick Reichenmiller, *Tightening TRIPS: The Intellectual Property Provisions in Recent US Free Trade Agreements* (Washington, DC: World Bank, 2005).

39 Karl Polanyi, *The Great Transformation: The Political and Economic Origins of Our Time* (Boston, MA: Beacon Press, [1944] 2001), 146.

40 Teivo Teivainen made the visible hand analogy in a personal conversation in 2010.

41 Ford, *A Social Theory of the WTO: Trading Cultures*; Williams, "Contesting Global Trade Rules: Social Movements and the World Trade Organization"; von Bülow, *Building Transnational Networks: Civil Society and the Politics of Trade in the Americas.*

42 Rorden Wilkinson, "Of Butchery and Bicycles: The WTO and the 'Death' of the Doha Development Agenda," *The Political Quarterly* 83, no. 2 (2012): 397.

43 Ford, *A Social Theory of the WTO: Trading Cultures.*

44 WTO, *Ministerial Declaration*, T/MIN(01)/DEC/1, 2001.

45 See Crawford Young, "In Search of Civil Society," in *Civil Society and the State in Africa*, ed. John W. Harbeson, Donald Rotchild and Naomi

Chazan (Boulder: Lynne Rienner Publishers, 1994), 33–50; and Michael Bratton, "Civil Society and Political Transition," in *Civil Society and the State in Africa*, ed. John W. Harbeson, Donald Rotchild and Naomi Chazan (Boulder, CO: Lynne Rienner Publishers, 1994), 51–81.

46 Thomas Callaghy, "Civil Society, Democracy and Economic Change in Africa: A Dissenting Opinion on Resurgent Societies," in *Civil Society and the State in Africa*, 237.

47 Jan Aart Scholte, "The WTO and Civil Society," *Trade Politics*, ed. Brian Hocking and Steven McGuire (London: Routledge, 2004), 150.

48 Hannah, "NGOs and the European Union: Examining the Power of Epistemes in the EC's TRIPS and Access to Medicines Negotiations."

49 Amina Mama and Ayesha Imam, *The Role of Academics in Limiting and Expanding Academic Freedom* (Kampala: CODESRIA Symposium on Academic Freedom, Research and the Social Responsibility of the Intellectual in Africa, 1990), 21.

50 John Harbeson, "Civil Society and Political Renaissance in Africa," in *Civil Society and the State in Africa*, ed. John Harbeson, Donald Rotchild and Naomi Chazan (Boulder. CO: Lynne Rienner Publishers, 1994), 3.

51 See Hobson, "Part 1—Revealing the Euro-centric foundations of IPE: A Critical Historiography of the Discipline from the Classical to the Modern Era"; Hobson, "Part 2—Reconstructing the non-Eurocentric Foundations of IPE: From Eurocentric 'Open Economy Politics' to Inter-Civilizational Political Economy."

52 Harbeson, "Civil Society and Political Renaissance in Africa," 7–8.

53 See Robert Hudec, "'Circumventing' Democracy: The Political Morality of Trade Negotiations," *New York University Journal of International Law and Politics* 25, no. 2 (1993): 311–22; Daniel Esty, "The World Trade Organization's Legitimacy Crisis," *World Trade Review* 1, no. 1 (2002): 7–22; Quan Li and Rafael Reuveny, "Economic Globalization and Democracy: An Empirical Analysis," *British Journal of Political Science* 33, no. 1 (2003): 29–54; Ernesto López-Córdova and Christopher Meissner, *The Globalization of Trade and Democracy, 1870–2000* (Cambridge: National Bureau of Economic Research, 2005); B.S. Chimni, "The World Trade Organization, Democracy and Development: A View From the South," *Journal of World Trade* 40, no. 1 (2006): 5–36.

54 Timothy Shaw, "Africa in the Global Political Economy at the End of the Millennium: What Implications for Politics and Policies?" *Africa Today* 42, no. 4 (1995): 14.

55 Shaw, "Africa in the Global Political Economy at the End of the Millennium: What Implications for Politics and Policies?" 11.

1 Transformative agency in EPA negotiations

- **The Platform**
- **Impact of transformative participation on EPA negotiations**
- **Conclusion**

In this chapter, I analyze the Platform as a transformative actor in trade politics. Its configuration, EPA stance, internal proceedings, and campaign strategies grew out of West African activism on development cooperation and were consolidated over time during the EPA campaign. Their good access to the policy process helped the Platform to frame EPA debates in a way that was conducive to the politicization of trade. On the basis of their privileged position and the reframed debate, the Platform exercised concrete influence on negotiations.

The Platform

After the second negotiating phase of ECOWAS-EU talks from 2003 to 2005, which focused on stocktaking and preparatory work, negotiators have been drafting legal provisions since 2006. Since then, the Senegalese Platform member and international NGO ENDA has filled the civil society seat in ECOWAS' negotiating team. At the regional level, ENDA defends a common civil society position elaborated in the Platform. Platform members are responsible for lobbying at their respective national levels.

Origin and EPA stance

Historically, the Platform has grown out of civil society advocacy on the Cotonou Agreement between the late 1990s and the mid-2000s. When Cotonou negotiations were launched, so-called "national platforms of civil society organizations" working on ACP-EU relations

Transformative agency in EPA negotiations   33

formed in Benin, Burkina-Faso, Côte d'Ivoire, Ghana, Guinea, Mali, Niger, and Senegal between 1999 and 2001. They set up the Platform as their regional focal point and entrusted ENDA with its secretariat.[1] The network brought together "organizations who shared particular visions of economic policy [with the intention] ... to build a broader front of organizations with national ownership" (Platform representative 7).

Platform membership has fluctuated over time, but in 2009 consisted of 15 organizations from 11 countries, listed in Table 1.1.

The level of organization of the members varies. Four member organizations are national civil society platforms. The Platform of Civil Society Actors in Benin, for example, represents, among other groups, farmers' associations, local NGOs, trade unions, and women's rights groups.[2] Eight Platform member organizations are African development and/or global justice NGOs that are networked transnationally

Table 1.1 Platform membership in 2009

Country	Members
Benin	Groupe de Recherche et d'Action pour la Promotion de l'Agriculture et du Développement (GRAPAD)
	Plate-Forme des Acteurs de la Société Civile au Bénin (PASCIB)
Burkina-Faso	Organisation pour le Renforcement des Capacités de Développement (ORCADE)
	Secrétariat Permanent des ONG (SPONG)
Cape Verde	
Côte d'Ivoire	Réseau des Centrales Syndicales UE/ACP (RECSY UE-ACP)
The Gambia	World View
Ghana	General Agricultural Workers' Union (GAWU)
	Third World Network (TWN)
Guinea	Centre du Commerce International pour le Développement (CECIDE)
Guinea-Bissau	–
Liberia	–
Mali	Plateforme des Acteurs Non-Etatiques du Mali (CNP ANE AC)
Mauritania	–
Niger	Comité de Coordination des Organisations de la Société Civile Nigérienne Accord ACP/UE (CCOSCN/ACP/UE)
Nigeria	National Association of Nigerian Traders (NANTS)
Senegal	Conseil des Organisations Non-Gouvernementales d'Appui au Développement (CONGAD)
	ENDA Tiers Monde
Sierra Leone	–
Togo	Groupe d'Action et de Recherche sur l'Environnement et le Développement (GARED)

34 *Transformative agency in EPA negotiations*

and enjoy international visibility. Two members are trade unions. The National Association of Nigerian Traders (NANTS) is a traders' organization and as such representative of the private sector. The NANTS Secretariat is, however, politically autonomous and has decided to engage in the EPA campaign in coalition with civil society groups (Platform representative 3). Reportedly, civil society is poorly organized on trade issues in Cape Verde, Guinea-Bissau, Liberia, and Sierra Leone (Platform representative 1). In countries experiencing political turmoil, Platform members have disappeared during the EPA campaign. Until the 2008 military coup, for example, the Association Mauritanienne des Femmes Juristes and the Association Mauritanie 2000 represented Mauritania in the Platform.[3]

Platform organizations initially launched the Cotonou campaign with two overarching objectives in mind: to "promote the democratic definition of the economic policies of West African States" and to "promote alternatives which favor sustained socio-economic development."[4] They identified economic and trade cooperation as their primary campaign interest at a gathering on EU-ACP relations in 2002. Throughout 2003, the network raised awareness for EPA-related issues among civil society across the region.[5] At that time, the Platform also forged links with European organizations such as Christian Aid, Oxfam UK and the Friedrich Ebert Foundation, which became crucial in funding campaigning activities later (Platform representative 3).

In early 2004, the Platform hosted a regional strategic planning seminar on EPA with the help of their global North partners.[6] The seminar aimed to "exchange on the state of the EPA and WTO negotiations; encourage the greater involvement of platforms and other non-state actors in EPA negotiations; organize consultations and capacity building activities at national level and the elaboration of national positions," and "organize the preparation of analytical documents on the following themes: Impact of EPA on agriculture regional integration as well as trade and development."[7] The ACP Secretariat and the European Commission subsequently granted ENDA funding to coordinate a capacity-building exercise on EPA throughout West Africa in 2004 and 2005. The exercise produced three chief results, namely the rejection of the EU's EPA proposal among West African civil society actors, the consolidation of the Platform as the central West African civil society EPA network, and the connection of the Platform to other EPA-critical networks, such as the European STOP EPA campaign and Africa Trade Network (ATN).[8]

The Platform's trade political stance indicates that the simple categorization of trade political preferences into protectionist and free trade attitudes does not capture the nuances at play in global economic governance today. Doubting that West African economies could benefit from the EU's EPA demands for opening ACP market access in goods and services and WTO+ rules on trade-related issues, the Platform denounced the global trade agenda and criticized asymmetrical power relations in the global economy. In 2004, for example, Nancy Kachingwe affirmed in a briefing paper for Platform member TWN Ghana: "Adhering to WTO, World Bank and IMF policies is a questionable path if the end result is the death of the agricultural sector as a result of free-for-all imports. The emphasis on exports may make sense on paper, but it may be much more beneficial for us to focus on domestic and regional markets, rather than international markets only."[9]

When asked whether Platform member TWN Ghana supported protectionist policies during an interview with the Accra-based radio station CITI-FM 97.3 in 2004, spokesperson Kwasi Gyan-Apenteng replied that trade itself was not at issue, but that the way in which the global trade regime was organized created inequality and hardship. "Africa and Europe have traded for 500 years," he explained, "and every time we have lost. Why is it that we, the continent that produces everything that people want to survive, are the poorest?"[10] This was at the same time a point of convergence and divergence between public trade officials and transformative civil society in West Africa. There was consensus among all of my interviewees that one goal of EPA talks was to arrange the ECOWAS-EU trade regime in a way that would help the region to escape from its dire socio-economic reality. Profound disagreement, however, prevailed over how trade policy should be set in order to serve this purpose.

As I analyze in more detail below, exchanges over the merits of different strategies were politicized. The Nigerian organization NANTS argued that the extensive trade reforms that the EU pursued would lead to "loss of government revenue, influx of goods and import surge, capital flight, de-industrialization, labor dislocation and job losses, insecurity, and poverty escalation" in West Africa.[11] Suggesting inconsistencies in EU foreign policy, NANTS further declared: "if the EC is honest with the EPA, the likes of [Peter] Mandelson [then EU trade commissioner] should be more concerned with the livelihoods of the people of whom 70 per cent depend on subsistence agriculture, he should be more concerned therefore with the protection of food security, he should be more concerned with the right to freedom of expression especially on an issue that relates to the economic future of the poor, more concerned with the protection of the various commitments under the United Nations Declaration on Human Rights which the EU member countries are signatories to."[12]

36   *Transformative agency in EPA negotiations*

The Platform further openly questioned the EU's policy goals. One Platform representative saw securing long-term market access, which was threatened by European producers' growing incapacity to compete with countries such as Brazil, China, and India, as the EU's hidden agenda behind its affirmation that market opening would be good for West African development (Platform representative 1). A European official defended the approach by explaining in my interview that it did not make sense for the EU to accept that third parties could get more favorable trade deals with African countries, if African countries wanted to maintain European free market access (European public official 3).

As a policy alternative for relying on EU trade, Platform organizations intended to transform the ways in which West Africa interacts with the world economy and saw regional integration as one tool to reach this goal. ENDA argued that the transformation of the region into a unified economic space would permit "exploiting economies of scale, strengthen the competitiveness of companies on the international level, access new technologies and investments while helping to protect against external shocks and internal deficiencies."[13] One Platform representative asserted in my interview:

> Our vision is ... that the problem of Africa is a particular location in the international economic order, a kind of commodity exporter who imports everything ... So the development challenge for us is to transform this structure ... Our analysis is that from the WTO Agreements ... to EPA, they take away the policy instruments that are needed for that transformation ... We are talking about the ability to use all the policy instruments for development that have been proven to be correct and useful in the history of modern economic development of ... Asia, Europe, and America, which is now being denied to African countries. But the starting point is that we need to acknowledge that ... we must transform our economic structure.
>
> (Platform representative 7)

Many Platform organizations considered democratization a remedy for perceived problems with trade policy formation. This attitude is typical for transformative actors in trade politics[14] and related to the Platform's perception that West African public trade officials have traditionally failed to act in the interest of their populations, as I discuss in Part II. Thus, ENDA representative Bibiane Mbaye Gahamanyi stated in a 2004 editorial of the ACP-EU Civil Society Information Network:

Transformative agency in EPA negotiations 37

regional institutions and the EU ... need to face up to the failures and shortcomings of economic liberalist free market theory. The engine of sustainable development is not to be found in a one-size-fits-all model imposed by the most powerful countries; new balances must be found in the share-out of responsibilities between State, market, and civil society organizations.[15]

Ken Ukaoha pointed out in a NANTS publication on parliament-led trade policy formation:

in the absence of the lawmakers' intervention, international trade would dance to the tune of market-determined prices based on factor endowments of each country. It is therefore the lawful duty of the Legislature to ensure that within their oversight function, policies that relate to trade are: i) not averse with the laws of the Country, ii) pro-poor and indeed seek to protect the livelihoods of citizens, iii) fair, just, and equitable both in formulation and implementation, iv) coherent with the needs of the population, v) taken in consideration of local realities, and, vi) in tandem with the overall development strategy.[16]

Although the Platform's EPA stance was transformative, it was not uniform. Some Platform members saw the goal of their participation in the EPA process to "minimize negative impacts on sustainable development" (Platform representative 3). From their perspective, this implied making sure that the West African EPA would not be a "strict free trade agreement" (Platform representative 6). At the same time, a number of Platform organizations took a rejectionist position. One Platform representative identified the break-down of EPA negotiations as the ultimate aim of the campaign. The interviewee saw the political leverage that participatory trade politics provided as a tool for pushing ECOWAS' negotiating position to a point where it would be unacceptable for the EU (Platform representative 7). The interviewee acknowledged: "There is a tension between people [in the Platform] who think that civil society must be there and those who say 'I'm not a fan of ECOWAS, I don't like them, the only reason why I wanna go to their meetings is to challenge their negotiations on EPA'" (Platform representative 7). Regardless of the tensions that could potentially result from clashes between reformative and rejectionist members, the Platform had reportedly always succeeded in reaching agreement on a common negotiating position through its internal proceedings and campaign strategies (Platform representatives 1, 3, 6, 7, 8).

38 *Transformative agency in EPA negotiations*

Internal proceedings and campaign strategy

After each negotiation meeting with the EU, the Platform representative circulated minutes to report from the negotiating room. In addition, Platform interviewees stressed the importance of their biannual meetings, the so-called "Regional Dialogues," held since 2005, for animating their network (Platform representatives 3, 6, 7, 8). During Regional Dialogues, to which global North partner organizations as well as public officials were typically invited, members exchanged information and broadened the scope of arguments and viewpoints available on EPA (Platform representative 3). They also brought concerns from the local and national levels to the Platform's attention. The EPA's gender impact was provided as one example for an issue that had been brought up from the grassroots in this way (Platform representative 1).

During Regional Dialogues, Platform members adopted a common position in the form of a declaration that subsequently became "the framework for the position that individual members adopt nationally and defend in ECOWAS" (Platform representative 7). One representative explained that different views on certain points were discussed until a common position emerged. Where consensus was not reached, diverging opinions could be noted in the declaration (Platform representative 4). Overall, Platform representatives confirmed in 2009 that the approach worked out to their satisfaction and could not recall an instance where it had failed (Platform representatives 1, 3, 6, 7, 8).

Furthermore, the Dialogues allowed Platform members to nurture personal relationships. They had learned during previous campaigning that "relationships between people are important in order to establish common work" (Platform representative 2). Close networking and good personal relations also helped the Platform to make sure that all members followed democratic principles in their work. As one representative pointed out, there was not necessarily a correlation between the most democratically organized and the best-funded organizations. Thus, being knowledgeable about partners' work patterns and funding opportunities was an important element in developing a campaign that was both credible and sufficiently resourced (Platform representative 2).

Interviewees also highlighted the importance of networking for the process of learning about the value and effectiveness of any chosen strategy. Developing and deploying lobbying strategies in interaction with the actions of the governments that are being challenged is typical for transnational advocacy[17] and the Platform was no exception. For several organizations, building a network had been one of their first campaign strategies on the Cotonou Agreement and the EPA. The dialogue with other civil society groups helped organizations to draft their campaigns and find their position. One Platform representative explained that civil society groups initially recognized that "we couldn't do everything but everything was important." During the dialogues that were subsequently held, "the positions of the various parties allowed us to agree on how to move ahead" (Platform representative 8).

By 2009, the Platform campaign relied on a number of activities including: participating in institutions of trade policy-making at the national, regional and bilateral level; advocating policy alternatives on the basis of scientific research; organizing capacity-building and dialogue workshops for public officials and civil society actors in West Africa and across EPA regions; informing the public on EPA with the help of the media, crucially also in local languages; and engaging in public pressure campaigns (Platform representatives 1, 3, 4, 6, 7, 8). One representative explained that the different campaigning methods and tools "are the key elements of the weapons in the arsenal and you fight and deploy them at particular times ... This is something we discovered through doing" (Platform representative 7). The Platform representative summed this up with the words: "The moment gives you the task" (Platform representative 7).

Several Platform interviewees highlighted the importance of explaining what was at stake in EPA negotiations to the broader public and of educating parliamentarians on the issues. One persistent problem was that important parts of West African populations do not speak European languages or are illiterate, which make access to information on trade negotiations even more difficult than is the case elsewhere. The problem is compounded by the fact that European languages are the official languages of West African governments,[18] which means that information in local languages on EPA or trade more generally is not readily available. The Platform actively attempted to fill citizens' information gaps not only by reporting back to the public from policy-making sessions, but also by spreading information about EPA negotiations in local languages via local media (European civil society representative 3, Platform representative 4).

Once created, the Platform served as a focal point where organizations exchanged knowledge and resources to create a common understanding of trade policy and to forge common campaigns as a network. In addition to exchanging results from research and national views on EPA, Platform organizations pooled funding and engaged in jointly identified research topics based on the common fund (Platform representative 3). Over time, the Platform became central from the point of view of their global North partner organizations. One

40 *Transformative agency in EPA negotiations*

representative of a European NGO explained that by 2009, the organization did not provide funding for individual West African NGOs campaigning on EPA anymore, but cooperated with the Platform, which allocated sources across its membership (European civil society representative 2). The practice gave the Platform a very dominant role among citizen associations, social movements, and civil society groups in the region. As I discuss in Part II, this strengthened its effectiveness in trade campaigning. On the other hand, the privileged position played into perceptions of self-appointment and feeble grassroots links which fed into concerns about the Platform's representativity.

Assessments of the Platform's grassroots links remain contradictory. While some interviewees suggested that the Platform collectively represented several hundreds of thousands of individuals, others maintained that there were no strong grassroots connections (Platform representatives 1, 3, 6, 7, 8). All Platform interviewees explained that grassroots work was the responsibility of Platform members in their respective countries. At the same time, the Platform makes efforts to foster citizen organization around trade in countries where it remains informal, for example by organizing seminars, diffusing information and providing assistance for grassroots groups interested in EPAs (Platform representatives 1, 3, 6, 7, 8).

One Platform representative suggested during my interview that "the Platform does not have conflicts on substantial issues, but tensions may have arisen over who does what" (Platform representative 3). Another Platform representative looked back on 2007 as a year when "there was tension in the Platform between organizations who wanted to be part of negotiations and organizations who wanted to challenge negotiations" (Platform representative 7). At the time, ECOWAS tried to set up a separate platform to fill the society seat at the negotiating table provided for in the Negotiating Roadmap. According to ECOWAS officials, their intention had been to resolve issues of civil society representation as the grassroots connections of the Platform became doubtful (West African public official 1). According to Platform members, ECOWAS' intention had been "to mute [our] campaign" (Platform representative 7). The attempt fueled existing internal divisions as Platform members saw their privileged access to EPA decision-making and negotiations threatened and began to challenge ENDA's leadership role in the network.

Platform interviewees argued that debates on the negotiating substance helped to overcome tensions over representation and coordination in the network. One Platform representative explained in my interview: "the way we resolved [internal tensions] was to continue having a common position all the time and forcing everybody to respond to that" (Platform representative 7). The issues of the Platform's standing in the negotiating structure and ENDA's leading role in the Platform were settled during a Regional Dialogue that ENDA organized in Dakar in March 2008. An ENDA representative explained during my interview that the organization invited both Platform members and national and regional public officials with several strategic goals in mind. ENDA saw the Dialogue as an opportunity to restate its technical position on EPA as negotiations continued after having missed the 31 December 2007 deadline. The second goal was to expose contradictions in public negotiators' attitude towards the Platform, based on the idea that if officials attended the workshop, they would factually acknowledge the legitimacy of the Platform as a trade political actor through this behavior. ENDA felt that officials could subsequently no longer deny the Platform its key status in EPA negotiations. The third goal was to resolve the internal problems of the network.

According to the ENDA representative, the workshop was a success. The representative argued that the Platform won clout in the eyes of negotiators because the participation of public officials from ministerial levels, notably by ministers from Côte d'Ivoire and Senegal, showed that the network enjoyed political support from the highest level. At the internal Platform meeting following the workshop, ENDA opened the question of Platform leadership. The representative recalled that the past conflicts were openly discussed at this occasion and that the Platform came to the decision that ENDA should maintain the role of Platform coordinator, due to its perceived high level of expertise and wide transnational support network. At the same time, the Platform decided to improve internal communication and refine methods for reaching common positions. The regional civil society representative subsequently sent a common declaration to ECOWAS in order to improve the transparency of the Platform from the point of view of public officials (Platform representative 1).

In the next section, I show how the Platform, as part of broader West African and transnational civil society, translated participation into influence and helped to shape the evolution of ECOWAS-EU trade talks during a seven-year campaign.

Impact of transformative participation on EPA negotiations

Participatory practices in West African trade policy-making during EPA negotiations changed the quality of interaction between the different sets of actors and had consequences for policy outcomes. All of

42 *Transformative agency in EPA negotiations*

my interviewees in principle agreed that West African civil society had influence on EPA negotiations. More specifically, one Platform representative argued that "many dimensions ... are being considered now, that were not there in the beginning, likely because people said 'hey, think again!' ... because people are asking questions, people are demanding accountability, people are demanding responsibility ... people say ... 'your decisions have implications on the welfare of the people'" (Platform representative 3). European Commission officials testified that the presence of these groups at the negotiating table "has quite an important impact on the course of the negotiation. A lot depends on the level or preparedness of the ... civil society representative ... and they are quite active in these negotiations. They act and they participate as if they were full members of the ECOWAS Commission" (European public official 1).

The Platform's campaign developed alongside, and partly in coordination with, other transformative organizations and broader societal movements that were critical of ECOWAS-EU trade talks both in Africa and in Europe. Despite difficulties in disentangling Platform achievements from the campaign successes of the general STOP EPA movement, a number of Platform initiatives played an important role in the EPA process. By bringing civil society actors and trade policymakers together in workshops and conferences, Platform organizations facilitated dialogue among various public and civic organizations. The meetings provided an opportunity to alter the terms of the EPA debate and introduce issues that the Platform perceived as important. Below, I trace how Platform organizations helped to turn EPAs into a development issue. This shifted EPA talks away from the allegedly politically neutral terrain of technical trade negotiations and brought the debate into the uncertain waters of appropriate policy recommendations for development. I then show how Platform members could impact the West African negotiating position, and subsequently the course of negotiations, directly, building on their institutional access and the topical shift in the debate.

Framing the debate

The Platform and the transnational transformative coalition in which it was embedded challenged the separation between trade and development policies established in the Cotonou Agreement. By introducing uncertainty over the underlying assumptions of EU-promoted trade and development strategies into EPA debates, they blurred the line between allegedly neutral, technocratic trade talks and politically and

Transformative agency in EPA negotiations 43

historically charged development assistance. It led to increased uncertainty, and hence politicization of the negotiating process, because it stripped EPAs of their purely technical nature as trade agreements and shifted them onto the slippery terrain of economic policy recommendations for development.

As outlined in the Introduction, the European Commission initially favored a "pure trade deal,"[19] in line with Article XXIV of the GATT and Article V of the General Agreement on Trade in Services (GATS). Contrary to WTO practice, where developing country members receive Special and Differential Treatment (SDT) that provides them with flexibility in the application of trade rules, EPAs were not supposed to include a specific development component outside of the framework of asymmetrical market opening discussed below.[20] A firm belief in trade liberalization's ability to alleviate poverty marked the EU's initial approach. Then trade commissioner Peter Mandelson expressed this view to the European Parliament Development Committee in 2005: "My overall philosophy is simple: I believe in progressive trade liberalization. I believe that the opening of markets can deliver growth and the reduction of poverty."[21]

Since the EU had not revised its international commitment to development, the coherence of EU policy towards the ACP was hinging on Mandelson's philosophy to prove correct. Empirical evidence from world politics on the trade and development nexus is, however, mixed. In fact, the socio-economic impact of trade reform is highly context-dependent and can be negative.[22] A large coalition of ACP and European civil society organizations as well as the European Parliament and the member states Denmark, the Netherlands, Sweden, and the United Kingdom, hence challenged Mandelson's view from early on in the EPA process.[23]

In a declaration entitled "Six Reasons to Oppose the EPA in their Current Form," ACP and European organizations explained:

> It is increasingly recognized that when countries apply trade liberalization before they have consolidated strong economies and institutions, de-industrialization often takes place ... the EC's own mid term report on Sustainability Impact Assessment warns that EPAs "might accelerate the collapse of the modern West African manufacturing sector" and could also "further discourage the development of processing and manufacturing capacity in the ACP countries in export oriented and other industries."[24]

The Platform echoed these concerns in the West African EPA debate. TWN claimed in 2005: "If EPAs continue to develop along their current course they are a clear threat to the development of ACP countries and

44 *Transformative agency in EPA negotiations*

the people living in these countries. They go against the international commitment of the EU to promote sustainable development and poverty reduction."[25] As part of their campaign, Platform organizations specifically warned about the impacts of the global trade agenda. NANTS predicted in the Nigerian newspaper *This Day* in May 2006 that the level of liberalization requested by the EU "would endanger the local industries that will become unprotected and therefore strip the economy of employment opportunities."[26]

The Platform further highlighted inconsistencies in the EU's EPA discourse in order to expose the feeble foundations of Mandelson's philosophy. Reporting from a press conference at the European Delegation in Accra in June 2006, where deputy general director of trade Karl Falkenberg advocated the inclusion of trade-related investment rules in EPAs, TWN noted:

> Asked to explain how liberalized rules which actually make capital outflow a lot easier would reverse West Africa's export of capital, Falkenberg could only repeat the mantra that "the investment will create additional jobs ... other than in cocoa" ... He did not respond to the challenge ... "how do you [build our own domestic markets] and build our supply side capacity if you have an investment agreement that allows European businesses to relocate here as if they were in domestic markets."[27]

ENDA representative Bibiane Mbaye Gahamanyi characterized a 2006 EPA impact assessment as "anachronistic" in the Senegalese newspaper *Le Quotidien*: "They predict a fall in public investment, in regional trade and in fiscal revenue," she explained, "and they want to make us believe that this will lead to a rise in household income and in wealth in the countries."[28]

As part of dismantling the EU's trade and development vision, Platform organizations also denounced European negotiating strategies and questioned the EU's stated commitment to foster development in the West African region. NANTS representative Ken Ukaoha explained in the Nigerian newspaper *This Day* in May 2006:

> Three years after the start of the negotiations [in October 2003], one would have expected an emerging consensus between the parties on the practical way forward to integrate the development dimension into EPAs. Yet, at the eve of substantive negotiations on the content of EPAs, sharp differences prevail on the approach to development in the context of the negotiations, creating tensions

and frustrations among the parties ... The way in which some fundamental questions such as development issues, the consolidation of regional integration, the choice of joint thematic groups as well as ACP-EC cooperation in international bodies, are dealt with perfectly illustrates this dichotomy, the European Commission's unstable language and the liberal free-market orientation which prevails in the ongoing discussions.[29]

Transformative organizations accused Europe of hidden self-interest behind altruistic policy advice and referred to negative past experiences with economic policy recommendations from the international community in order to mount opposition to EPA. In a document entitled "Forward with the Struggle to Stop EPAs," ATN declared in December 2006: "Over the past two decades, this right of African countries to pursue their own individual and collective developmental agenda has been attacked and subverted by the countries of the north that dominate the world economic system, as part of their never-ending attempts to further open up the economies of African and other developing countries for the benefit of their transnational corporations." The network explained: "The so-called Economic Partnership Agreements ... are set to be even more restrictive of the policy choices and opportunities available to our governments, and even more severe in their impacts than the World Bank/International Monetary Fund (IMF) structural adjustment policies as well as the WTO agreements."[30] In June 2006, West African and European groups adopted the Niamey Declaration under the umbrella of the francophone network Réseau des ONG de Développement et des Associations de Droits de l'Homme et de la Démocratie (RODDADH, Network of Development NGOs and Human Rights and Democracy Associations). It stated: "Neither EPAs nor the 10th EDF as presently conceived can realistically be favorable to Africa's development ... We reaffirm that development cannot come out of trade only."[31]

In its reaction to these claims, the EU held on to the view that its trade policy recommendations would lead to economic growth and presented a viable policy choice for development. In October 2007, then trade commissioner Peter Mandelson and then development commissioner Louis Michel explained in an open letter in *The Guardian* newspaper that skeptical voices "are not only wrong. They also undermine those in Africa and other ACP countries who are seeking to work constructively for economic reform." By doing so, the commissioners held, they were "playing poker with the livelihoods of those we are trying to help."[32] In declaring that it was pushing for trade reform in ACP countries in order to help, however, the European Commission

46   *Transformative agency in EPA negotiations*

locked itself into a negotiating position that became increasingly difficult to reconcile with technocratic market-opening ambitions. As Ole Elgström notes, "In its efforts to defend its negotiation position, the Commission increasingly began to emphasize its positive attitude towards development-oriented agreements ... Proclaiming EPAs a tool for development made it more difficult to withstand ACP and Member State demands for an unambiguous development profile in the agreement."[33]

Overall, the European Commission gradually changed its perception of EPAs during the course of negotiations and by 2009 saw them as "partnership agreements founded on the shared goal of development that make trade the servant of this objective not the reverse."[34] When compared to Mandelson's philosophy announced in 2005, the statement that then trade commissioner Catherine Ashton made to the European Parliament in 2009 captured the discourse shift that occurred within the Commission during this time. If according to the EU, trade liberalization was an end in itself that had the beneficial side effect of bringing development in 2005, by 2009 development was the end and trade, not trade liberalization, one means of achieving it.

West African trade officials confirmed in interviews that the EU's negotiating position had gradually evolved towards ECOWAS' stance on the development question in 2009. One official explained: "today, the European side is aware of the fact that it cannot approach an EPA without having also dealt with the development dimension" (West African public official 2). At the same time, all West African public negotiators whom I interviewed confirmed that it was the merit of civil society to have insisted on the development dimension of EPAs since the start of negotiations (West African public officials 1, 2, 3, 5, 6, 7, 8). European Commission officials also perceived civil society groups as having played a key role in raising development concerns in the West African EPA debate. The head of cooperation of the European Commission Delegation in Ghana stated in 2006:

> Through the works of Civil Society Organizations ... we do understand the development concerns of ECOWAS states and the negative effects the EPAs will have on their economies. But we are hoping that before the EPAs are fully implemented, these concerns would have been addressed. We are working to ensure the minimization of the losses and the maximization of the benefits.[35]

One West African official speculated: "If you had left [the development question] to government people, they would have talked about it superficially" (West African public official 1).

Transformative agency in EPA negotiations 47

While the campaign to turn EPAs from a technical trade issue into a development issue did not directly result in a tangible negotiating outcome, it changed the terms of the EPA debate within West Africa and the overall negotiating climate of the ECOWAS-EU EPA. Since there is no consensus on the best economic policy strategy for development, it introduced a level of uncertainty into the policy process that had not been previously present. This benefited Platform organizations because in the situation of uncertainty, information and expertise gained new centrality.

Altering the course of negotiations

Since no final EPA text had been agreed at the time of writing, the extent to which Platform input will feature in a potential ECOWAS-EU agreement remained an open question. The region's refusal to sign an EPA on 31 December 2007 despite the fact that the EU was pushing strongly for the deadline was nonetheless one achievement that the Platform and its allies recorded early in the campaign. As negotiations continue, ECOWAS further defends a number of negotiating positions against the opposition of the EU that rely on the Platform's policy proposals.

As mentioned in the Introduction, it had become obvious in the aftermath of the *EC-Bananas* dispute that the EU's unilateral trade preferences for ACP countries were incompatible with WTO law.[36] Article 37 of the Cotonou Agreement therefore posited: "Economic Partnership Agreements shall be negotiated during the preparatory period which shall end by 31 December 2007 at the latest ... the new trade arrangements shall enter into force by 1 January 2008, unless earlier dates are agreed between the Parties." In order to avoid a series of dispute settlement proceedings at the WTO, the EU negotiated a so-called waiver for the negotiating period in the multilateral system, during which the Lomé arrangement continued to apply. The waiver was set to expire on 31 December 2007.

Platform representatives reported that the European Commission applied political pressure to push ACP governments into signature throughout 2007 (Platform representative 1). Other observers confirmed that the European Commission strongly pursued the deadline across the six EPA regions.[37] When it became clear that most ACP countries would not be ready to sign a deal by the end of 2007, the EU suggested that regions should adhere to interim EPAs which would secure trade-in-goods market access under Article XXIV of the GATT and contain *rendez-vous* clauses[38] to continue negotiations on comprehensive EPAs, including WTO+ provisions on services, intellectual property and the Singapore Issues.[39]

48 *Transformative agency in EPA negotiations*

Article 37.6 of the Cotonou Agreement stipulated that the EU would examine possibilities to maintain favorable EU market access in cases where countries decided that they were "not in a position to enter into economic partnership agreements." Despite the clause, then development commissioner Louis Michel advised ACP ambassadors in October 2007 that "there is no plan B" for EPAs.[40] Due to the expiry of the Cotonou waiver at the WTO, the European Commission announced that all ACP countries that had not signed interim agreements by the 31 December would fall back on the EU's ordinary GSP. It was common understanding that the EU's GSP, and crucially also its EBA initiative for LDCs, were less generous than previous Lomé-based preferential access. Although EBA in principle grants duty-free, quota-free access, many argued that it would have negative impacts on LDC trade flows due to its less advantageous rules of origin provisions. A Platform representative argued in 2011 that these fears had not proven to be justified in retrospect (Platform representative 1).

When ECOWAS ministers demanded in 2006 that the 31 December 2007 deadline should be extended by three years, several NGO reports cited a European Commission letter to West African negotiators in which the Commission explained: "the only tariff regime that will be in place on 1 January 2008 will be the GSP. The exports of the West African non-LDCs to the EU will be seriously affected. More than €1 billion of non-LDC exports to the EU, or 9.5 per cent of their total exports, will be submitted to higher tariffs, and will face direct competition with exports from other developing countries."[41] In a declaration adopted during an ACP Council of Ministers meeting in Brussels on 13 December 2007, ACP ministers "deplore[d] the enormous pressure that has been brought to bear on the ACP States by the European Commission to initial the interim trade arrangements."[42]

In West Africa, interviewees were divided in their assessment of the role that civil society actors played in the region's ability to resist such pressure. Some observers were convinced that without civil society intervention, the agreement would have been signed at the end of 2007 (European civil society representatives 1, West African civil society representative 2, West African journalist). West African public officials rejected this assessment and pointed out that both regional and national administrations had made recommendations not to sign the EPA before the civil society campaign against the deadline had gotten off the ground (West African public officials 4, 9).

My evidence suggests that Platform lobbying and broader public mobilization against the deadline strengthened the position of those public officials in West African institutions who found the deadline premature, against those officials who favored a deal with the EU. This indicates that trade institutions are not unified actors but that internal politics matter for trade policy outcomes. Platform impact was mediated through advocacy-based interaction with trade officials and the mobilization of and participation in broader social resistance over several years. The opposition to the 31 December 2007 negotiating deadline therefore provides one example for a case where the Platform successfully applied what its members called "the insider-outsider approach" to advocacy, which I discuss in detail in Chapter 3.

Contrary to the perceptions of some West African trade officials, Platform organizations started to position themselves on the question of the 31 December 2007 deadline relatively early in the EPA process. At the TWN/General Agricultural Workers' Union (GAWU)-organized national stakeholders' workshop in Ghana in 2004, for example, "a consensus emerged that the timelines are too short for the country to undertake meaningful negotiations, and there is a need to slow the process down, particularly to make informed decisions about the positions that the country should take."[43] In Senegal, ENDA reached similar conclusions in 2005:

> The EPA negotiating and implementation timetables (signing of EPAs in December 2007 and liberalization by 2020) have been determined arbitrarily and are unrealistic, their sole aim being GATT Article 24 conformity. This approach is bad because the timetable of the EPA process must respect the imperatives resulting from the fight against poverty, development, availability of sufficient resources to address production constraints and necessary adjustments, as well as the capacity of the countries and the ACP region to master problems related to institutional reform.[44]

Francophone Platform organizations from Benin, Burkina-Faso, Côte d'Ivoire, Guinea, Mali, Mauritania, Senegal and Togo demanded in the Niamey Declaration in 2006 "a postponement of the EPA signing date ... to favor a real debate on development priorities."[45]

In the two years before the deadline, the signals coming out of ECOWAS on the region's willingness to sign were mixed. In 2006, West African press announced that West African trade ministers had endorsed the 2007 deadline.[46] In February 2007, the news agency Reuters reported that the region's negotiators had confirmed the end-of-year deadline in a joint declaration with the EU.[47] Within one month, however, ECOWAS asked for the extension of the deadline, to no avail.[48] Internal frictions on the feasibility of the deadline within ECOWAS

50 *Transformative agency in EPA negotiations*

became apparent around that time. Platform organizations and certain West African officials started publicly condemning the 31 December 2007 deadline. The TWN Ghana head of programme Tetteh Hormeku and the Nigerian director general of customs Jacob Gyeke Buba, for example, jointly called on the EU to extend the deadline in March 2007.[49]

Nonetheless, Platform members that followed internal ECOWAS proceedings showed themselves as pessimistic on ECOWAS' ability to resist the EU's timetable. Hormeku told Ghana News Agency in May 2007: "From all indications there is that willingness of our government officials and negotiators to follow religiously the timetable of negotiations set out by the EU and we can all but agree that it will culminate in the signing of the agreement."[50] Over the months, the consensus came under increasing stress. In June 2007, the Prime Minister of Burkina-Faso Tertius Zongo declared in a press interview: "going straight to EPAs is not the solution."[51] In July 2007, the head of the international negotiations division at the Senegalese Ministry of Commerce Amadou Ba told Inter Press Service: "I don't know if a winner will emerge from the signing of the Economic Partnership Agreement under the current conditions but I know for sure that Africa cannot be the winner."[52] At the same time, Platform organizations reported from internal ECOWAS meetings that there was divergence among public officials on the question of the deadline.[53] Throughout 2007, public officials and non-state actors started to rally around the idea of rejecting the deadline, as "governments, policy analysts, regional economic groups and civil society organizations are increasingly speaking with one voice: the Economic Partnership Agreements … must be significantly modified to safeguard those countries' prospects for development."[54] In October 2007, West African trade ministers decided at a Ministerial Monitoring Committee meeting in Abidjan that the region would not sign an EPA on 31 December 2007 (Platform representative 1).

My evidence suggests that Platform organizations and their allies played a role in fostering the emerging consensus. In February 2007, for example, the West African peasant movement Réseau des Paysans et des Producteurs Agricoles de l'Afrique de l'Ouest (ROPPA), which had been charged with drafting a list of sensitive agricultural products by the regional trade institutions, announced that it was unable to conclude its assessment in time to meet the deadline.[55] A Senegalese official recalled in a personal interview that in the run up to the EU-sponsored mid-term evaluation of the negotiating process, Platform organizations stressed the necessity to carry out an independent evaluation of the economic impact of EPA. The Platform argued that the EU-funded, joint EU-West Africa evaluation that the European Commission had

Transformative agency in EPA negotiations 51

proposed would not be objective. They expressed concern that an EU-funded impact assessment would be biased on the question of the deadline's feasibility.

The official explained that the Platform's insistence on an independent evaluation led to the freeing of public funds for such an exercise. The subsequent study declared the 31 December 2007 deadline premature. According to the official, transformative organizations had thus mounted the political pressure to convince the state to conduct independent research. On the basis of this research, West African public officials recommended withholding signature to the region's decision-makers (West African public official 4). The West African press shared the assessment that civil society participation changed the dynamics of EPA negotiations when compared to other ACP regions. In November 2007, as ECOWAS and the EU were deadlocked over the West African demand to negotiate a new waiver at the WTO, a West African journalist commented: "The talks with West Africa, which include oil-exporting heavyweight Nigeria and many of the world's poorest countries, are the most difficult of all the EU negotiations, thanks to the pressure civil society groups are exerting on their governments."[56]

Regional and national trade policy processes and street politics were also intermingled at the end of 2007 and the beginning of 2008. On the one hand, Platform members participated in public protests alongside other civil society groups and social movements. At the EU-AU Lisbon summit in December 2007, then Senegalese president Abdoulaye Wade followed the South African and Nigerian examples and announced his intention not to sign an EPA by 31 December 2007.[57] Several marches were subsequently organized in Dakar and Brussels to protest against the EPA process. Some interviewees felt that demonstrations of this magnitude could only be mounted with support from the Senegalese government, which was suspected of having orchestrated the protests (European civil society representative 1, West African journalist).

On the other hand, opposition started to emerge from the cultural realm. In December 2007, the Senegalese artist Didier Awadi launched the song "On ne signe pas" (We won't sign), in which West African artists connect a trade agreement with the EU with poverty and clandestine emigration to Europe. The song accuses the EU of a neo-colonial mindset and compares EPAs to the historical experience of transatlantic slave trade. The accusations were not lost on the negotiating partner. A European official explained in an interview that West African civil society at times "launched forceful attacks" against the EU, and rejected accusations of neo-colonialism as unfounded (European public official 3).

52 *Transformative agency in EPA negotiations*

On the song's website, the EPA is portrayed as "a weapon of mass destruction for African economies."[58] Platform members ENDA, Groupe de Recherche et d'Action pour la Promotion de l'Agriculture et du Développement (GRAPAD), GAWU and Centre du Commerce International pour le Développement (CECIDE), along with partner organizations such as ROPPA and ATN, signed the critical EPA declaration on the website. In my interview, the artist explained that it had been his intention to support West African civil society organizations' struggles against EPA by raising awareness for and resistance to the negotiating process among West African populations with the song. He identified references to slave trade and clandestine migration as a way of raising people's sensitivities. This in turn helped to bring the message across that trade politics concerned everybody (West African singer).

During my interviews, all West African actors agreed that strong civil society opposition, both in political institutions and in the streets, made it politically possible for West African governments to resist European and WTO pressure to sign a trade agreement on 31 December 2007 with their most important trade and development cooperation partner. As one Senegalese trade official put it, "In the nightclubs, people were dancing to 'no to EPA'. It gave us a basis to say at the WTO: 'we would like to [sign EPAs], but it's not possible'" (West African public official 10).

Examples for other fields of influence given during interviews included input on the drafting of the sensitive products list,[59] the ECOWAS common external tariff,[60] the so-called EPA Development Programme[61] and resistance to the inclusion of Singapore Issues,[62] notably competition and investment, on the negotiating agenda. The West African market access offer constituted one of the most compelling examples of direct Platform influence on ECOWAS negotiating positions. In this instance, the Platform used their good access to decision-makers in order to present an alternative interpretation of applicable WTO law which altered the course of negotiations.[63] During EPA negotiations, some Platform members started doubting the EU's insistence that Article XXIV of the GATT, which regulates the establishment of free trade areas and customs unions among WTO members, requires 90 percent average liberalization between EPA parties. The Platform subsequently commissioned a study on the conditions outlined by Article XXIV of the GATT to the international trade law expert El Hadji Diouf, who was at the time in charge of the Regionalism and EPA program at the Geneva-based International Centre for Trade and Sustainable Development.

In a systematic legal analysis, Diouf demonstrated that no standard interpretation of the provision exists among WTO members or in the jurisprudence. Members' practice to the contrary leaves room for flexibility on the level and modalities of market opening. The study particularly validated the point that ECOWAS could open its market at 60 percent, seeing as the EU had already made a 100 percent market access offer.[64] The EU had denied across all EPA regions that anything less than 90 percent average market access between both sides would be compatible with WTO obligations.[65]

Through its good institutional access, the Platform introduced the study into the course of negotiations. The move changed the negotiating dynamics on this topic. A West African public official described the impact with the following words: "Before, it was the EU that asked what the scientific basis [of our position] was, but now it's us" (West African public official 7). After a negotiating round in Abidjan in September 2009, ECOWAS commissioner for industry and trade Mohammed Daramy explained to West African journalists that negotiations were deadlocked over the West African market access offer, which the EU deemed too low and ECOWAS refused to revise. West African press cited Daramy as follows: "Mr. Daramy said ECOWAS could give 'at most' 70 per cent of its market under the terms and in return would demand commitment of the EU to support EPA development programs."[66] The European Commission rejected the demand in all other ACP regions. It accepted it in principle in an ECOWAS-EU negotiating session in May 2010.[67]

In his statement, Daramy added that "West Africa is not negotiating for time—we are concerned with reducing poverty and development of our people." He concluded that ECOWAS was in the "driver's seat" of EPA negotiations and that the region "will negotiate for the next 20 years if that is how long it will take to get our concerns addressed."[68] At the time of writing, ECOWAS has revised its market access offer to 70 percent, but the matter remains a contentious issue in West African EPA talks. While the outcome of negotiations is uncertain, ECOWAS is using its low market access offer as a negotiating chip to reach compromise on other EPA policy goals.

As negotiations continue into 2013, they remain blocked over West Africa's market access offer. Currently, the region is continuing negotiations with the option that a regional EPA would replace the existing EU-Côte d'Ivoire and EU-Ghana agreements, which would in turn facilitate regional integration. The EU envisages negotiating comprehensive EPAs including not only trade in goods but topics such as service trade, trade-related intellectual property and trade-related

54 *Transformative agency in EPA negotiations*

investment matters, competition and public procurement, trade-related aspects of environmental and social policies, and personal data protection, but these topics will not be addressed until a trade-in-goods interim EPA is signed. As EU-West African trade arrangements are in their sixth year of hovering in a legal and political grey zone, the future of the negotiation process is uncertain.

While transformative agency thus had impact on the course of EPA talks, my data also reveals that political tensions between the various actors characterized participatory trade politics in West Africa. A West African journalist specializing in trade issues pointed out during my interview that public officials initially rejected Platform organizations (West African journalist). West African negotiators held that the Platform had been too dogmatic at the beginning of negotiations and had not been making meaningful contributions (West African public officials 1, 7, 8). If West African public officials, like their counterparts in trade institutions across the world, were once skeptical of transformative civil society actors, the question arises of how trade politics evolved in the region to become participatory. If participatory mechanisms reintroduce previously excluded political contestations into the policy process, for example in the form of competing visions of the trade and development linkage, why does participation occur in some trade institutions but remain exclusive in others?

Conclusion

The Platform is a network of West African civil society organizations that grew from regional advocacy on Africa-EU cooperation and was consolidated around mobilization on the Cotonou Agreement in the early 2000s. It adopted a transformative stance on trade issues and notably on EPAs from the early days of its Cotonou campaign. The Platform gradually developed its campaign strategies over time, but by 2006 adopted a variety of techniques geared at both West African trade institutions and the general public. Since then, the Platform featured on the West African negotiating team in EPA talks, with ENDA occupying the role of coordinator. Occasional tension within the network was mediated through its internal proceedings. Regional Dialogues, in which the Platform debated and formulated its view on specific aspects of the agreement, also helped to improve its at times strained relations with West African public officials.

Thanks to their privileged institutional access to decision-makers, Platform organizations, in tandem with broader West African, ACP, and European civil society, altered the course of trade negotiations

Transformative agency in EPA negotiations 55

during a seven-year campaign. On the one hand, they emphasized the necessity to consider the development dimension of EPAs and in doing so challenged the view that the global trade agenda had positive implications to address economic and social hardship in the region in and of itself. Once the EPA was reframed as a trade and development agreement, rather than a pure trade deal, the Platform forged certain ECOWAS negotiating positions directly, notably through devising policy alternatives that according to the EU did not exist.

In the next chapter, I argue that the trade literature is in need of redesigning its methodological tools to theorize participatory trade politics and its potential and real transformations. The way in which most trade scholars today analyze trade policy-making hinders us from recognizing broader societal interests as trade political actors. Real life trade politics unfolds in ways that challenge our currently predominant thinking about trade.[69]

Notes

1 ENDA, *Capacity Building in Support of the Preparation of Economic Partnership Agreement (EPAs)* (Dakar: ENDA, 2002).
2 PASCIB, *Recueil des Documents de Position* (Cotonou: PASCIB, 2007).
3 Platform, *Concertation annuelle de la plate-forme de la société ouest africaine sur l'Accord de Cotonou* (Dakar: ENDA, 2008).
4 Platform, *Concertation annuelle de la plate-forme de la société ouest africaine sur l'Accord de Cotonou*, 7.
5 Bibiane Gahamanyi, *West Africa in the EPA Negotiations with the European Community* (Dakar: ENDA, 2004).
6 Platform, *Rapport du Programme Cotonou 2003* (Dakar: ENDA, 2003).
7 Platform, *Rapport du Programme Cotonou 2003*, 3.
8 Third World Network (TWN) Africa created ATN in 1998. ATN has 25 members from 15 African countries today and holds observer status with the African Union and the UN Economic Commission for Africa. It describes itself as "a long standing network of civil society organizations, working on economic justice. The network covers African social, labor, women, faith-based, developmental, farmers, environmental, human rights, and other organizations working on the role and effects of international trade and trade agreements in relation to Africa's needs and aspirations at national, regional and continental level." ATN 2011, *ATN*, twnafrica.org/index.php?option = com_content& view=category&id=47&Itemid=72.
9 Nancy Kachingwe 2004, *Ghana National Trade Policy and Economic Partnership Agreement*, twnafrica.org/index.php?option=com_content& view=article&id=91:ghana-national-trade-policy-and-economic-partnership-agreements-&catid=41:occasional-papers&Itemid=97.
10 TWN 2004, *STOP EPA Launched at Africa Social Forum*, www.twnafrica.org/index.php?option=com_content&view=article&id=89:stop-epa-launched-at-africa-social-forum& catid=43:press-releases&Itemid=101.

56 *Transformative agency in EPA negotiations*

11 Ken Ukaoha, "Reasons Why Nigeria Could Not Sign the EPA," *Trade Policy Monitor* 1, no. 2 (2008): 5.

12 Ukaoha, "Reasons Why Nigeria Could Not Sign the EPA," 11.

13 Cheikh Tidiane Dièye, "Introduction: Quel futur pour l'intégration et le commerce intra-régional en Afrique de l'Ouest?" in *Le Futur du Commerce Intra-Régional en Afrique de l'Ouest*, ed. Cheikh Tidiane Dièye (Dakar: ENDA, 2010), 14.

14 Jan Aart Scholte, "The WTO and Civil Society," in *Trade Politics*, ed. Brian Hocking and Steven McGuire (London: Routledge, 2004), 146–61.

15 Gahamanyi, *West Africa in the EPA Negotiations with the European Community*, 4.

16 Ken Ukaoha, *The Imperative of Parliamentary Interventions on Trade Policy* (Abuja: NANTS, 2009), 2.

17 Donatella Della Porta and Sidney Tarrow, *Transnational Protest & Global Activism* (Lanham, MD: Rowman & Littlefield, 2005).

18 The official language of Mauritania is Arabic. The other 15 countries have European languages as their official languages, namely: French (Benin, Burkina-Faso, Côte d'Ivoire, Guinea, Mali, Niger, Senegal and Togo); English (The Gambia, Ghana, Liberia, Nigeria and Sierra Leone); and Portuguese (Cape Verde and Guinea-Bissau).

19 During empirical research, Elgström found: "Among DG Trade officials, EPAs were widely seen as 'just another free trade agreement.' They tended to conduct the negotiations as if they were 'a traditional trade negotiation.' ... This framing reflected the organizational culture of this General Directorate. It also mirrored a normative conviction ... DG Trade's approach came, however, as a shock to many ACP representatives, who were used to the more development-friendly and accommodative negotiation mode in DG Development ... DG Trade was perceived as a confrontational negotiator that paid little attention to development concerns while pushing the developing countries to open their markets to EU exports." Ole Elgström, *Trade ... and Aid? EU Policy on Economic Partnership Agreements*, Working Paper 13 (Dublin: UCD Dublin European Institute, 2008).

20 Ole Elgström, "Images of the EU in EPA Negotiations: Angel, Demon—or Just Human?" *European Integration Online Papers-Eiop* 12, no.5 (2008): 1–12.

21 Peter Mandelson 2005, *Statement to the Development Committee of the European Parliament*, ec.europa.eu/commission_barroso/ashton/speeches_a rticles/sppm019_en.html.

22 Dani Rodrik, *The Global Governance of Trade: As if Development Really Mattered* (New York: United Nations Development Programme, 2001); UNDP, *Making Global Trade Work for People* (London: Earthscan, 2003); Joseph Stiglitz and Andrew Charlton, *Fair Trade for All: How Trade Can Promote Development* (Oxford: Oxford University Press, 2005); Clive George, *The Truth about Trade: The Real Impact of Liberalization* (London: Zed Books, 2010).

23 Elgström, *Trade ... and Aid? EU Policy on Economic Partnership Agreements*.

24 TWN 2005, *Six Reasons to Oppose EPAs in their Current Form*, twnafrica.org/index.php?option=com_content&view=article&id=287:six-reasons-to-oppose-e pas-in-their-current-form&catid=34:economic-partnership-agreement&Item id=81.

Transformative agency in EPA negotiations 57

25 TWN, *Six Reasons to Oppose EPAs in their Current Form.*

26 Ken Ukaoha, "EPA as Impediment to Nigeria's Development Strategy," *This Day*, 18 May 2006.

27 TWN 2006, *No EPA Without Investment Rules and Full Reciprocity, Falkenberg Insists!*, www.bilaterals.org/spip.php?article5206.

28 Olivier Monnier, "APE entre l'UE et la CEDEAO: La société civile maintient son opposition," *Le Quotidien*, 15 November 2006.

29 Ukaoha, "EPA as Impediment to Nigeria's Development Strategy."

30 ATN, *Forward with the Struggle to Stop the EPAs: Declaration of the 9th Annual Meeting of the Africa Trade Network* (Accra: ATN, 2006).

31 RODDADH, *Déclaration de Niamey* (Niamey: RODDADH, 2006), 3.

32 Peter Mandelson and Louis Michel, "This is Not a Poker Game," *The Guardian*, 31 October 2007.

33 Elgström, *Trade ... and Aid? EU Policy on Economic Partnership Agreements*, 18.

34 Catherine Ashton 2007, *Economic Partnership Agreements: Remarks to the European Parliament*, ec.europa.eu/commission_barroso/ashton/speeches_articles/spca009_en.htm.

35 Jonathan Adabre, "EU Begins to Soften its Position on EPA Negotiations," *Public Agenda*, 14 August 2006.

36 Appellate Body Report on *European Communities—Regime for the Importation, Sale and Distribution of Bananas*, WT/DS27/AB/R, adopted 9 September 1997.

37 Dot Keet, *Economic Partnership Agreements (EPAs): Responses to the EU Offensive against ACP Developmental Regions* (Amsterdam: Transnational Institute, 2007); Mari Griffith and Sophie Powell, *Partnership under Pressure: an Assessment of the European Commission's Conduct in the EPA negotiations* (Action Aid, CAFOD, Christian Aid, Tearfund and Traidcraft, 2007); Oxfam, *Partnership or Powerplay? How Europe Should Bring Development into its Trade Deals with Africa, Caribbean, and Pacific Countries* (London: Oxfam International, 2008).

38 This implies that while no explicit agreement is reached in the text of an interim EPA on anything but trade in goods, both parties agree to continue negotiating on other items covered under *rendez-vous* clauses, namely trade in services and so-called trade-related topics, with a view to reaching a comprehensive EPA that includes all components.

39 ECOWAS, *Ministerial Monitoring Committee Meeting Conclusions and Recommendations* (Abidjan: ECOWAS, 2007).

40 Debra Percival, "'No Plan B' for Free Trade Accords, says Commissioner Louis Michel," *The Courier*, 20 January 2007.

41 Oxfam, *Breaking the Spirit of Cotonou: A Critique of the EC's Approach to the Economic Partnership Agreement Negotiations with ACP Countries* (London: Oxfam International, 2007), 6; Griffith and Powell, *Partnership under Pressure: an Assessment of the European Commission's Conduct in the EPA Negotiations.*

42 ACP, *Declaration of the ACP Council of Ministers at its 86th Session Expressing Serious Concern on the Status of the Negotiations of the Economic Partnership Agreements* (Brussels: ACP Council of Ministers, 2007), 1.

43 Nancy Kachingwe 2004, *Ghana National Trade Policy and Economic Partnership Agreement*, twnafrica.org/index.php?option=com_content&view=article&id=91:ghana-national-trade-policy-and-economic-partnership-agreements-&catid=41:occasional-papers& Itemid=97.

58 *Transformative agency in EPA negotiations*

44 ENDA, *Revue des APE au niveau national: Contribution des organisations de la société civile* (Dakar: ENDA, 2005), 6.

45 RODDADH, *Déclaration de Niamey*, 3.

46 Suleiman Mustapha, "Pressure Groups to Hold Mass Protest at AU Summit," *The Statesman*, 26 June 2006.

47 Ingrid Melander, "W. Africa Accepts Year-End EU Trade Deal Deadline," *Reuters*, 6 February 2007.

48 David Cronin 2007, *No Postponement of EPA Deadline—EU*, allafrica. com/stories/200710191115.html.

49 "Extend Deadline on Partnership Pact", *Daily Graphic*, 14 March 2007.

50 Ghana News Agency, "EPAs Could be Signed by December," *The Statesman*, 29 May 2007.

51 ROPPA, *Manifeste des organisations de la société civile du Burkina au sujet des négociations des APE* (Ouagadougou: ROPPA, 2007).

52 Hamadou Sy 2007, *Africa Will Not be the Winner of the EPAs*, mg.co.za/ article/2007-07-18-africa-will-not-be-the-winner-of-epas.

53 H.A. Djiwan, "Bénin: la société civile se mobilise à Cotonou," *Fraternité*, 30 July 2007.

54 Gumisai Mutume, "Africans Fear 'Ruin' in Europe Trade Talks. Opposition Grows to More Inequitable Trade Liberalization," *African Renewal*, July 2007.

55 Panapress, "Le ROPPA rejette de calendrier des négociations sur les APE," *Panapress*, 4 February 2007.

56 Amos Safo, "EU Trade Negotiations Heading for a Stalemate," *Public Agenda*, 23 November 2007.

57 Afrol News 2007, *Senegal Opposes EPA*, www.afrol.com/articles/27433.

58 Awadi featuring Kirikou 2008, *On ne signe pas*, awadimusic.com.

59 Since ACP countries are not expected to provide 100 percent market access for EU products, the region can exclude sensitive products from liberalization. To the extent that the sensitive products lists lock West African countries into a specific production and exchange pattern with the EU, they raise further doubts about the claim that EPA will help the region to develop.

60 Because ECOWAS intends to consolidate its customs union before finalizing the EPA with the EU, its common external tariff is a key component of negotiations. Otherwise, an EPA would block regional integration because a unified trade regime with the outside world is one constitutive element of a customs union (Platform representative 1).

61 Under the EPA Development Programme, ECOWAS asks the EU to commit to €9.5 billion in additional aid, in order to cushion EPA-related adjustment shocks. Although initially not in favor of the Development Programme, the Platform has since suggested that West African tariff liberalization steps should be tied to aid delivery, which has become an official ECOWAS negotiating position (Platform representative 1).

62 According to the WTO Dictionary of Trade Policy Terms, the Singapore Issues are "so named because they entered the WTO work program through the declaration issued by the Singapore Ministerial Conference. The issues are trade and investment, trade and competition, transparency in government procurement and trade facilitation." Walther Goode, *Dictionary of Trade Policy Terms* (Cambridge: Cambridge University Press, 2007).

63 See Silke Trommer, "Legal Opportunity in Trade Negotiations: International Law, Opportunity Structures and the Political Economy of Trade

Transformative agency in EPA negotiations 59

Agreements," *New Political Economy*, DOI: 10.1080/13563467.2012.753520 (2013).

64 El Hadji Diouf, *Article XXIV of GATT and the EPA: Legal Arguments to Support West Africa's Market Access Offer* (Dakar: ENDA, 2009).

65 Oxfam, *Breaking the Spirit of Cotonou: A Critique of the EC's Approach to the Economic Partnership Agreement Negotiations with ACP Countries.*

66 Peace FM 2009, *EPA Negotiations in Limbo*, news.peacefmonline.com/news/200909/27912.php.

67 ECDPM, "The West Africa EPA Development Programme: Between Conservatism and Innovation," *Trade Negotiations Insights* 9, no. 5 (2010): 1–4.

68 Peace FM, *EPA Negotiations in Limbo.*

69 For a similar conclusion, although on different premises, see William Ethier, "The Theory of Trade Policy and Trade Agreements: A Critique," *European Journal of Political Economy* 23, no. 3 (2007): 605–23.

2 Beyond trade economism

- **Three dimensions of trade economism**
- **A history of trade policy formation theory**
- **Conclusion**

The literature has produced analytical tools for studying transnational trade advocacy, for explaining why civil society groups, and particularly trade critics, fail to influence trade institutions, and for arguing in favor of or against the lack of voice. West African participatory trade politics, however, draws attention to the fact that no coherent analytical framework is at our disposal for explaining why civil society advocacy on trade succeeds. Scrutinizing dominant trade policy formation theories' inability to capture West African participatory trade politics is an important intermediary step in my overall argument, because the exercise illustrates the roots of our difficulties in resolving the efficiency/legitimacy deadlock in trade debates. It feeds into my argument that overcoming the deadlock requires reconsidering the way in which we theoretically frame questions of who makes trade policy decisions, through which mechanisms, and why trade policy-making practices change, or resist change.

In this chapter, I argue that variable, logical, and historical dimensions of economism affect existing frameworks for conceptualizing the processes through which trade policy decisions are made. As a result, theory cannot include non-state, non-corporate groups, never mind transformative actors that oppose the global trade agenda in the pictures that it draws of trade political mechanisms. Economistic trade policy formation theories are unsuitable for explaining the attitudinal change from a situation where trade officials were skeptical towards civil society actors to a situation where both sides discussed and defended a common trade policy line in negotiations with the EU.

Meanwhile, economistic foundations distort broader political economy and global governance debates by supporting the normative claim that

Beyond trade economism 61

the trade political sphere should remain free from broader societal demands against it in order for trade policy outcomes to be efficient. They obscure the fact that the intellectual supremacy of this argument was constructed on the deliberate, and contested, methodological choice first made by Frank William Taussig[1] at the end of the nineteenth century to focus exclusively on industries in order to determine the effects of trade measures on society. The narrow focus on this specific type of social and economic agent was necessary to resolve the longstanding free trade vs. protectionism controversy in political economy in favor of free trade. Trade economism thus not only rests on a tautology, but hampers our capacity to reflect on responses to current trade governance challenges that lie outside of the status quo.

Three dimensions of trade economism

Commenting on the existing challenges in political economy studies of trade, Helen Milner urges us to recognize that "a better understanding of how political leaders form their trade preferences and how these preferences are connected to societal ones is essential."[2] The variable, logical, and historical dimensions of trade economism inherent in currently dominant theoretical approaches to trade policy formation present obstacles to such a rounded understanding of trade policy choices. Trade economism also prevents scholars from conceptualizing transformative agency in trade politics.

Variable trade economism

Variable economism is based on "the overestimation of the political influence of economic variables, which are taken to be exogenous and hence independent of political variables and ... the underestimation of the influence of political variables in the determination of political outcomes or effects."[3] Most trade policy formation theories contain a specific reading of the economic, which includes the idea that welfare and rationality hinge on utility maximization, defined as rising capital endowment or access to goods and services. In her review of the political economy literature on trade, Milner summarizes the chief explanatory factor for policy preferences across the literature in the following way: "groups seek protection or liberalization because such policies increase their income."[4]

Under this view, non-state actors that are not directly participating in global markets are typically conceptualized as consumers. This can explain why transformative organizations lack direct impact on trade

62 *Beyond trade economism*

policy. The absence of immediate significant economic pay-off causes consumers difficulties in adopting effective long-term strategies on trade policy. Since material gains and losses from trade mainly affect importing and exporting interests as trade barriers vary, it is argued that corporate agents' monopoly of political influence over trade policy-making follows from the nature of the policy field.[5] Why groups that represent broader societal interests appear in trade politics in the first place, and why they challenge the political monopoly of corporate groups, is left unquestioned. Why an actor like the Platform pursues certain specific policy goals rather than others also cannot be explained. The narrow understanding of welfare implies that analytical frameworks discard social and environmental dimensions of individual and communal life experience, as well as the impact of trade rules on these categories, from the outset.

The assumption that rational self-interest strives for maximizing material possession supports the narrow notion of welfare. Benjamin Cohen explains: "for anyone trained in neoclassical orthodoxy, utility is instinctively defined simply in terms of real economic welfare—a term synonymous with the amount of goods and services available for final use."[6] The definition works "to the exclusion of all other possible values or goals. While consumers seek to maximize their consumption, producers seek to maximize their net income in order to gain the greatest possible command over goods and services ... The sole interest of the state is or should be to gain the greatest possible income for society. All else, in the eyes of the economist, is irrational."[7]

Due to these assumptions, variable trade economism disqualifies less easily quantifiable forms of rationality or motivations for human behavior, such as the pursuit of Milner's "societal interests," from the realm of trade policy. By definition, transformative groups cannot be adequately factored into economistic theories because their motivations and political demands either escape or contradict the normative preferences of theory's conceptual foundations. As I show in Part II, however, Platform organizations pointed to the interconnected nature of economic, social, and political organization and underlined solidarity and responsibility as important mechanisms for integrating society across time and space. Under the narrow lens of current trade policy formation theories, such demands appear irrational, although theory leaves obscure why it may be irrational to fight poverty, social injustice or environmental degradation.

Interestingly, trade policy formation theories limp behind the discipline of economics on this point. Within economic theory, debates on welfare and motivations for human behavior are a lot more complex

Beyond trade economism 63

than Cohen's dichotomy proclaims.[8] Attempts to come to terms with the limits of individualistic and utilitarian notions in economics have, however, not caught on in trade policy formation theory. This supports my argument that the connections between neoclassical trade economics and political economy studies of trade are predominantly methodological. As becomes apparent below, they consist of a number of assumptions and models that economics imperialism transported into political economy in the 1970s.

International Relations scholars of course recognize that trade political actors pursue other goals than pure utility maximization. However, even in the IR literature, ambitions to maximize welfare in the narrow sense are typically assumed to monopolize the core of the trading activity. It is only in a second step that trade interests may or may not interact with other policy goals and political mechanisms. Realists differentiate between the pursuit of political influence—power—and the pursuit of material gain—wealth. They conceptualize trade as a means towards wealth, but one that interacts with the pursuit of power.[9] Referring to political stability, domestic distribution or even cultural autonomy as goals that states may pursue, regime theorists introduce the role of ideas and causal beliefs into the study of trade policy.[10] They analyze how governments create governance systems to reconcile potential gains and losses from trade under what John Ruggie calls "embedded liberalism."[11] Institutionalists study policy-making processes in order to understand how formal structures and procedures of government impact on interactions between trade political actors.[12]

As Trentmann argues, while this "goes beyond rational choice, it continues to separate ideas from interests" and therefore neglects the fact that "interests are not pre-social but are embedded in society and culture."[13] The point is crucial since it signals that there can be limits to actors' self-reflectivity on their trade political interests. This is not to say that individuals err in what they think motivates them in becoming politically active. It does mean, however, that there can be limits to actors' awareness of the social and cultural short- and long-term processes that shape their understanding of a given trade policy context and of their own role within this context. As I argue in Part II, competing normative preferences for trade policy-making result in part from variations in individual and social understandings of political realities and events, both in the present and the past. Theoretical frameworks that sideline social and historical dimensions therefore by definition miss important underlying dynamics of long-term trade political processes.

Under variable economism, trade policy formation theories further underestimate the fact that no interest exists as an "unambiguous,

64   *Beyond trade economism*

separate group, but an interest in conflict with and part of other social roles."[14] Just as much as "everyone and at the same time no one is a 'consumer',"[15] producers, trade unionists, and state actors also fulfill other social roles. The politics of trade for which transformative actors strive specifically unfold in the interplay between social agents' multiple, conflicting identities and interests, which expand well beyond rational self-maximizing concerns. Taking multiple identities into account, it is unclear why trade officials should have static attitudes towards transformative actors and could not come to perceive societal concerns as legitimate claims in trade policy.

Logical trade economism

Logical economism refers to "the reduction of the practical analytical framework of political action to the framework of economic action."[16] Economics imperialism in trade policy formation theory is one expression of logical economism. The term "economics imperialism" denotes the tendency of neoclassical economics to export its methodology and fundamental assumptions rooted in deduction and abstract reasoning to the other social sciences.[17] Under logical trade economism, trade policy formation scholars use abstract modeling for analyzing international and domestic trade policy formation processes.

In his book *Commerce and Coalitions*, Ronald Rogowski develops a trade political model based on the Stolper-Samuelson theorem to show how trade policy preferences form in domestic politics.[18] He relies on three factors of production, namely capital, land, and labor, and assumes that they exist at varying levels of abundance in different countries. Depending on a country's factor endowments, Rogowski predicts that exposure to trade encourages either class conflict or urban-rural conflict in a given society.[19] The causal connection between factor endowment and trade policy preference is expected to be direct and automatic. "If all factors were (temporarily) abundant relative to the rest of the world," Rogowski explains, "the society would unanimously embrace free trade; if all were scarce, it would agree on protection."[20] Non-economic societal values and concerns are presumed to have no impact on trade policy choices. The model is also unable to take complex internal socio-political structures into consideration, as have arisen in West Africa since colonization. I return to both points in Chapter 5.

Under logical trade economism, the invisible hand of the neoclassical market mechanism appears to guide trade policy-making. Scholars routinely refer to actors and institutions of trade policy as the supply side and the demand side of trade politics. Policy decisions are

Beyond trade economism 65

conceptualized as a political equilibrium. Policy outcomes are judged in terms of gains or benefits and losses. As a consequence, trade policy formation theories understand trade measures as commodities that trade political actors swap and exchange on the marketplace of trade political forums.[21]

Logical trade economism therefore reproduces the fragmented view on society that variable trade economism provokes. Applying deductive methods and abstract reasoning not only relies on utility maximization as the basis of welfare and rationality, but also reinforces the seeming accurateness of the notions. Despite historical evidence to the contrary, the theoretical expectation arises that trade political concepts are not subject to variations in meaning and that the same forces, namely competing ambitions to maximize capital endowment and consumption levels, guide trade policy process everywhere in accordance to a given set of universally valid rules.

As a result, all political action that cannot be subsumed under the neoclassical framework cannot be appreciated in theory. Trentmann explains that this reduces trade policy-making "to an individualist act of assessing the sectoral costs and benefits of trade policy," which "brackets the collective dimension of politics" such as "party allegiance, mobilization, social solidarity, and discursive practices."[22] The denial of collective dimensions encourages the view that regulatory activity in the field of trade is an apolitical, neutral, and scientific matter. On this point, trade policy formation theories are dramatically out of touch with trade political practice. As I highlight in Part II, the history of the global trading system instead suggests that trade policy-making has never been apolitical or neutral. One would equally be hard pushed to find a trade official who would think of trade negotiations as an apolitical process.

Although not all transformative actors are necessarily opposed to market economy or global economic integration, their concerns arise from the consequences of the global market economy that they deem to be unjust and unsustainable. Such variation in appreciation of economic and political terms cannot be reflected in models that construe politics itself as a neoclassical market mechanism. The methodological choice implies that trade scholarship under logical trade economism deprives itself of the opportunity theoretically to ask political questions that transcend utility maximizing efforts within the global trade agenda. This point is crucial, since the question of global trade's purpose and effects on the world is one of the core questions with which critics of the global trade agenda approach global trade politics. Trade scholars struggle to understand this point, as evidenced by the

66 *Beyond trade economism*

complaint that critics of the global trade agenda do not represent a united force in trade politics. If scholars adopt a methodological approach that prevents asking the question of the purpose and effects of trade policy-making in society theoretically, they are bound to be blind to real and potential transformations in global trade politics.

Historical trade economism

Historical economism is not primarily a theory of knowledge but "a social syndrome ... involving a double limiting of state practice and international political theory in the joint reproduction of an econo-mistic social order."[23] According to Ashley, historical economism is the result of a gradual historical development and typical amongst advanced capitalist states. Historical economism occurs when "the modern capitalist state has assumed the task of sustaining the accu-mulation process, that social practices have become habituated to this expectation, and ... with time, the state has come to find a primary justification in its performance of this task."[24] Perceptions of increasing scarcity, Ashley argues, accelerate and deepen the process. Ultimately, historical economism:

> asserts the state's own determinate economic interests—as one more participant depending upon economic success—in the deter-minate matrix of international economic relations. As a result, interstate practice is increasingly tightly and visibly coupled to the immediate, quasi-physical collisions and interactions of globally determinate economic interests. The tighter the coupling, the more the state becomes a technical rational actor finding its legitima-tions within the logics of economy, and the less the modern state system possesses the independent capacity to adapt creatively in response to crisis.[25]

As a correlation with this phenomenon, social theorists "naturalize and universalize the given order, regarding it as an unsurpassed condition of necessity."[26] During this process, variable and logical economism not only come to appear as the sole theoretical approach to economic policy, but the political is denaturalized and the term politics acquires a multitude of specific meanings. At the same time, theory's own nor-mativity makes it incapable of reflecting on anything that lies outside of its own preferences for social and political organization. Through this mechanism, theory takes on the political role of justifying resistance to transformations in the existing order.

Beyond trade economism 67

Building on variable and logical trade economisms, theorists under historical trade economism do not understand politics as an ordinary social phenomenon of competing normative preferences for society. Instead, the fact that differing normative claims compete in trade politics appears as an abnormality or as a disturbance. "Rarely in the economics profession do we encounter greater dissonance between what we are taught in principle and what we observe in practice [than in international trade]," Cohen writes, "and try as we might to find logical reasons for all this in the tenets of our own discipline, ultimately we are tempted simply to throw up our hands and proclaim: 'It's all politics!'"[27] What sources of political power and popular movement exist in trade policy-making other than the desire to maximize capital endowment and access to goods and services, however, remains unquestioned.

Under the fragmented view of reality, transformative claims against trade policy appear as puzzling. David Robertson notes that transformative actors "seek access to WTO meetings to redress 'labor conditions, development problems, environmental damage, consumer protection and gender irregularities'—none of which is WTO's business."[28] However, the perceptions of increasing negative impacts of trade policy choices on these areas, coupled with a corporate monopoly over trade policy-making, are precisely the reason why transformative groups approach trade institutions.[29] Economistic theories cannot appreciate such historical transformations in the politics of trade, because they cannot allow for variations in the way in which trade rules interact with broader social and political organization. Economistic trade policy formation theories therefore implicitly assume what Polanyi calls "a mystical readiness to accept the social consequences of economic improvement, whatever they may be."[30] In other words, under historical trade economism, we are prone to underestimating social reactions to the far-reaching economic and political consequences of the expansion of the trade agenda in real life.

The problem arises because historical trade economism tends to conflate ontological and normative dimensions of the trade political debate. The assumption that trade policy *is* about maximizing (narrowly construed) welfare that *does* take place in an isolated economic sphere encourages scholars to analyze trade policy-making as if it were a neoclassical market mechanism, thus creating a false ontology. The assumption leads scholars to argue that this is how it *should be* if trade policy is to be effective, thus creating a normativity that is represented as a technical reality and implies that the view of trade politics as special politics cannot be reversed. In the next section, I trace

68 *Beyond trade economism*

the historical origins of our current thinking about trade in order to strengthen my overall argument that our economistic foundations can and should be corrected.

A history of trade policy formation theory

Trade has been a central subject of inquiry for political economy since the discipline's origin. During its historical trajectory, trade scholarship partakes in and replicates epistemological, conceptual and methodological shifts that are ongoing within the history of ideas. Methodological controversy marks trade theoretical debates within the discipline for close to two centuries. In the 1970s and 1980s, current theories, including their assumptions and methods, come to dominate trade scholarship. Trade policy formation theories thus depend on historical and social contexts.

The classical school

Since the classics, the question of whether free trade or protectionism is favorable bugs trade theory. In the nineteenth century, trade scholars focus their analysis on governmental levying of customs tariffs on internationally traded goods. Trade theory is a relatively heterogeneous field, both in terms of analytical methods and in terms of its verdict on the object and purpose of trade policy. Trade scholarship mirrors broader attempts in classical political economy to examine the nature and causes of wealth, and its distribution across society. Early thinkers such as Adam Smith, John Stuart Mill, Thomas Malthus, or Karl Marx understand political economy as a unified social science that inquires into the economy as part of a broader social context and that incorporates elements that are today placed in other analytical realms, such as sociology, history, or psychology. The classics use a mix of deductive and inductive method and incorporate historical elements in their analysis of economic relations which they conceptualize as being inseparable from other social relations.[31]

In terms of methods of analysis, trade scholars at the end of the nineteenth century differ widely in their approaches. Some theoretical tools resemble current trade policy theories, including domestic and foreign policy perspectives inherent in IR and institutionalist approaches. Frederick Clow, for example, discusses the relationship between trade policy choices and geopolitical considerations.[32] Other writers apply less familiar methods. Taussig delves into an analysis of agricultural traditions and growing methods in order to reach policy

Beyond trade economism 69

recommendations for the various products under his scrutiny.[33] Analyzing the tariff levels of the Australian territories of New South Wales and Victoria, Perry Powers relies on a broad variety of social and economic indicators, including population numbers, infrastructure, savings rates, labor conditions, purchasing power, industrial capacities across economic sectors, trade flow statistics, and mortgage rates, in order to evaluate the benefits of trade policy choices.[34]

Irrespective of the methods that trade scholars apply, the general aim of their inquiry is to establish whether free trade or protectionist policies are more advantageous for society. In doing so, they observe the key role that political actors play in tariff setting. In a discussion of US trade policy, William Hill notes that "an explanation of the causes of American tariffs which leaves the politicians out of consideration is no explanation," and accords high tariff levels to demands for protectionism from "farmers, merchants and laborers, as well as from manufacturers."[35]

On the whole, the literature does not analyze questions of trade policy formation separately from the broader social outcomes of trade policy choices. Rather, scholars expect trade policy-making processes to have profound political and social implications. In addition, the belief that "there is other wealth that transcends economic wealth" underlies trade debates.[36] Scholars see tariffs primarily as a source of public revenue and they perceive struggles over appropriate trade policy measures as being intermingled with other social and political struggles.[37] Émile Levasseur cites nineteenth-century French merchants "declaring that 'prohibition is a matter of political and social right'."[38] Trade analysts further comment on distributional aspects of trade policy: "From the standpoint of production commerce has certainly made material civilization possible," Lindley Keasbey writes in 1898, "but from the point of view of distribution it has undoubtedly accentuated the inequality of wealth."[39]

In general, trade theory remains embedded in an analysis of the specific historical circumstances in which trade policy formation takes place. Socialist analysts, for example, see the prevalent free trade vs. protectionism debate as clearly connected to capitalist social organization. "If the proletariat becomes victorious," Karl Kautsky declares, "it will establish social institutions under which the question of free trade versus protection will not appear any more, or at any rate, will not appear any more in its present form."[40]

Around the turn of the century, the unresolved nature of the free trade vs. protectionism debate starts to causes frustration. While some scholars follow Alexander Hamilton and Friedrich List in favoring

70 *Beyond trade economism*

protectionism,[41] others advocate free trade on the basis of the theories of Ricardo and Mill.[42] At the beginning of the twentieth century, Taussig rejects the use of historical and statistical evidence for reaching a verdict on the free trade vs. protectionism controversy. "After all," he writes, "that account tells us chiefly of the externals of the movements, – how it came about that one policy or other was followed by England or Germany or the United States ... But it throws little light on the heart of the problem, – what were the results of the policy adopted."[43] Subsequently, a number of scholars turn to analyzing the effect of adopted tariff levels on domestic economic indicators such as wage and price. On the basis of the change in analytical perspective—from the policy-making process to the repercussions of the adopted policies on specific economic indicators—they begin to recommend free trade.[44]

The argument leaves many trade scholars and practitioners of the era unimpressed. Following the Great Depression of the late nineteenth century, industries continue to push for protectionism.[45] Scholars present classical analyses of trade measures.[46] Taussig's attack on classical methods is, however, part of a profound transformation in the history of economic thought.

The marginalist revolution

In the 1880s, the famous *Methodenstreit* opposes the marginalist Carl Menger and the leader of the German Historical School Gustav Schmoller, in a controversy over the relative merits of induction and deduction as scientific method. The *Methodenstreit* starts a long theoretical debate through which consecutive but interrelated methodological shifts establish economics as an independent field of inquiry. The relevance of the social for studying the material is one important bone of contention in the debate. For Schmoller, "the common element which relates each economic individual or nation is not only the state, but is something deeper: the common language, history, memories, morals, and ideas."[47] Scientific inquiry into the economy therefore demands historical and social observation.

Marginalism, on the other hand, combines Ricardo's deductive method with Benthamite utilitarianism. Marginalists sacrifice the labor theory of value for the sake of a value theory based on utility maximization at the margin. With this shift, the individual becomes the basic unit of analysis and utility its main motivation for behavior, despite the fact that the new methodology sidelines the role of ideas and values as triggers for human behavior. Methodological individualism, according to which the whole can be explained by the sum of its parts, further encourages formalism and the eventual shift to a science of choice under conditions of scarcity. As Dimitris Milonakis and Ben Fine explain, "the concept of marginal utility ... gave great impetus to the mathematization of economics ... second, it gave a rationale for narrowing the scope of economic investigation to the study of the problem of allocation under scarcity and the determination of prices, by focusing on market relations treated in isolation from their social and historical context."[48]

Driven by frustrations about the unresolved nature of the free trade vs. protectionism controversy, Taussig presents one of the first attempts to demonstrate the effects of tariff legislation in the United States from 1830 to 1860 on the economic conditions prevalent within the country, rather than using these conditions as explanatory factors for given tariff levels.[49] Reviewing Edward Stanwood's (1903) *American Tariff Controversies in the Nineteenth Century*, Taussig comments:

> in the main the volumes are confined to the legislative history of tariff bills and acts: to the votes and manoeuvres in Congress, the connection with the general political situation, the intrigues and combinations that affected the various measures, and the parts played by the presidents, secretaries, chairmen of committees and other political leaders in shaping and enacting them ... the economic history of the country, and that of the particular industries most affected by the tariff, receive scant attention.[50]

With a pronounced ambition to resolve the free trade vs. protectionism controversy, Taussig advocates a change in analytical perspective. He declares: "Clearly these [the economic history of the country and of the particular industries] are subjects much more important than legislative and political detail for reaching an opinion on the merits of the [free trade vs. protectionism] controversy."[51] He therefore recommends using the economic situation of a country's industries as indicator for the impacts of trade politics on society. As I argued above, the assumption that narrowly construed economic operators are the appropriate proxy for evaluating the impacts of trade policy choices on society at large continues to inform trade policy formation theories today.

Others follow Taussig to evaluate the effect of tariff on production.[52] Commenting on Francis Bastable's (1887) *Theory of International Trade*, John Clark describes how the new perspective impacts on political discourses about trade. "The preliminary demonstration of the gain that is inherent in international trade," he notes, "enables the reader to approach the study of protective tariffs from a direction opposite to that from which, in popular discussion, an American is

72 *Beyond trade economism*

usually invited to approach it."[53] At the same time, the "preliminary demonstration" is based on a new methodology that "proceeds from assumed conditions so simplified as to resemble the facts of life only at a single point, and gradually introduces complicating elements until the essential conditions of actual trade are included in calculations."[54]

Inspired by the methodological evolutions in political economy, marginalist trade scholars adopt the assumption that utility is the sole basis of the theory of value. The new focus on individual utility permits abstract modeling. In the United States, the systematic recording of trade flows and returns by the US Bureau of Statistics since the late nineteenth century further facilitates the application of deductive methods.[55] In trade theory, they are subsequently used to prove the overall positive impact of free trade. William Jevons declares that the benefits from free trade "are to be believed because deductive reasoning from premises of almost certain truths leads us confidently to expect such results."[56] Clark adds that the conceptual and methodological adjustment results in "a new illustration of the faultlessness of the logic of free trade as a permanent international policy."[57] Bastable shows that international trade facilitates "a gain in utilities and a saving of sacrifices; the parties get more and work less by reason of the transactions between them."[58] This reasoning confirms scholars in their decision to exclude questions of the distribution of the gains from trade from their analysis. While questions of growth and distribution fade into the background under the marginalist revolution, the methodological adjustment exacerbates the distance between trade theory and trade politics. It also cements the fusion between the assumption that trade impacts on economic operators only and deductive methodology relying on abstract modeling, which causes problems for theorizing transformations in trade politics today.

At the turn of the century, the new-found insights encourage frustrations with the politics of trade among scholars and practitioners, thus foreshadowing today's problematic relationship between theory and real life trade politics. John Cummings argues that the setting of tariffs "can be undertaken in accordance with some underlying principle, rather than with a view single to satisfying local or special interests." In his opinion, this would contribute to "opening the way in the future to a scientific handling of our tariff schedules."[59] Others recommend "tak[ing] the question of tariffs out of politics and put[ting] it on a business basis," which they expect to guarantee the neutrality and fairness of the policy-making process.[60] The ambition also relates to broader attempts to turn the social sciences into a pure science. Rivalries among academic disciplines strengthen marginalism against more traditional

Beyond trade economism 73

approaches in political economy. According to Joseph Schumpeter, efforts to ground economic analysis in philosophy, psychology and sociology are responsible for endless quarrels within the discipline, which he perceives as being inferior to the "exact sciences."[61]

Ambitions to mirror the exact sciences distance economic analysis further from moral inquiry and ethics. As Léon Walras holds, "the distinguishing feature of pure science ... is the complete indifference to consequences, good or bad, with which it carries on the pursuit of truth."[62] Following the rise of marginalism, normative evaluations split from allegedly scientific, value-neutral analysis.[63] Analysts sacrifice questions of what "ought to be" for predictions of "what will happen if we do certain things."[64] If scholars initially neglected trade policy-making processes in order to overcome the free trade vs. protectionism controversy, the emerging conclusions encourage their growing hostility towards the political struggles that continue to dominate real life trade politics. From the marginalist perspective, the politics of trade policy formation begins to appear as a disturbing factor in the application of the theoretical insights derived from deductive reasoning.

As in general political economy, the initial popularity of the new school in trade theory is short-lived. During World War I and in the interwar period, protectionism is the dominant trade policy choice both in theory and practice.[65] Commenting on the legislative process preceding the US 1922 Tariff Act, Arthur Cole finds "in the place of order, confusion; in the place of seclusion ... the hubbub and constant interruptions of visiting delegations ... urging preferential treatment of this, that, and the other item ... Neither in committee nor upon the floor of the Senate was much consideration given to a scientific revision of the tariff."[66] Among trade theorists, the utilitarian value theory causes controversy. Allyn Young refers to the "method of representing utility as a general function of varying combinations of commodities" as having "great attractions to the mathematician; but it seems less adapted to express the everyday facts of economic life."[67] Milonakis and Fine highlight that marginalist economics fail to expel those committed to historical and social methods from the realm of political economy from the 1870s until the 1950s. Similarly, trade scholars continue to analyze trade policy-making using the methods of the classical school.[68]

Meanwhile, marginalist scholars continue to refine their models in order to advocate free trade. They replace simplifying assumptions in Ricardian trade theory with real life complexities.[69] Enrico Barone introduces Alfred Marshall's twin concept of consumer and producer surplus to demonstrate the losses from protection.[70] Previously

74   *Beyond trade economism*

neglected questions such as domestic distribution of the gains from trade return to the research agenda.[71] As basic numerical models prove unsatisfactory, abstract mathematics is introduced into trade analysis.[72] The rise of econometrics, that is to say the reliance on mathematical and statistical models for theoretical purpose originating in the 1930s,[73] supports these efforts. However, at the end of World War II, free trade is marginalized in trade circles. In a review of Margaret Gordon's (1941) *Barriers to World Trade: A Study of Recent Commercial Policy*, Percy Bidwell writes: "The idea of free trade, i.e., of the exchange of goods between countries unrestricted except by revenue duties, has gone to the limbo where hover the shades of laissez faire and rugged individualism."[74]

Instead, scholars of the 1940s and 1950s highlight the need for international policy cooperation in the field of trade.[75] They explain that the charter of the proposed International Trade Organization "provides not so much a set of rules for world trade as a forum in which world trade practices can be discussed."[76] In contradiction with the prominent discourse around the historical origins of the WTO today, Jacob Viner comments in *Foreign Affairs* during GATT negotiations: "there are few free-traders in the present day world, no one pays any attention to their views and no person in authority anywhere advocates free trade."[77]

The economics of trade politics

Spurred by the US government's ambition of expanding trade volumes, the GATT is signed in Geneva in 1947.[78] It becomes the first international multilateral forum for trade decision-making in history. During the 1950s, scholars pay little attention to questions of trade policy formation. As the Cold War unfolds, the political economy research agenda turns to newly arising questions such as centrally planned economies and economic development. As neoclassical economics develops out of marginalism, its underlying assumptions encourage reliance on methodological formalism even if theoretic representations typically have little in common with real life economics.[79] Following the decoupling of economic analysis from its social and historical context, universal rules for an economy that is thought to have individual utility at its core can be theoretically constructed. Through the process of desocialization and dehistoricization, the categorization into alleged economic and non-economic inquiry establishes boundaries between the social sciences and completes the transformation from classical political economy to economics.[80]

Beyond trade economism 75

During the 1960s and 1970s, the economic theory of politics develops as one expression of economics imperialism. Based on the work of authors such as James Buchanan, Mancur Olson and Gordon Tullock, it builds the methodological and conceptual foundations of economistic trade policy formation theories by treating trade politics as a marketplace construed in isolation from other fields of political and social life. In one of the early contributions of the economics of trade politics, Richard Caves explains: "economists have expanded their interest in public policy from purely normative prescriptions to models explaining the decisions reached by democratically elective governments, bureaucracies, and public corporations."[81] In 1971, George Stigler puts forward a demand and supply theory of economic policy-making.[82]

Economistic trade policy formation theories first develop within the discipline of economics in the 1970s, but subsequently branch out into the discipline of political science. In 1976, Caves presents three models of the process of political choice to explain tariff variations on Canadian manufactured products. To explain trade political outcomes, he relies on the economic costs and benefits of political organization.[83] Drawing on Olson, William Brock and Stephen Magee establish "The Economics of Special Interest Politics." They hypothesize that corporate actors invest in advocacy in order to maximize their net economic returns. Politicians "weigh the favorable effects of special interest money against the unfavorable association with the lobby and the social cost of the redistributive policy."[84] Robert Baldwin analyses how particular characteristics of industries affect patterns of protection.[85] Arye Hillman and Wolfgang Mayer devise economistic models of domestic tariff preference formation.[86] Howard Marvel and Edward Ray and Daniel Trefler show how specific characteristics make industries more likely to seek protection and to pressure governments to provide it.[87] Kent Jones, James Cassing and Arye Hillman, and Dani Rodrik analyze the choice of different trade policy measures on the basis of the economic theory of trade policy.[88] Hillman argues that decision-makers chose protection levels to maximize political support.[89] During the 1980s, political scientists start to analyze trade policy formation processes based on the new theory.[90]

With the launch of the Uruguay Round in the mid-1980s, real life trade politics, however, transcends the scope of tariff levying on goods to include services, investment rules, intellectual property rights and other fields. It is commonly recognized that the Uruguay Round reforms of the trading system encourage transformative actors to enter the trade policy stage in the mid-1980s. They introduce resistance to economistic perspectives on trade to the realm of real life trade politics at the historical

76 *Beyond trade economism*

moment when the economistic view comes to dominate academic thinking about trade politics. Despite important changes in the dynamics of global trade politics since the advent of the WTO, most of trade theory has not revisited its underlying (economistic) assumptions about trade.

Neoclassical trade economics are not adaptable to the new kinds of trade reform.[91] The issues escape the Ricardian rationale underlying the traditional free trade argument. This has several repercussions for trade theory. First, trade policy recommendations relying on neoclassical assumptions become ever less convincing. Second, in as far as the economistic view on trade has historically evolved with the pronounced intention to advance free trade on the basis of neoclassical theory, the inapplicability of this theory to the new trade politics makes questions about the appropriateness of current trade policy formation theories ever more pressing. Third, as trade policy expands and threatens broader societal interests ever more visibly, real life trade politics becomes more confrontational.

The current trade political debate is deadlocked in a state where many demands for the democratization of trade politics operate on the basis of the same circular argument as the trade economism they (mostly implicitly) criticize. Some might argue that environmental protection groups should be involved in trade policy-making because trade impacts on the environment, or that global justice organizations should make contributions to trade policy formation, because global trade rules impact on poverty. Others might argue that trade politics is about integrating the global economy and should thus be done with economic operators in mind. All these statements contain political weight and are what struggles over global trade are currently about—that is to say competing normative preferences for how the world should be governed and to what effect.

However, by incorporating such reasoning in theoretical frameworks, important aspects of trade policy formation theories rely on unfalsifiable hypotheses of the type "because trade policy is about X, those who have a stake in X should participate in trade policy-making." They stand in the way of imagining alternative forms of trade politics both in practice and in the realm of theory. In Part II, I strengthen existing analytical frameworks for trade policy formation to move our discussions beyond trade economism.

Conclusion

Inquiries into how trade policy decisions are made currently overemphasize the importance of economic dimensions, defined to refer to rising capital endowment and access to goods and services and construed as

Beyond trade economism 77

neoclassical market mechanisms, in social and political outcomes. Seen through the lens of trade economism, corporate groups appear as the principle actors in the current global trading order since they carry out import-export activities and, unlike the final consumer, are thought to experience immediate costs and benefits from trade policy choices. At the same time, the view that trade policy-making consists of corporate actors and public officials swapping trade policy preferences on the market place of trade institutions is naturalized and presented as inevitable.

Economistic approaches to trade policy formation neglect the social dimensions of the trading activity as a result of the historical evolution of the discipline. Construing trade political agency on the basis of "diffuse costs or benefits,"[92] or on "the polarization between free traders and protectionists with clear and fixed interests,"[93] conditions our thinking about possible interactions between trade officials and transformative actors. Such constellations are far from natural and unalterable. Instead, they rely on assumptions and causal beliefs that have been built over centuries of scholarly inquiry and are based on a set of intellectual and theoretical constructions that contain specific normative preferences for the world.

Two key, unquestioned assumptions are that the principal objective of trade policy is the pursuit of wealth understood as access to goods and services and the conflation of the impact of trade on society policy with its impact on the corporate sector. Based on this view, scholars can explain why critics of the global trade agenda fail in their attempts to influence trade policy, thus confirming current political practice. Nonetheless, they are ill-equipped to ask, never mind answer, questions of why trade institutions are open to transformative actors and why transformative advocacy on trade succeeds.

This is strange seeing as the literature on trade's legitimacy crisis recognizes that critical actors approach trade institutions because trade politics impacts on policy areas such as environment, labor, health, food security, etc. Despite the acknowledgement that the trading activity and the rules that guide it internationally affect numerous other policy areas, the literature on the more narrow question of how trade policy forms within a given global or domestic institution has not critically discussed its basic assumption that trade policy choices concern a limited number of social groups only. As a result, trade policy formation theories fail to provide us with a framework for explaining policy variation beyond their own theoretical assumptions.

Based on an economistic notion of the trading activity, there is a tendency to conflate the effectiveness of trade policy in advancing the

78 *Beyond trade economism*

global trade agenda with trade policy's legitimacy. The tendency elevates economic efficiency to the status of an indicator of good policy-making against which the democratic nature of a trade political process is expected to compete. At the same time, it fails to ask important questions as to for whom trade policy is effective, at the expense of whom, and how this affects broader socio-economic realities and other fields of global and domestic policy-making.

Taken together, the above suggests that the theoretical pre-legitimization of specific trade political actors and interests prevents scholars from asking deeper questions as to why trade policy formation is exclusive and privileges certain social actors over others at a given historical moment and in a given geographical context, why it changes in specific contexts and why it resists change in others. A growing body of literature finds trade politics to be constrained by dominant ideas about trade politics that draw the limits of what types of politics are believed possible. Meanwhile, the global trading system continues to involve ever more actors, issues and political forums. The rising substantial and institutional complexity of trade policy formation creates a multi-level, multi-issue policy field that is conducive to transformative advocacy. The literature on transnational studies in general and transnational trade coalitions in particular can help to understand the political opportunities that the new dynamics bring about.[94]

As I argue in the next part of the book, the key for understanding the evolution of West African participatory trade politics lies in grasping what economism obscures, namely the interactions between the material and the ideational world through which perceptions of legitimacy in trade policy-making can change over time. Instead of noting an interplay between interests, ideas and institutions in trade policy formation, I examine how these elements interacted across space and time, and use the patterns that arise from my analysis as explanatory factors for trade policy outcomes.

Notes

1 Taussig is considered to have built the foundations of neoclassical trade theory. Jacob Viner, one of the founding fathers of the Chicago School of Economics, wrote his doctoral dissertation under Taussig. Viner later influenced Milton Friedman, when the latter accomplished his Master of Arts in Economics at the University of Chicago.
2 Helen Milner, "The Political Economy of International Trade," *Annual Review of Political Science* 2 (1999): 111.
3 Richard Ashley, "Three Modes of Economism," *International Studies Quarterly* 27, no. 3 (1983): 466.

Beyond trade economism 79

4 Milner, "The Political Economy of International Trade," 95.
5 See Jeffrey Frieden and Ronald Rogowski, "The Impact of the International Economy on National Policies: An Analytical Overview," in *Internationalization and Domestic Politics*, ed. Robert Keohane and Helen Milner (Cambridge: Cambridge University Press, 1996), 25–47; Alasdair Young and John Peterson, "The EU and the New Trade Politics," *Journal of European Public Policy* 13, no. 6 (2006): 795–814; Andreas Dür and Dirk De Bièvre, "Inclusion Without Influence? NGOs in European Trade Policy," *Journal of Public Policy* 27, no. 1 (2007): 79–101.
6 Benjamin Cohen, "The Political Economy of International Trade," *International Organization* 44, no. 2 (1990): 271.
7 Cohen, "The Political Economy of International Trade," 271.
8 See Anthony Atkinson, "Economics as a Moral Science," *Economica* 76, no. 1 (2009): 791–804. I would like to thank Jamie Morgan, who pointed this out to me.
9 See Charles Kindleberger, "Dominance and Leadership in the International Economy: Exploitation, Public Goods, and Free Rides," *International Studies Quarterly* 25, no. 1 (1981): 242–54; Richard Rosecrance, *The Rise of the Trading State: Commerce and Conquest in the Modern World* (New York: Basic Books, 1986); John Conybeare, *Trade Wars: The Theory and Practice of International Commercial Rivalry* (New York: Columbia University Press, 1987); Robert Gilpin, *The Political Economy of International Relations* (Princeton, NJ: Princeton University Press, 1987); David Lake, *Power, Protection and Free Trade: International Sources of U.S. Commercial Strategy, 1887–1939* (Ithaca, NY: Cornell University Press, 1988).
10 See Lea Brilmayer, "Trade Policy: The Normative Dimension," *New York University Journal of International Law and Politics* 25, no. 2 (1993): 211–18; Thomas Howell, "Trade Protection: Rethinking the American Perspective," *New York University Journal of International Law and Politics* 25, no. 2 (1993): 251–62.
11 John Ruggie, "International Regimes, Transactions, and Change: Embedded Liberalism in the Postwar Economic Order," *International Organization* 36, no. 2 (1982): 379–415.
12 See Ann Capling and Patrick Low, *Governments, Non-State Actors and Trade Policy-Making: Negotiating Preferentially or Multilaterally?* (Cambridge: Cambridge University Press and World Trade Organization, 2010).
13 Frank Trentmann, "Political Culture and Political Economy: Interests, Ideology and Free Trade," *Review of International Political Economy* 5, no. 2 (1998): 233–34.
14 Trentmann, "Political Culture and Political Economy: Interests, Ideology and Free Trade," 223.
15 Claus Offe, *Contradictions of the Welfare State* (Cambridge, MA: MIT Press, 1984), 228.
16 Ashley, "Three Modes of Economism," 472.
17 Ralph Souter, "'The Nature and Significance of Economic Science' in Recent Discussion," *Quarterly Journal of Economics* 47, no. 3 (1933): 377–413; Talcott Parsons, "Some Reflections on 'The Nature and Significance of Economics'," *Quarterly Journal of Economics* 48, no. 3 (1934): 511–45; Gary Becker, "Gary S. Becker," in *Economics and Sociology: Redefining Their Boundaries. Conversations with Economists and Sociologists*, ed.

80 *Beyond trade economism*

Richard Swedberg (Princeton, NJ: Princeton University Press, 1990), 27–46; Edward Lazear, "Economic Imperialism," *Quarterly Journal of Economics* 115, no. 1 (2000): 99–146.

18 Ronald Rogowski, *Commerce and Coalitions: How Trade Affects Domestic Political Alignments* (Princeton, NJ: Princeton University Press, 1990). Interestingly, the trade economists Wolfgang Stolper and Paul Samuelson confirm in their paper "Protection and Real Wages," that "free trade," just like "protectionism," requires government intervention, although this is not how their paper is remembered in neoclassical macroeconomics today. Examining "the effects of international trade upon the relative remunerations of productive agencies," namely capital and labor, they find that the introduction of free trade "necessarily lowers the real wage of the scarce factor" of production. Wolfgang Stolper and Paul Samuelson, "Protection and Real Wages," *Review of Economic Studies* 9, no. 1 (1941): 58–66. Despite concluding "that there is a grain of truth in the pauper labor type of argument for protection," Stolper and Samuelson are "anxious to point out that … our argument provides no political ammunition for protectionists" (ibid., 73). Rather, they argue that "it has been shown that the harm which free trade inflicts upon one factor of production is necessarily less than the gain to the other. Hence, it is always possible to bribe the suffering factor by subsidy or other redistributive devices so as to leave all factors better off as a result of trade" (ibid., 73).

19 Rogowski, *Commerce and Coalitions: How Trade Affects Domestic Political Alignments*, 7–16.

20 Rogowski, *Commerce and Coalitions: How Trade Affects Domestic Political Alignments*, 13.

21 See Gene Grossman and Elhanan Helpman, "Protection for Sale," *American Economic Review* 84, no. 4 (1994): 833–50; Dirk de Bièvre and Andreas Dür, "Constituency Interests and Delegation in European and American Trade Policy," *Comparative Political Studies* 38, no. 10 (2005): 1271–96.

22 Trentmann, "Political Culture and Political Economy: Interests, Ideology and Free Trade," 222.

23 Ashley, "Three Modes of Economism," 484.

24 Ashley, "Three Modes of Economism," 487.

25 Ashley, "Three Modes of Economism," 490.

26 Ashley, "Three Modes of Economism," 490.

27 Cohen, "The Political Economy of International Trade," 261–62.

28 David Robertson, "Civil Society and the WTO," *The World Economy* 23, no. 9 (2000): 1122.

29 Rorden Wilkinson, "The Contours of Courtship: The WTO and Civil Society," in *Global Governance: Critical Perspectives*, ed. Rorden Wilkinson and Steven Hughes (London: Routledge, 2002), 193–211; Heinz Klug, "Law, Politics, and Access to Essential Medicines in Developing Countries," *Politics & Society* 36, no. 2 (2008): 207–46; Sylvia Ostry, "The World Trade Organization: System under Stress," in *Unsettled Legitimacy. Political Community, Power and Authority in a Global Era*, ed. Steven Bernstein and W. Coleman (Vancouver: University of British Columbia, 2009), 259–79; Marisa von Bülow, *Building Transnational Networks: Civil Society and the Politics of Trade in the Americas* (Cambridge: Cambridge University Press, 2010).

Beyond trade economism 81

30 Karl Polanyi, *The Great Transformation: The Political and Economic Origins of Our Time* (Boston, MA: Beacon Press, [1944] 2001), 35.
31 Dimitris Milonakis and Ben Fine, *From Political Economy to Economics: Method, the Social and the Historical in the Evolution of Economic Theory* (London: Routledge, 2009).
32 Frederick Clow, "South American Trade," *Quarterly Journal of Economics* 7, no. 2 (1893): 193–204.
33 Frank Taussig, "Some Aspects of the Tariff Question," *Quarterly Journal of Economics* 3, no. 3 (1889): 259–92.
34 Perry Powers, "The Australian Tariff Experiment," *Quarterly Journal of Economics* 3, no. 1 (1888): 87–98.
35 William Hill, "The American Commercial Policy: Three Historical Essays by Ugo Rabbeno," *Journal of Political Economy* 4, no. 2 (1896): 256.
36 W.G. Langworthy Taylor, "The Relative Importance of Our Foreign Trade," *Journal of Political Economy* 12, no. 1 (1903): 19.
37 See Léon Poinsard, *Libre Échange et Protection* (Paris: Firmin Didot et Cie, 1893).
38 Émile Levasseur, "The Recent Commercial Policy of France," *Journal of Political Economy* 1, no. 1 (1892): 22.
39 Lindley Keasbey, "L'Evolution du Commerce dans les Diverses races Humaines by Ch. Letourneau," *Political Science Quarterly* 13, no. 3 (1898): 542.
40 Karl Kautsky, *Protokoll über die Verhandlungen des Parteitags der Sozialdemokratischen Partei Deutschlands, abgehalten zu Stuttgart vom 3. bis 8. Oktober 1898* (Berlin: Expedition der Buchhandlung Vorwärts, 1898), 190.
41 See George Curtiss, *The Industrial Development of Nations: And a History of the Tariff Policies of the United States, and of Great Britain, Germany, France, Russia and Other European Countries* (Binghamton: George B. Curtiss, 1912).
42 See Charles Bastable, *The Theory of International Trade, with Some of its Applications to Economic Policy* (London: Macmillan, 1887).
43 Frank Taussig, "Schmoller on Protection and Free Trade," *Quarterly Journal of Economics* 19, no. 3 (1904): 503.
44 See Arthur Pigou, *Protective and Preferential Import Duties* (London: Macmillan and Co., 1906); John Robertson, *Trade and Tariffs* (London: Adam and Charles Black, 1908); Raymond Bridgman, *The Passing of the Tariff* (Boston, MA: Sherman, French & Co., 1909); Frank Taussig, *Free Trade, the Tariff and Reciprocity* (New York: The Macmillan Co., 1920).
45 See Alvin Johnson, "Protection and the Formation of Capital," *Political Science Quarterly* 23, no. 2 (1908): 220–41.
46 See George Fisk, "The Payne-Aldrich Tariff," *Political Science Quarterly* 25, no. 1 (1910): 35–68; Roy Blakey, "The Proposed Sugar Tariff," *Political Science Quarterly* 28, no. 2 (1913): 230–48; Bernhard Holland, *The Fall of Protection* (New York, Longmans: Green and Company, 1913).
47 Cited in Milonakis and Fine, *From Political Economy to Economics: Method, the Social and the Historical in the Evolution of Economic Theory*, 81.
48 Milonakis and Fine, *From Political Economy to Economics: Method, the Social and the Historical in the Evolution of Economic Theory*, 98.
49 Frank Taussig, "The Tariff, 1830–60," *Quarterly Journal of Economics* 2, no. 3 (1888): 314–46.
50 Frank Taussig, "American Tariff Controversies in the Nineteenth Century by Edward Stanwood," *Political Science Quarterly* 19, no. 2 (1904): 302–3.

82 *Beyond trade economism*

51 Taussig, "American Tariff Controversies in the Nineteenth Century by Edward Stanwood," 303.
52 See Edgar Johnson, "The Effect of a Tariff on Production," *Quarterly Journal of Economics* 18, no. 1 (1903): 135–37; Chester Wright, "Wool-Growing and the Tariff Since 1890," *Quarterly Journal of Economics* 19, no. 4 (1905): 610–47.
53 John Clark, "The Theory of International Trade with some of its Applications to Economic Policy by C. Francis Bastable," *Political Science Quarterly* 2, no. 3 (1887): 525.
54 Clark, "The Theory of International Trade with some of its Applications to Economic Policy by C. Francis Bastable," 524–25.
55 Worthington Ford, "Official Tariff Comparisons," *Political Science Quarterly* 13, no. 2 (1898): 273–85.
56 William Jevons, *The Theory of Political Economy* (New York: Augustus M. Kelley, [1871] 1957), 19.
57 Clark, "The Theory of International Trade with some of its Applications to Economic Policy by C. Francis Bastable," 526.
58 Clark, "The Theory of International Trade with some of its Applications to Economic Policy by C. Francis Bastable," 525.
59 John Cummings, "Cost of Production as a Basis of Tariff Revision," *Journal of Political Economy* 17, no. 3 (1909): 153.
60 C.C. Arbuthnot, "The National Tariff Commission Convention," *Journal of Political Economy* 17, no. 4 (1909): 225.
61 Joseph Schumpeter, *Das Wesen und der Hauptinhalt der theoretischen Nationalökonomie* (Leipzig: Duncker & Humbolt, 1908).
62 Léon Walras, *Elements of Pure Economics* (London: Augustus M. Kelley, [1874] 1954), cited in Milonakis and Fine, *From Political Economy to Economics: Method, the Social and the Historical in the Evolution of Economic Theory*, 95.
63 Gunnar Myrdal, *The Political Element in the Development of Economic Theory* (London: Routledge, 1953).
64 Richard Lipsey, *An Introduction to Positive Economics* (London: Weidenfeld and Nicolson, 1989), xvii.
65 See J.A. Hobson, *The New Protectionism* (London: T. Fisher Unwin, 1916); Abraham Berglund, "Our Merchant Marine Problem and International Trade Policies," *Journal of Political Economy* 34, no. 5 (1926): 642–56.
66 Arthur Cole, "The Textile Schedule in the Tariff of 1922," *Quarterly Journal of Economics* 37, no. 1 (1922): 30.
67 Allyn Young, "Marshall on Consumers' Surplus in International Trade," *Quarterly Journal of Economics* 39, no. 1 (1924): 147.
68 See Orville McDiarmid, *Commercial Policy in the Canadian Economy* (Cambridge, MA: Harvard University Press, 1946); Perdo Abelarde, *American Tariff Policy Towards the Philippines* (New York: King's Crown Press, 1947).
69 See Frank Taussig, *International Trade* (New York: Macmillan, 1927); Gottfried Haberler, *Der Internationale Handel* (Berlin: Julius Springer, 1933); Jacob Viner, *Studies in the Theory of International Trade* (New York: Harper and Brothers, 1937).
70 Enrico Barone, *Principi di Economia Politica* (Rome: Athanaeum, 1913).
71 See Eli Heckscher, "Utrikhandelns verkan på inkomstfördelningen," *Ekonomisk Tidskrift* II (1919): 1–32; Bertil Ohlin, *Interregional and International Trade* (Cambridge, MA: Harvard University Press, 1933).

Beyond trade economism 83

72 See Wassily Leontief, "The Use of Indifference Curves in the Analysis of Foreign Trade," *Quarterly Journal of Economics* 47, no. 3 (1933): 493–503.
73 Harold Davis, *The Theory of Econometrics* (Bloomington, IN: Principia Press, 1941).
74 P.W. Bidwell, "Barriers to World Trade: A Study of Recent Commercial Policy by Margaret S. Gordon," *Journal of Political Economy* 49, no. 5 (1941): 769.
75 See Herbert Feis, "Suggested Charter of an International Trade Organisation of the United States," *Journal of Political Economy* 55, no. 1 (1947): 84–85; Michael Heilperin, *The Trade of Nations* (New York: Alfred A. Knopf, 1947).
76 Charles Kindleberger, "The United States and the Restoration of World Trade by William Adams Brown, Jr.," *Journal of Political Economy* 59, no. 1 (1951): 79–80.
77 Viner, *Studies in the Theory of International Trade*, 613.
78 D. Gale Johnson, "Reconciling Agricultural and Foreign Trade Policies," *Journal of Political Economy* 55, no. 6 (1947): 567–71.
79 Mark Blaug, "Disturbing Currents in Modern Economics," *Challenge* 41, no. 3 (1998): 11–34. De Vroey argues that neoclassical economics came to dominate the social sciences precisely because it appears to be value-neutral and factually strengthens the existing social order. Neoclassical economics, he explains, "was especially attractive because it looked as scientific as the natural science theories, while it eluded the dangerous topics of class interests and transformation of the system ... It provided tools for the management of the economy in the framework of the existing social order, as if this was the only possible object of economics." Michel de Vroey, "The Transition from Classical to Neoclassical Economics: A Scientific Revolution," *Journal of Economic Issues* 9, no. 3 (1975): 415–39.
80 Michel de Vroey, "The Transition from Classical to Neoclassical Economics: A Scientific Revolution"; Milonakis and Fine, *From Political Economy to Economics: Method, the Social and the Historical in the Evolution of Economic Theory.*
81 Richard Caves, "Economic Models of Political Choice: Canada's Tariff Structure," *Canadian Journal of Economics/Revue Canadienne d'Economique* 9, no. 2 (1976): 279.
82 George Stigler, "The Theory of Economic Regulation," *Bell Journal of Economics* 2, no. 1 (1971): 359–65.
83 Caves, "Economic Models of Political Choice: Canada's Tariff Structure."
84 William Brock and Stephen Magee, "The Economics of Special Interest Politics: The Case of the Tariff," *American Economic Review* 68, no. 2 (1978): 246.
85 Robert Baldwin, "The Political Economy of Protection," in *Import Competition and Response*, ed. Jagdish Bhagwati and Thirukodikaval Srinivasan (Chicago, IL: University of Chicago Press, 1982), 263–86.
86 Arye Hillman, *The Political Economy of Protection* (London: Harwood, 1982); Wolfgang Mayer, "Endogenous Tariff Formation," *American Economic Review* 74, no. 5 (1984): 970–85.
87 Howard Marvel and Edward Ray, "The Kennedy Round: Evidence on the Regulation of Trade in the US," *American Economic Review* 73, no. 3 (1983): 190–97; Daniel Trefler, "Trade Liberalisation and the Theory of

84 Beyond trade economism

Endogenous Protection: An Econometric Study of U.S. Import Policy," *Journal of Political Economy* 101, no. 1 (1993): 138–60.

88 Kent Jones, "The Political Economy of Voluntary Exports Restraints," *Kyklos* 37, no. 1 (1984): 82–101; James Cassing and Arye Hillman, "Political Motives and the Choice between Tariffs and Quotas," *Journal of International Economics* 19, no. 3–4 (1985): 279–90; Dani Rodrik, "Tariffs, Subsidies and Welfare with Endogenous Policy," *Journal of International Economics* 21, no. 3–4 (1986): 285–99.

89 Arye Hillman, "Declining Industries and Political-Support Protectionist Motives," *American Economic Review* 72, no. 5 (1982): 1180–87.

90 See Stephen Magee and Leslie Young, "Endogenous Protection in the US," in *US Trade Policies in a Changing World Economy*, ed. Robert Stern (Cambridge, MA: MIT Press, 1987), 145–95; David Lake, "The State and American Trade Strategy in the Pre-Hegemonic Era," *International Organization* 42, no. 1 (1988): 33–58; Frieden and Rogowski, "The Impact of the International Economy on National Policies: An Analytical Overview"; Kenneth Scheve and Matthew Slaughter, "What Determines Individual Trade-Policy Preferences?" *Journal of International Economics* 54, no. 2 (2001): 267–92.

91 Carsten Fink and Patrick Reichenmiller, *Tightening TRIPS: The Intellectual Property Provisions in Recent US Free Trade Agreements* (Washington, DC: World Bank, 2005).

92 Erin Hannah, "NGOs and the European Union: Examining the Power of Epistemes in the EC's TRIPS and Access to Medicines Negotiations," *Journal of Civil Society* 7, no. 2 (2011): 183.

93 Von Bülow, *Building Transnational Networks: Civil Society and the Politics of Trade in the Americas*, 197.

94 Silke Trommer, "Activists beyond Brussels: Transnational NGO Strategies on EU-West African Trade Negotiations," *Globalizations* 8, no. 1 (2011): 113–26.

Part II

Transformations in trade politics

3 The historical evolution of West African participatory trade politics

- **The political environment of West African EPA negotiations**
- **Trade political agency**
- **Conclusion**

My evidence suggests that attitudinal change was an important factor in the evolution of West African participatory trade politics and validates von Bülow's invitation to pay analytical attention to this point.[1] Several interviewees reported that West African trade institutions were initially hostile towards civil society participation in the EPA process (Platform representatives 1, 3, 4, 6, 7, 8, West African civil society representatives 2, 3, West African journalist, European civil society representative 1). Although West African trade officials rejected the term "hostility" in interviews, some remembered "from what was said in ministry corridors at the time" that the groups were seen as "dogmatic" and mounting poorly argued, "ideological" opposition to the agreements at early stages of negotiations (West African public officials 1, 4, 7, 8, 9). According to a Platform representative, at the beginning of the negotiating process, Platform organizations "were not invited to the first meetings … we were chasing information and funds to go to meetings in order to be included" (Platform representative 7). Confrontational attitudes, however, eased over time. Although specific aspects of participatory trade politics remained contested, as I discuss in the next chapter, public officials described the experience as on the whole positive during my interviews (West African public officials 10, 15). One trade official recalled that although having initially been skeptical of the Platform, he had changed his mind in 2009 (West African public official 9).

In this chapter, I reproduce and analyze the answers that interviewees provided to my question of how participatory trade politics evolved in West Africa between the start of negotiations in 2002 and the consolidation of participatory policy-making practices in 2008. I

88 *The evolution of participatory trade politics*

understand participatory trade politics to be consolidated in West Africa at that time because my evidence suggests that by then all actors at least in principle acknowledged that EPA negotiations would be carried out through the mechanisms described in Part I. My interviewees collectively pointed to six elements that played a role in the emergence of participatory trade politics in the region, namely: 1 the Marrakesh Agreements; 2 the Cotonou Agreement; 3 the West African socio-economic context; 4 previous trade advocacy experience; 5 the technical knowledge that the Platform provided; and 6 individual activism.

I treat the first three elements as structural explanations, because they appeared as a factual reality to actors at the start of EPA negotiations and characterized the political environment in which West African EPA negotiations took place. I treat the last three elements as trade political agency, because they arose from transformative campaigning on trade issues. As becomes clear throughout the chapter, the various elements were related in the sense that structural factors influenced actors' perceptions of feasible trade political mechanisms and presented political opportunity for putting participation into practice. Also, through political agency, the perceptions of some of the structural factors changed in a way that made them conducive to participation. As my analysis shows, appearing as a factual reality and constituting a factual reality is not always the same thing. Transformations in West African trade politics precisely emerged through the interplay of ideas and interests within this grey zone, and the types of attitudinal changes that the process provoked.

The political environment of West African EPA negotiations

West African participatory trade politics evolved through a series of political contestations between the launch of EPA negotiations in 2002 and the consolidation of the practice in 2008. During this period, the political environment of West African trade politics was favorable to transformative actors' efforts to influence EPA talks. At least three factors set the stage for quarrels around both the content of EPAs and the political process through which it should be established, namely: 1 the political experience following the signing and implementation of the Marrakesh Agreements; 2 the legal rhetoric of participation anchored in the Cotonou Agreement; and 3 the socio-economic context of the West African region.

The Marrakesh Agreements

Together with their ACP and EU counterparts, West African economic justice organizations in the late 1990s reportedly became convinced of

The evolution of participatory trade politics 89

the need to engage in trade advocacy in order to make sure that their governments' trade policy choices would not undermine development efforts (Platform representatives 2, 9, European civil society representatives 1, 2). My interviewees connected this directly to the fact that at that time, many global South countries started to feel the negative socio-economic impacts of the implementation of the Marrakesh Agreements. The Marrakesh Agreements concluded the Uruguay Round and established the WTO on 1 January 1995. They did not reflect the interests of global South countries.[2] To the contrary, current trade rules tilt the world trading balance towards industrialized countries' interests.[3]

Michael Finger argues that the implementation cost of the obligations and standards under the new agreements were excessive and led to misguided domestic policy reform, with damaging economic effects in the long run. In terms of trade in goods, he finds that Southern countries did not make any gains through the tariff cuts agreed at the conclusion of the Uruguay Round.[4] In addition, for ACP countries, the Round led to preference erosion, that is to say a relative loss in competitive advantage on the European market compared to developing countries that did not enjoy Lomé preferences, due to multilateral tariff cuts.[5]

West African public officials shared this assessment of the Uruguay Round outcomes in my interviews (West African public official 4). Civil society interviewees explained that the full extent to which WTO Agreements hampered development efforts only became obvious to African countries when their governments started implementing the new obligations in the late 1990s. At the time, organizations concerned with economic justice, development, and social issues became suspicious that their governments "did not know what they were signing" in Marrakesh (European civil society representative 1, West African citizen). The literature confirms this view. Commenting on the Uruguay Round outcomes, Sylvia Ostry explains that "the deal was pretty much take it or leave it for the Southern countries. So they took it but, it's safe to say, without a full comprehension of the profoundly transformative implication of this new trading system."[6] Monitoring the Uruguay Round and the Seattle Ministerial Conference in 1999, critical organizations such as ENDA began to express frustration about the fact that African countries were not adequately represented in the global trade institution and hence could not defend their interests during negotiations.[7]

An interviewee from one of the Platform's European partner organizations, who was an ECOWAS citizen, explained in my interview that in the aftermath of the WTO Agreements, West African civil society actors became convinced that "it was not safe to leave trade negotiations to governments, because they would come home with a bad deal"

90 *The evolution of participatory trade politics*

(European civil society representative 1). Using more subtle language, a West African trade unionist argued it was important to engage in trade advocacy because "the EU was applying political pressure [in EPA talks] and [West African] states, if left to themselves, have a habit of signing" (West African civil society representative 3). When EPA negotiations kicked off, the wording of the Cotonou Agreement provided a concrete opportunity for claiming a right to inclusion in the process.

The Cotonou Agreement

Many interviewees felt that the legal right to participation enshrined in the Cotonou Agreement constituted the political lever that enabled them to attend internal EPA meetings in public institutions at a time when West African public officials were resisting participation. As explained in Part I, the agreement sets out the fundamental principle of participation which is one novelty when compared with the Lomé Conventions. In line with the principle, the ACP Secretariat and the EU financially supported ACP civil society groups that were working on the Cotonou process. As outlined in Chapter 1, the Platform had been funded in this way in its early days (Platform representative 3). In addition to funding, "the legal opportunity provided by the agreement" was a key factor in enabling civil society to participate in EPA negotiations according to one interviewee (Platform representative 7).

Public officials explained during my interviews that the participatory approach had to be retained due to the region's international obligations resulting from the Cotonou Agreement (West African public officials 10, 15). They were generally under the impression that ECOWAS' Negotiating Roadmap was transposing the terms of the Cotonou Agreement when it established that civil society and private-sector representatives "participate" in West Africa's negotiating structure. Interestingly, and contrary to what many interviewees believed, no direct legal obligation to include civil society in EPA negotiations can be found in the Cotonou Agreement.

In total, the agreement makes reference to participation of civil society actors in the Cotonou process in 11 out of 100 Articles. All clauses on civil society participation feature in the general provisions of the agreement.[8] The general provisions spell out the objectives, purposes and principles of the partnership. To recall the wording of Article 2, Cotonou parties agree that "the partnership shall be open to different kinds of other actors," and list the private sector and civil society as such "other actors."

The evolution of participatory trade politics 91

In legal terms, the language "shall be open to" does not create a specific international legal right or obligation. More to the point, while Articles 4, 6 and 7 of the agreement stress the potential for non-state actors' contributions to development processes, no equivalent mention of civil society actors is made in its trade chapters. The negotiating history of the agreement supports the view that the parties had development cooperation in mind when using the term "participation." The legislative intent of the Cotonou Agreement was "to make EU-ACP development cooperation less centered on governmental relations by much wider inclusion in the process of non-state actors."[9] This reflects current consensus on good governance practice in development cooperation. Whether the intent also applies to the trade chapters of the Cotonou Agreement remains questionable, in particular seeing as there is no previous governance practice that confirms participatory approaches to trade policy-making. While many interviewees referred to the legal *right* to participation enshrined at the international level, the Platform representative cited above therefore very cunningly spoke of the legal *opportunity* that the agreement provided.

The West African Negotiating Roadmap, thus, went beyond the vague terms of the Cotonou Agreement by providing legal rights to participation. Although the exact origin of these rights is controversial, one interviewee provided a telling example for their role in bringing about participatory trade politics. As outlined in Chapter 1, the individual that had acted as regional civil society representative in the Regional Negotiating Committee left ENDA and the Platform in 2007. The new representative suspected ECOWAS officials of trying to seize the opportunity "to get rid of civil society" (Platform representative 1). The account merits reproduction in full because it illustrates how the Platform created political opportunity for participation using mixed strategies of claiming legal rights, access to campaign resources that allowed mobility, building on personal relationships, and threatening public officials with citizen action.

The representative explained: "Throughout the year 2007, there were a lot of tensions between official negotiators and the representatives of the Platform … There were even moments when ECOWAS negotiators—some ECOWAS officials, not all negotiators—managed to manipulate some Platform members to say that the Platform should reject that ENDA coordinates the Platform." While many Platform organizations continued to support the ENDA representative, arguing that ECOWAS could not impose its preferences on the Platform, the representative felt that the atmosphere of tension and contestation was one reason why

92 *The evolution of participatory trade politics*

the previous representative left ENDA and the Platform in October 2007. One month after taking on the role of regional civil society representative in November 2007, the representative recalled:

> there was a Ministerial Monitoring Committee meeting in Ouagadougou, and well, I did not receive an invitation. ENDA did not receive an official invitation ... but I went anyway ... I called the Senegalese trade minister, with whom we always had excellent relations, I told him that I will travel on my own expenses ... and since we were not invited, I went along as a member of the Senegalese delegation ... When I arrived, there were people that disagreed, that really still had problems with us ... There was a big discussion that caused a nearly one-hour delay. Some said "no, we don't accept that civil society is here" ... That was before the Europeans arrived. I told them: "only two things can make me leave this room. Either you bring ECOWAS heads of states and they come together to say we, the ECOWAS heads of states, decide that civil society is not part of negotiations anymore. I will leave the room, but I will not leave to go home. I will leave to call on the peoples of West Africa to tell them: your heads of states are fools because they do not have the right to reject our participation ... the second thing is if all those who negotiated the Cotonou Agreement come here to denounce the agreement ... As long as the Cotonou Agreement stands, I am a non-state actor, designated by a platform that I represent. I have more legitimacy than you do ... Go fetch the document that creates this regional negotiating committee." They went to fetch it and they said: "okay, this is what is written in the agreement." They read it and they said: "okay, your rights are established, nobody can deny that."
>
> (Platform representative 1)

While using the political leverage for participation resulting from the Cotonou process, Platform members also saw the participation principle in a critical light. One reason interviewees provided was that the participation principle was made effective through the EDF and remained ultimately EU-funded. One Platform representative recalled that this led to biased funding decisions and that financing had not been renewed to groups who had been seen as becoming "too political." From the interviewee's point of view, the EU generally favored "complementary" rather than "critical participation" by civil society actors in the region (Platform representative 2). The argument is compatible with the analytical limits to the term "civil society" in

The evolution of participatory trade politics 93

theorizing trade policy formation that I stressed in the introduction. As other scholars find in their research, public officials typically resist the inclusion of conformist, or "complimentary" actors less strongly than the inclusion of transformative, or "critical," actors in trade decision-making, irrespective of the type of interest that is being represented.[10]

Another Platform representative argued that the participation principle resulted from "an ideology of attack on the African states," according to which "the ACP state is useless [and] irresponsible" (Platform representative 7). The representative pointed out that civil society involvement in aid delivery was introduced in ACP-EU cooperation during the 1980s as a corollary to the conviction that ACP states had to withdraw from development policy in order to improve the effectiveness of the emerging "structural adjustment paradigm." In this view, the Lomé Conventions and the Cotonou Agreement presented "the lock in of a particular paradigm of development." The EU therefore committed to strengthen non-state actors in ACP countries which would be the new preferred channels for EU aid implementation and actively financed groups through the EDF (West African private-sector representative). The Platform representative held that this was a "politically dangerous proposal" because it implied "writ[ing] into an international agreement how the state should behave." The representative felt that the practice was factually "undermining the capacity of the state to be a state." While the EU reportedly presented the initiative as an attempt to support efficient development assistance by avoiding direct cooperation with dysfunctional ACP governments, the representative saw the initiative as "one-sided" as it only concerned the ACP parties to the Cotonou Agreement and not the EU (Platform representative 7).

In sum, the Cotonou Agreement presented an often-quoted, if factually and conceptually ambivalent factor for the emergence of transformative participation in West African trade politics. During the consolidation of participatory trade politics, Platform members and their allies framed EPA debates in a way that turned the legal opportunity into a legal right, and in this sense turned the perception of a political opportunity stemming from the international level into an existing political opportunity at the domestic and regional levels. The region's socio-economic context constituted a third structural element that EPA actors highlighted during my interviews.

The West African socio-economic context

In the West African context of generalized, strained socio-economic conditions, the question of how to improve people's lives underlies

94   The evolution of participatory trade politics

almost all policy debates. This benefited Platform efforts for political participation in at least three respects. First, under the given conditions, it was politically more difficult for public officials to distance themselves from transformative actors that campaigned on development issues than is the case for their counterparts in global North trade institutions. The Platform's credible warnings against the EPA's negative development impacts outlined in Part I made it hard for West African governments to circumvent these groups, irrespective of whether individual officials agreed or disagreed with the Platform's understanding of the trade and development nexus.

Internally, trade officials were not only initially skeptical of Platform organizations, but many officials also adhered to the free trade discourse that Platform organizations rejected (West African private-sector representative, West African public official 1, Platform representative 6). The differences led to intense policy debates on the regulation-deregulation mix that would be conducive to development within ECOWAS. In fact, some interviewees pointed out that the internal debates among West African actors were often more heated than negotiations with the European Commission (West African public official 2).

This connects with the second repercussion of West Africa's socio-economic context for the emergence of participatory trade politics. Their socio-economic reality, particularly when compared to the socio-economic context of the negotiating partner, allowed West Africans to forge a sense of solidarity among trade officials and transformative voices, which did not exist on the European side of the negotiating table. Irrespective of whether West African actors came from public or private institutions or were adherents or opponents of the global trade agenda, emphasizing development impacts sent the signal that "we're all sitting in the same boat" (West African public official 2). My interviewees confirmed that despite fundamental disagreements over appropriate trade policy lines, they regularly managed to elaborate a common position with a view to finding the best possible compromise for the region. One trade official explained that officials and the Platform "work together to arrive at an agreement as opposed to working against each other fighting over a theoretical issue" (West African public official 2).

When asked how compromise was brought about, one West African public official replied that it was possible to agree on common positions "because we have one goal in mind: the welfare of West Africa" (West African public official 2). I argue in the next two chapters that the sense of unity and solidarity among the West African negotiating team implied in the above statements was one element that enabled trade political actors of different normative convictions to continue cooperating

The evolution of participatory trade politics 95

on trade issues. At the same time, it allowed framing the EU as the other in EPA talks. When asked how the West African state and non-state actors overcame their differences, one Platform representative recalled: "I told them [i.e. West African public trade negotiators]: 'What unites us here is much more important than our little quarrels, we want to defend the interests of our regions. You should not look at me as your opponent and I should not look at you as my opponent. Our opponent is the European Union'" (Platform representative 1).

Third, issue linkage between trade and development reinforced references to both the lax terms of the Cotonou Agreement and what is generally acknowledged to constitute good governance practice on development. NANTS representative Ken Ukaoha highlighted this point in 2006. "The saliency of stakeholders' participation in the [EPA] process should be enhanced and is imperative for the attainment of authentic development," he explained. "The raison d'être," he continued, "is that participatory development planning and administration by the people in the institutions and systems, which govern their lives, is a basic human right and also essential for the realignment of political power in favor of disadvantaged groups and for social and economic development."[11]

As stated above, in the Cotonou Agreement, the participation principle was only explicitly mentioned in the general provisions. Presenting trade and development as inseparably connected policy areas encouraged the view that Cotonou provisions should be interpreted in a way to apply the participatory principle to EPA negotiations also, although this is not explicitly mentioned in the legal text. A Platform representative explained in an interview that one important goal for the organization was to put the message across that trade was not only about exchanging goods, but was rather directly connected to questions of poverty reduction and development. Therefore, civil society needed to participate in the EPA process, because trade rules, the representative explained, were part of the key rules that determined individual access to economic opportunity (Platform representative 2). Thus, because Platform organizations had an inclusive vision of development, and the link between trade and development was, in their view, direct, trade politics needed to be inclusive also. The episode shows how Platform organizations created political opportunity for participation in trade policy-making by combining and manipulating the broader context in which EPA negotiations were placed. By referring to one set of structural conditions, namely the region's socio-economic context, they reinforced the perception of another aspect of the EPA's political environment, namely the wording of the Cotonou

96 *The evolution of participatory trade politics*

Agreement, as a factual reality structuring the talks. Thus, the specific type of trade political agency present in West Africa played an important role in bringing participatory trade politics about.

Trade political agency

One Platform representative explained in my interview that West African transformative civil society organizations "had to negotiate the negotiating structure and its practical application little by little [with public officials]." The representative recalled: "it was an effort of constructing [the Platform's] credibility and we had to establish a working relationship ... Once we had credibility, we could insert ourselves in the [decision-making] structure, that is to say put the structure into practice" (Platform representative 8). In this section, I discuss the three types of trade political agency that contributed to the consolidation of participatory trade politics in West African EPA, namely: 1 advocacy experience from previous campaigning; 2 creating and supplying trade expertise; and 3 the individuals involved in West African EPA negotiations and their personal relationships.

Trade advocacy experience

Associational life has a long tradition in West Africa.[12] Civil society organizations on economic justice issues in particular are progressive and strong when compared to other regions of sub-Saharan Africa.[13] As pointed out above, these organizations took an interest in trade issues in the late 1990s during the implementation phase of the Uruguay Round results. When EPA negotiations were launched, regional civil society was hence already organized around trade issues on the local, regional, and transnational levels. One Platform representative argued that West African civil society managed to participate in EPA negotiations due to "a history of struggle around Cotonou and Lomé ... which is also informed by the struggle around structural adjustment and WTO, ... [that is to say due to] a history of collective action around trade" (Platform representative 7).

Numerous channels and networks had structured West African collective action on trade since the late 1990s. Among the various initiatives, mobilization prompted by the Global Coalition for Africa, ATN, and the Cotonou network became particularly relevant for the evolution of participatory trade politics. The Platform members ENDA and TWN ran joint campaigns against structural adjustment policies under the Global Coalition for Africa in 1997. Raising themes that would

The evolution of participatory trade politics 97

later reappear during the EPA campaign, these campaigns worked to "challenge ... the notion of participation, the notion of economic, the notion of development ... [by] combining resistance to the imposition of economic policy from the North" (Platform representative 7). Already in the late 1990s, stressing variations in the meanings of terms was therefore an important strategy for West African civil society organizations working on economic policy.

In addition, ATN members became convinced in the late 1990s that the issues of structural adjustment, ACP-EU relations, and WTO negotiations were interrelated and decided to harmonize trade policy campaigns (Platform representative 7). The network subsequently engaged in building trade expertise among regional civil society groups, connecting African movements to global WTO mobilization, and organizing WTO-based campaigns. ATN was, for example, a key organization in the advocacy and campaigning of African civil society groups around the Seattle Ministerial Conference in 1999.[14] As highlighted in Chapter 1, organizations started to organize around Cotonou negotiations at about the same time. They adopted a focus on trade and were able to campaign on it as a visible social force.

The Platform developed from all three channels that presented important precedents for African trade and economic justice campaigning. One Platform representative pointed out that local campaigns on issues such as trade or labor helped to establish a relatively far-reaching regional network when the EPA campaign was launched. "It wasn't very difficult to mobilize [grassroots organizations]," the representative recalled, "because prior to this time we already had groups working ... on the [Cotonou] Agreement ... Local set-ups ... were already organized in different ways, doing different things ... so when there was the call ... mobilizing them wasn't so difficult" (Platform representative 3). The representative added that the same was true for African networks such as ATN and international networks with NGOs from the global North, which already existed when EPA negotiations were launched. The North-South networks in turn provided important sources of funding and trade expertise (Platform representative 3). In this sense, framing EPA as a development issue had been an important strategy, also because it enlarged the number of organizations and movements that shared a common interest in the topic and could pool resources.

In addition to previous initiatives, a West African official recalled that trade institutions in countries such as Nigeria, Ghana, and Senegal had recognized the importance of civil society engagement with policy-making early on (West African public official 6). The Senegalese

98 *The evolution of participatory trade politics*

government, for example, established a National Committee of International Trade Negotiations in 2001. It constituted a forum for consultation and coordination between the government, the private sector, and civil society on trade issues. Former trade minister of Senegal Aicha Pouye explained in my interview that she had created the Committee due to a belief that all three parties needed to be strongly involved in order to be able to formulate legitimate, well-informed, and welfare-enhancing trade policy positions (Former Senegalese trade minister).

Although being scattered, national practices gave Platform organizations political clout at the regional level, when ECOWAS officials were skeptical of their participation at the start of EPA negotiations. One Platform representative highlighted in my interview that the multiplicity of the EPA process, including decision-makers on the national and the regional policy levels, helped them to secure their chair in the policy-making process (Platform representative 7). Another Platform representative added that it had been an explicit strategy of the Platform to create political support for their member organizations at the domestic level in order to back their standing with ECOWAS trade officials (Platform representative 1). The account is compatible with von Bülow's argument that transformative actors chose their lobbying path in response to their perceptions of their political environment.[15] It also points to the importance of considering all levels of political activity in our analytical frameworks for transnational advocacy.[16]

The experience gathered during previous campaigns held important lessons for Platform organizations when EPA negotiations were launched. During my interviews, West African actors identified the so-called Cotton Initiative at the WTO as their first significant achievement in trade advocacy. The episode provided two important lessons: namely, that actors with limited economic weight could use contradictions in the trading system and the world economy in order to challenge powerful countries on their policies, and that transformative actors could give important impulses to such developments.

Speaking for the Central and West African region, Benin, Burkina-Faso, Chad, and Mali presented the *Sectoral Initiative in Favor of Cotton* to the WTO Committee on Agriculture on 16 May 2003.[17] At the time, cotton accounted for approximately 30 percent of total exports of the four countries and assured the livelihood of millions of farmers.[18] The region was the world's second largest cotton exporter after the United States, which heavily subsidized its cotton producers, thus driving down world market prices.[19] In their initiative, the four countries called on the WTO to recognize "the strategic nature of

The evolution of participatory trade politics 99

cotton for development and poverty reduction in many LDCs," and insisted on the "phase-out of support measures for the production and export of cotton."[20] In addition, they demanded financial compensation for cotton producers for the income losses that would persist during the transition period towards the new regime.[21]

The multilateral trading system has so far failed to produce satisfactory solutions for the cotton issue.[22] The initiative was nonetheless remarkable because it "pitted some of the most politically and economically vulnerable states in the world against the most powerful, and resulted in US concessions."[23] Despite the limited political leverage that these countries traditionally have in international trade negotiations, cotton subsidies became one of the key issues of the Doha Round and played an important role in shifting the attention of WTO negotiations to the development question.[24]

The Cotton Initiative not only demonstrated "the possibilities for politically weak developing countries, in the right conditions, to turn multilateral institutions against their more powerful creators."[25] Because it effectively started at the grassroots level, it was also an impressive demonstration of the types of political opportunity structures that multi-level, information-driven governance contains for trade advocacy. In 2001, local producers' organizations, notably in Burkina-Faso, issued the initial warning about links between subsidization practices of Northern countries and the economic situation of West African cotton farmers. Via the internet, they connected with producers' organizations and other groups across West and Central Africa.[26]

At a regional civil society meeting in Dakar in February 2002, West and Central African cotton producers' associations and regional NGOs announced their intention to pursue the cotton issue in regional and international trade negotiations, thus starting the campaign that culminated in the four governments acting on cotton at the WTO.[27] The network included organizations such as ROPPA and ENDA, which would later cooperate on EPA issues. To the extent that the first impulses came from global South organizations, the Cotton Initiative confirms von Bülow's view that the literature's tendency to focus on civil society organizations and social movements based in the global North misrepresents the dynamics at work in world politics.[28] Even before EPA negotiations took off, the Cotton Initiative already provided evidence for the fact that civil society initiatives in global South countries can have impacts on global economic policy-making.

The Cotton Initiative had additional lessons in store for transformative organizations in West Africa. It indicated "the inconsistency of trade policies and development policies of several of the countries of

100 *The evolution of participatory trade politics*

the North" and pointed "to the limits of globalization, whose alleged positive impacts have yet to materialize for several of the countries of the South."[29] Furthermore, the Cotton Initiative also exposed internal divisions in industrialized countries' governments[30] and showed that states are not unified actors. While West African organizations mounted the Cotton Initiative with the financial support of the French Ministry of Foreign Affairs, which should have been pleased with campaigning success, the French Ministry of Agriculture was opposed to the demands that West Africans made in the WTO due to the challenges brought to the EU's Common Agricultural Policy.[31]

West African civil society organizations perceived the Cotton Initiative as a starting point for continuous trade and development advocacy. As François Traoré, president of the African Cotton Producers Association, said in an interview with ENDA in 2005: "I think that the cotton example has allowed [civil society actors] to raise other subjects [on international trade], around which civil society will continue to mobilize."[32] A Platform representative explained in an interview that the Platform saw itself as carrying out the function of a "regional trade policy watchdog." The representative argued that its member organizations started taking on this role during the Cotton Initiative and subsequently carried it over to EPA, thus again highlighting the importance of the existence of multiple policy-making levels for trade policy formation (Platform representative 3). Pointing to the potential for multiple alliances that global economic governance holds, Eric Hazard explains in an ENDA policy paper: "States did not shy away from nurturing new alliances with industrial representatives, producers organizations and maybe even non-governmental organizations ... the cooperation allowed, in the long run, a considerable reinforcement of the capacities of producers, industrials, non-governmental organizations, but also of the various representatives of African States."[33]

In addition, European and African organizations learnt to cope with the difficulties of transnational North-South lobbying during the Cotton Initiative. Transnational North-South advocacy carries the risk of reproducing the power asymmetries present in the global economic system and can provoke tensions between North and South activists.[34] This is often one concern that observers raise in relation to NGO participation in the WTO. West African participatory trade politics suggests that this is not inevitably the case. During the EPA campaign, civil society actors built on the lessons learnt from previous campaigning. Two interviewees from a European ally of the Platform, for example, explained that it was important for their organizations not to make any public statements in the name of the Platform during the

The evolution of participatory trade politics 101

EPA campaign, in order to demonstrate respect for the Platform's political autonomy and to avoid jeopardizing its credibility (European civil society representatives 2, 3, 4).

Previous trade advocacy therefore provided numerous networks and invaluable lessons on which the EPA campaign could build. Initially difficult relations between public officials and critics of the global trade agenda started further improving when the Platform began providing technical knowledge on trade questions during 2007.

Technical knowledge

Preventing the signing of an EPA at the 31 December 2007 negotiating deadline set in the Cotonou Agreement had been the Platform's primary campaign goal in the first phase of its campaign. To this end, a Platform representative reported, the network mainly used political declarations, public mobilization, and broad, overall impact assessments of the EPA in order to present arguments that would stop the region from adhering to an ECOWAS-EU trade deal (Platform representative 1).

As mentioned in Chapter 1, civil society had long been advocating for regional integration based on the assumption that creating a regional market would be a better economic strategy than remaining locked into commodity-centered trade with the EU. When the non-LDCs Côte d'Ivoire and Ghana initialed individual, goods-only interim EPAs in late 2007 over concerns of European market access loss, this forced the Platform to choose between its no-to-EPA stance and its yes-to-regional-integration stance. Realizing that the region now had to sign an EPA if it wanted to foster a regional market, many organizations chose a third path and moved their attitude from "no to EPA because of development" to "EPA only if it is good for development" (Platform representative 1). One Platform representative recalled in my interview that at a Ministerial Monitoring Committee in Ouagadougou in November 2007, trade ministers for the first time spoke about a "development EPA" and mandated the Regional Negotiating Committee to negotiate an EPA that had a "distinct development component" (Platform representative 1). In an effort to reflect on the specific clauses that a development EPA needed to contain, Platform organizations subsequently began to carry out technical research (Platform representative 1).

According to all West African interviewees, the move had considerable impact on Platform members' interaction with trade officials. It improved the relationship between trade officials and transformative actors and, in the view of all Platform interviewees, was the main

102 *The evolution of participatory trade politics*

reason for their EPA campaigning successes. The Platform conducted or commissioned studies on various EPA topics such as market access, sensitive products, services, coherence with the multilateral trading order, EPA implementation, and policy alternatives. Through their institutionalized access to the decision-making process, they passed their results as well as analysis that partner organizations in the global North provided to public officials.

The decision to produce technical knowledge had two main repercussions. During the process, Platform organizations expanded their own knowledge on trade and developed new perspectives that they had not initially considered. One Platform member explained:

> You get better at what you do by ... engaging with the process. There are many things that we didn't know before, but during the debate issues come up. Dimensions get into it that you need to ... investigate. And in investigating that, you come to conclusions that you didn't know before ... sometimes someone comes into a meeting and asks a seemingly stupid question. And the seemingly stupid question brings out all new dimensions of the topic ... new dimensions are coming into the picture by every day debate ... and of course that has enhanced the capacity of those who are involved in the debate.
>
> (Platform representative 3)

As part of the new strategy of providing technical expertise, Platform members educated their staff on trade issues, notably with the help of their Northern partners (European civil society representative 1).[35] West African public officials confirmed that the strategic adjustment impacted on the way in which they perceived Platform organizations and civil society in general. Officials had initially felt that there were large gaps between their own training on trade issues and activists' perceived lack of information. They explained that transformative organizations initially rejected EPAs on purely ideological grounds. Once civil society groups had acquired trade expertise, officials argued, a dialogue was possible (West African public officials 1, 2, 3, 5, 6, 7, 8, 10). One official explained: "Now they are more appreciated and valuable partners to the negotiating process as opposed to earlier stages where it was just rhetoric and lack of substance. Now they are more appreciated as members of the negotiating team" (West African public official 2).

In addition, trade officials argued that the new approach made Platform organizations more nuanced in their positions. They felt that

The evolution of participatory trade politics   103

as "the level of rhetoric comes down ... [it] has ... opened them up to consider what the EPA entails in detail rather than just looking at the EPA from the outside without even knowing what's in the EPA on the inside. They are more informed to actually contribute as to what is good and what is bad as opposed to just collectively saying no, we don't want any of it" (West African public official 2). This was seen as politically useful, because "the devil is in the detail. So once you look in the detail we can now have a more elaborate and informed debate on what's an EPA" (West African public official 2). In fact, public officials and civil society reported that by 2009, both sides solicited one another for information and exchange on EPA (West African public official 10, Platform representative 4). This confirms Williams's argument that transparency and openness improves relations between trade institutions and their critics to the benefit of both sides.[36]

One open question is whether the change of strategy influenced the Platform's trade political attitude in the long run. My data suggest that the Platform perceived trade officials to be most open to technical language, and saw the capacity to master this language as one basic requirement for entering into trade policy debates. One representative explained: "Technocrats ... are the most difficult [actors] to convince ... they don't tackle political questions although we were facing a political choice" (Platform representative 8).

Other Platform members argued that when they engaged in technical discussion, trade officials had to take them seriously (Platform representatives 1, 2, 3, 6, 7, 8). According to one Platform representative, "things changed because we're not just engaging in demonstration and confrontation, we're giving ... [West African trade officials] the facts, the evidence, the analysis." As a result, the representative argued, "the government and the institutions were more receptive of our input ... When we had strong arguments, it couldn't be resisted" (Platform representative 3). One Platform representative felt that if civil society did not have this "added value" to bring to negotiations, they would not be represented at the negotiating table today (Platform representative 4).

At the same time, the Platform saw knowledge production as a tool for "counterbalancing technical arguments and political pressure" in EPA negotiations (Platform representative 7). According to Platform representatives, combining confrontational and capacity-based strategies required understanding the technical needs of negotiators and the factual needs of the people and adjusting their campaigning with a view to bringing both elements together. In this sense, the Platform was attempting to unpack the political content of technical language and began expressing its own political concerns in technical language at the

104 *The evolution of participatory trade politics*

same time. They reportedly spread the different roles among the Platform's various national organizations according to individual members' capacities and special characteristics (Platform representative 8). One representative insisted: "what you do technically is for one audience. What you do politically is for another audience. But you need to do both." The representative called it "a different kind of campaign that focuses on different levels of people" (Platform representative 7). This is different from trade advocacy in the global North, where civil society organizations working on trade issues tend to choose between providing technical expertise and participating politically in public debates.

The Platform saw both avenues for campaigning as complementary. Platform interviewees insisted that it was the combination of strategies, which they also referred to as "the insider-outsider approach," that had led to their campaign successes (Platform representatives 1, 3, 6, 7). West African participatory trade politics therefore confirms evidence from other policy contexts suggesting that "confrontational and participatory modes of policy work are not mutually exclusive." Rather, "expertise and mobilization play an equally important role in the best advocacy."[37] While the approach was highly effective, Platform members did not see the insider-outsider approach as opportunistic. One Platform representative argued: "You can be an activist and professional at the same time," because EPAs "interest us as citizens and … as Platform members" (Platform representative 4). The statement underlines the relevance of individuals' multiple identities in trade politics. As argued in Chapter 2, any theoretical attempt to construe social agents as consumers only, state officials only, or private-sector representatives only, is arbitrary and brackets political dimensions that arise from overlapping identities in real life situations.

In 2009, Platform representatives had thus not started to perceive themselves as forming a community of experts with trade officials. Rather, in their view, their involvement with trade policy-making remained fundamentally political. They continued to see trade officials as decision-makers whose positions they were trying to influence according to their own trade policy preferences. A Platform representative summed this up in the following words:

> Civil society … cannot always be confrontational. We need to engage with the process through the insider-outsider approach … You need to befriend the government, you need to lobby them … in order to put your position through … and then while you're doing that you need to generate evidence, you need to generate

The evolution of participatory trade politics 105

facts to back up your position ... within the friendly relationship, and sometimes ... you think ... "if I don't put pressure through the people, through mobilizing, ... [trade officials] will not really listen to me when I'm talking" ... But when they see ... people marching on the street ... they think ... "let's get their [i.e. civil society's] position on board." And at this point in time we could say that whatever be the positioning of ECOWAS ... they would think twice about what civil society actors have to say ... in terms of showing analysis, in terms of providing alternatives, in terms of enhancing consultation.

(Platform representative 3)

The political environment of EPA negotiations arguably played a role in the attitudinal change that the provision of expertise prompted. West African trade institutions lack trade policy and negotiating capacity when compared with the EU. In terms of negotiating capacity, the EU entered EPA talks with a considerable advantage in resources and experience. European countries have been driving members of multilateral trade rounds since the establishment of the GATT in 1947. As a result, European trade negotiators have clearly formulated their understanding of Europe's trade interests and are currently pursuing it in numerous bilateral trade agreements in parallel with multilateral and EPA talks. While the extent of capacity varies across West Africa, information on the domestic economic situation is not always systematically available. In addition, certain prerequisite policy processes for establishing a free trade area with the EU had not been accomplished in the region. The fact that the ECOWAS customs union was not consolidated by 2009 presented one important missing element. Defining what a development EPA was and which concrete clauses it required added a further challenge. In the ensuing situation of institutional strain, providing free, alternative, and independent expert opinion turned Platform actors into valuable allies for West African governments and trade institutions that did not necessarily have the resources to produce relevant studies (European civil society representative 3). As a Platform representative explained, "[West African trade officials] need somebody who knows ... it doesn't matter if the guy is a civil society actor or a government person" (Platform representative 3).

Overall, when I conducted my interviews, all West African trade officials valued the Platform's input as analytically sound and politically useful (West African public officials 1, 2, 3, 5, 6, 7, 8, 10). One official explained that Platform involvement at the technical level occurred at a time when West African trade institutions had developed

106   *The evolution of participatory trade politics*

an ambition to re-claim policy autonomy on trade vis-à-vis the international community. The official said: "I think we've gone beyond the stage where we simply accept [a trade policy line] because it's given to us ... government had already put in mechanisms and structures to ensure we have quality personnel and staff to analyze and make counter-proposals and then obviously we also appreciate different perspectives from civil society" (West African public official 2). This supports my argument in Chapter 1 that critical actors strengthened the position of those public officials within the ranks of the West African negotiating team that were critical of the global trade agenda. It confirms that the state is not a unified actor for the purpose of trade policy but that variations in normative preference exist among the people that make up institutions.

Interviewees further stressed the lesson from the Cotton Initiative that filling capacity gaps in under-funded global South public institutions turned transformative trade political actors into attractive allies because they could provide technical trade expertise in a fast and independent manner (West African public officials 4, 10). One specific advantage of cooperating with the Platform from the point of view of officials lay in the fact that "civil society can free resources and conduct research much more quickly than we can" (West African public official).

Taken together, the statements show how radically the view that trade officials had on transformative organizations changed during the consolidation of participatory trade policy-making. Being on good terms with public officials enhanced the quality of the Platform's EPA campaign, because it gave them access to internal information at both regional and national levels (Platform representative 6). One observer reported that especially in the early days of the campaign, Platform members receiving financial contributions from European NGOs were suspected of representing European interests (West African journalist). Conducting scientific research, sharing the results with public officials, and speaking a technical language eased underlying communication problems about transformative actors' understandings, motivations, and policy goals in West African trade policy. My evidence thus indicates that understandings of what trade policy is about and who should be included in trade decision-making are not static, but can evolve over time.

From the perspective of officials, the fact that Platform organizations hired individuals with similar educational backgrounds as West African public officials helped to create a level of confidence among the actors that had previously not been present. As one trade official noted: "We all studied together, we hold the same degrees" (West African public official 10). Interestingly, the regional civil society representative also

The evolution of participatory trade politics   107

highlighted the role that education played in efforts to break into EPA decision-making. In order to gain respect for his position in the West African negotiating set-up, he recalled telling officials: "I claim the status of expert amongst you because I hold a PhD in Development Studies. I will not accept being told that I don't understand things" (Platform representative 1). At the same time, some civil society actors perceived this as a problem. A representative of ROPPA criticized in my interview that individuals came from the same school of thought and insisted that the system needed to change (West African civil society representative 1). The specific nature of individual activism and personal relationships therefore also characterized the trade political agency through which West African participatory trade politics emerged.

Individual activism

Individual activism was important for creating and seizing the political opportunity that enabled transformative participation in trade policy-making in the region. Scholars acknowledge that individuals matter for the outcome of a campaign.[38] In West Africa, individuals who decided to get involved in trade campaigning provided momentum that led to political agency. One Platform representative explained in my interview: "one of the things that happened in West Africa which ... did not happen in other [EPA] regions is that the West African civil society used the provisions of the Cotonou Agreement to assert their role ... and to say to ECOWAS: 'we can't just come to the Ministerial Meetings and just see you talk ... the agreement provides for our active contribution and we demand it be recognized as such'" (Platform representative 3).

When asked about the origins of participatory trade politics, many Platform interviewees suggested that they quite simply got involved with EPA campaigning because they felt that they should. One representative of a Platform organization recalled that civil society realized in 2002 that "we can't just be observers ... there is reason for us to be actively involved. And that led to all kinds of coalitions" (Platform representative 3). These coalitions within and across regions played a crucial role in bringing about transformative participation in West African trade politics. Commenting on ATN, one observer noted that the network "galvanized the campaign around the region to create a particular energy and that was what transformed the relationships that were being built around West Africa into a very potent policy-demanding platform in West Africa" (Platform representative 7).

108 *The evolution of participatory trade politics*

Arguably, the energy resulted from a conscious decision by individuals then involved with the various groups "to find ways of influencing the evolution of [EPA] policy" (Platform representative 7). One Platform representative pointed out that the creation and enlargement of policy space for civic participation was one of the long-term goals of the organization's campaign. For this reason, Platform members wanted to "give a civic and political meaning to the term participation" from the early days of the Cotonou process (Platform representative 2). In addition, one representative argued, "one major goal had been to change the way that civil society is perceived ... they are responsible people who are capable of making a contribution" (Platform representative 1). Another representative argued that West African trade politics became participatory, partly because the Platform claimed a right to the legal opportunities provided in the Cotonou Agreement, which transformative groups in other EPA regions simply did not do (Platform representative 7).

As the example of the regional civil society representative's re-establishment in the Ouagadougou Ministerial Monitoring Committee Meeting in December 2007 showed, the quality of personal relationships played a role in the evolution of West African participatory trade politics. Platform members not only used good connections to establish their participatory rights against resistance from West African trade officials, but also from European officials. One representative recalled that the European Commission had tried to prevent civil society participation in one negotiating meeting. It had reportedly informed the West African negotiating team that the meeting room was too small to hold all representatives. ENDA subsequently contacted the Senegalese trade minister "who had worked with ENDA since the Cotonou Agreement ... He said: 'If one member of the delegation is not invited, Senegal will not participate.' The Commission gave in" (Platform representative 8). Interviewees further pointed out that good personal relations between the Platform members were one key political condition for the development of a successful strategy, notably also in terms of mediating between Francophone and Anglophone groups (Platform representative 2).

Finally, individuals mattered because their personal level of activity and engagement changed the nature of trade politics in West Africa. One European actor closely involved with the West African EPA process felt that transformative participation was partly the personal merit of the Platform civil society representative (European civil society representative 1). Similarly, a West African public official explained that the behavior of the Platform representative in negotiations had a

The evolution of participatory trade politics 109

decisive impact on the way in which both negotiations and participatory trade politics evolved (West African public official 5). European Commission officials cited the replacement of the regional civil society representative in 2007 as a case in point. One member of the EU negotiating team explained: "At the beginning of negotiations the civil society representative was totally silent in the meeting but active outside the meetings. She was more an observer, but helped to prepare the positions before the meetings. And now it is really the opposite, he's very, very present in the meetings and on all the issues. So he is really negotiating" (European public official 1). Because there was only one civil society representative included in the West African negotiating team, the behavior of the individual filling the role had a bearing on the way in which other negotiators perceived civil society at the table and on the level of influence that was exercised during negotiations.

One European civil society representative who had been closely cooperating with Platform organizations in West Africa expressed the view that it had been positive for the Platform's campaign that the first regional civil society representative had fulfilled a more observational role. The interviewee felt that trade officials on both sides needed to get used to the idea of transformative participation in trade negotiations at the beginning of the EPA process and that too pro-active involvement on the part of the regional civil society representative at that time could have jeopardized the standing of the Platform in the negotiating structure. The interviewee believed that the initial restraint had provided the groundwork for the considerable freedom of expression that the second regional civil society representative enjoyed with trade officials (European civil society representative 4).

Conclusion

Although one Platform representative qualified government-civil society relations in West Africa during the early stages of EPA negotiations as "confrontational" (Platform representative 3), the way in which the political environment interacted with trade political agency in the West African EPA context led to the consolidation of transformative participation in the trade policy formation process during the year 2008. Negative experience with the outcomes of the Uruguay Round motivated citizens in the region to organize around trade issues several years prior to EPA negotiations. When EPA talks began, the wording of both the Cotonou Agreement and the ECOWAS Negotiating Roadmap opened the possibility for civil society participation because both texts explicitly referred to the term. The West African

110 *The evolution of participatory trade politics*

socio-economic context further created a political situation in which public officials, the corporate sector, and civil society shared one very fundamental, long-term policy goal, namely the development of the West African region. The notion provided a basis for dialogue among actors that had initially been skeptical of each other's policy goals.

In addition, previous trade campaigns, notably the WTO Cotton Initiative, had equipped West African NGOs with campaigning experience, trade policy expertise, and regional and transnational networks on which they could build for the EPA campaign. One of the lessons from the Cotton Initiative was that expressing a trade political position in technical language and backing it up with scientific evidence could turn critics of the global trade agenda into attractive trade political allies for public officials. The scientific expertise and technical know-how that Platform members began to provide around 2007 was therefore another important source of their influence on the negotiating substance. What was additionally necessary for participatory trade politics to emerge were actors that were able to recognize political opportunity when it presented itself and that had the human and financial resources both to seize and expand on it. In this sense, personal agency was crucial in bringing about participatory trade politics. As one representative of a Platform organization put it, "Recognizing that [political opportunity] is a major thing" (Platform representative 3).

Despite the fact that all actors accepted participatory trade politics as a characteristic of West African EPA policy-making by 2009, one West African journalist working on trade questions since 2003 explained in my interview: "relations [between public officials and civil society] are less harsh [in 2009], but there is still mistrust" (West African journalist). Cleavages were at times visible from the other side of the negotiating table and were thought to affect negotiations. One European Commission official testified: "the representatives of the private sector and of civil society ... have their own views on the different issues, so it can make the negotiations maybe more difficult to progress because they might have some diverging views from ECOWAS" (European public official 1).

Both statements suggest that participatory trade politics not only emerged through struggle for participation, as I have shown in this chapter. Contestations did not fade when participatory trade politics was consolidated in 2008. Instead, contestations over EPA substance and decision-making mechanisms continued to mark the West African trade policy formation process on EPA. Therefore, the question is not only how participatory trade politics evolved historically, but also why ECOWAS continued to apply it, bearing in mind that the former gives partial answers to the latter.

Notes

1 Marisa von Bülow, *Building Transnational Networks: Civil Society and the Politics of Trade in the Americas* (Cambridge: Cambridge University Press, 2010).

2 For example, Thomas W. Hertel, Bernard M. Hoekman and Will Martin, "Developing Countries and a New Round of WTO Negotiations," *The World Bank Research Observer* 17, no. 1 (2002): 113–40; Aaditya Mattoo and Arvind Subramanian, *The WTO and the Poorest Countries: The Stark Reality* (Washington, DC: International Monetary Fund, 2004); and Michael F. Jensen, "African Demands for Special and Differential Treatment in the Doha Round: An Assessment and Analysis," *Development Policy Review* 25, no. 1 (2007): 91–112.

3 For example, Dani Rodrik, *The Global Governance of Trade: As if Development Really Mattered* (New York: United Nations Development Programme, 2001); Paul Brenton, "Integrating the Least Developed Countries into the World Trading System: The Current Impact of European Union Preferences Under 'Everything But Arms'," *Journal of World Trade* 37, no. 3 (2003): 623–46; William R. Cline, *Trade Policy and Global Poverty* (Washington, DC: Institute for International Economics, 2004); and Rorden Wilkinson, "The Problematic of Trade and Development Beyond the Doha Round," *Journal of International Trade and Diplomacy* 3, no. 1 (2009): 155–86.

4 Michael J. Finger, "Implementation of Uruguay Round Agreements: Problems for Developing Countries," *The World Economy* 24, no. 9 (2001): 1097–108.

5 Richard Gibb, "Post-Lomé: The European Union and the South," *Third World Quarterly* 21, no. 3 (2000): 457–81.

6 Sylvia Ostry, "The Uruguay Round North-South Grand Bargain: Implications for Future Negotiations," in *The Political Economy of International Trade: Essays in Honor of Robert E. Hudec*, ed. Daniel L.M. Kennedy and James D. Southwick (Cambridge: Cambridge University Press, 2002), 287.

7 Eric Hazard, *Négociations commerciales internationales et réduction de la pauvreté: Le livre blanc sur le coton* (Dakar: ENDA, 2005).

8 Namely Articles 1, 2, 4, 6, 8, 10 and 11.

9 Stephen Hurt, "Co-operation and Coercion? The Cotonou Agreement Between the European Union and ACP States and the End of the Lomé Convention," *Third World Quarterly* 24, no. 1 (2003): 172.

10 Laura Macdonald and Mildred A. Schwartz, "Political Parties and NGOs in the Creation of New Trading Blocs in the Americas," *International Political Science Review* 23, no. 2 (2002): 135–58; Holly Jarman, "The Other Side of the Coin: Knowledge, NGOs and EU Trade Policy," *Politics* 28, no. 1 (2008): 26–32; and Erin Hannah, "NGOs and the European Union: Examining the Power of Epistemes in the EC's TRIPS and Access to Medicines Negotiations," *Journal of Civil Society* 7, no. 2 (2011): 179–206.

11 Ken Ukaoha, "EPA as Impediment to Nigeria's Development Strategy," *This Day*, 18 May 2006.

12 Adebayo Olukoshi, *West Africa's Political Economy in the Next Millennium: Retrospect and Prospect* (Dakar: CODESRIA, 2001).

13 Sophie Melief and Paul van Wijk, *Order Out of Chaos: Mapping the Complexity of Pan African Civil Society. Two Thematic Mappings by Region and Their Pan-African Linkages* (Den Haag: Oxfam Novib, 2008).

112 *The evolution of participatory trade politics*

14 ATN 2011, *ATN*, twnafrica.org/index.php?option=com_content&view=cat egory&id=47&Itemid=72.
15 Von Bülow, *Building Transnational Networks: Civil Society and the Politics of Trade in the Americas.*
16 Kathryn Sikkink, "Patterns of Dynamic Multilevel Governance and the Insider-Outsider Coalition," in *Transnational Protest & Global Activism*, ed. Donatella Della Porta and Sidney Tarrow (Lanham, MD: Rowman & Littlefield, 2005), 151–73.
17 WTO, *Poverty Reduction: Sectoral Initiative in Favour of Cotton*, Joint Proposal by Benin, Burkina Faso, Chad and Mali, TN/AG/GEN/4, 16 May 2003.
18 Daniel A. Sumner, "Reducing Cotton Subsidies: The DDA Cotton Initiative," in *Agricultural Trade Reform and the Doha Development Agenda*, ed. Kym Anderson and Will Martin (Washington, DC and New York: The World Bank and Palgrave Macmillan, 2006), 271–92.
19 Elinor L. Heinisch "West Africa versus the United States on Cotton Subsidies: How, Why and What Next?" *Journal of Modern African Studies* 44, no. 2 (2006): 251–74.
20 WTO, *Poverty Reduction: Sectoral Initiative in Favour of Cotton*, 2.
21 WTO, *Poverty Reduction: Sectoral Initiative in Favour of Cotton*.
22 Donna Lee, "Poverty and Cotton in the Doha Development Agenda," in *Trade, Poverty, Development: Getting Beyond the WTO's Doha Deadlock*, ed. Rorden Wilkinson and James Scott (London: Routledge, 2013), 72–90.
23 Heinisch, "West Africa versus the United States on Cotton Subsidies: How, Why and What Next?" 270.
24 Sumner, "Reducing Cotton Subsidies: The DDA Cotton Initiative."
25 Heinisch, "West Africa versus the United States on Cotton Subsidies: How, Why and What Next?" 252.
26 Hazard, *Négociations commerciales internationales et réduction de la pauvreté: Le livre blanc sur le coton.*
27 Hélène Seignier and Marc Lévy, *Le coton à Cancun: Un bon exemple d'articulation entre influences des acteurs sociaux et gouvernance d'état* (Paris: Réseau IMPACT, 2004); and Denis Pesche and Kako Nubukpo, "L'Afrique du coton à Cancún: Retour sur la genèse d'une négociation," *AGRIDAPE* 24, no. 1 (2008): 15–17.
28 Von Bülow, *Building Transnational Networks: Civil Society and the Politics of Trade in the Americas.*
29 Hazard, *Négociations commerciales internationales et réduction de la pauvreté: Le livre blanc sur le coton*, 149.
30 Hazard, *Négociations commerciales internationales et réduction de la pauvreté: Le livre blanc sur le coton.*
31 Seignier and Lévy, *Le coton à Cancun: Un bon exemple d'articulation entre influences des acteurs sociaux et gourvernance d'état.*
32 Hazard, *Négociations commerciales internationales et réduction de la pauvreté: Le livre blanc sur le coton*, 17.
33 Hazard, *Négociations commerciales internationales et réduction de la pauvreté: Le livre blanc sur le coton*, 149.
34 Seignier and Lévy, *Le coton à Cancun: Un bon exemple d'articulation entre influences des acteurs sociaux et gouvernance d'état*; Shareen Hertel, *Unexpected Power: Conflict and Change among Transnational Activists* (Ithaca, NY: Cornell University Press, 2006).

The evolution of participatory trade politics 113

35 One ENDA member, for example, underwent trade policy training at ICTSD in Geneva. ICTSD describes itself as an "independent, non-profit and non-governmental organization" aiming to "influence the international trade system such that it advances to the goal of sustainable development." Since the organization "empowers stakeholders in trade policy through information, networking, dialogue, well-targeted research, and capacity building" and "identifies knowledge gaps in international trade rule- and policy-making from a sustainable development perspective," ICTSD can be categorized as an organization with a reformist stance towards the global trade agenda. See ICTSD 2011, *About*, ictsd.org/about/.
36 Marc Williams, "Contesting Global Trade Rules: Social Movements and the World Trade Organisation," in *Global Tensions: Challenges and Opportunities in the World Economy*, ed. Lourdes Benería and Savitri Bisnath (London: Routledge, 2004), 193–206.
37 Caroline Harper, "Do the Facts Matter? NGOs, Research, and International Advocacy," in *Global Citizen Action*, ed. Michael Edwards and John Gaventa (London: Earthscan, 2001), 249.
38 Matthew J.O. Scott, "Danger-Landmines! NGO-Government Collaboration in the Ottawa Process," in *Global Citizen Action*, ed. Michael Edwards and John Gaventa (London: Earthscan, 2001), 121–33.

4 Actors' assessments of West African participatory trade politics

- Merits of participation
- Challenges of participation
- Conclusion

Actors' assessments of West African participatory trade politics shared two common features that point to the importance of their double embeddedness in social networks and political environments and of their varying interpretations of these realities. On the one hand, international economic institutions today emphasize the importance of good governance, especially in the context of global South policy-making, and there is broad consensus that the term includes criteria such as transparency and accountability.[1] It would therefore have been difficult for my interviewees to condemn West Africa's transformation towards more inclusive trade policy-making practices per se. Instead, they broadly agreed that civil society participation in trade politics was in principle positive.

On the other hand, open and hidden contestations among public officials and transformative organizations characterized participatory trade politics as a day-to-day policy-making process. While one West African negotiator qualified the negotiating set-up as "a big success" (West African public official 1), the interviewee, like all public officials interviewed, identified room for improvement in the practice. Similarly, although Platform representatives were on the whole satisfied with the level of influence reached, doubts remained about the longevity of the participatory mechanism. One Platform representative explained: "we have not sufficiently advanced, I think, to appear as essential and to enjoy significant attention ... We are doing this work to enlarge democratic space ... I think we have advanced a little, but not very well" (Platform representative 2).

Assessments of participatory trade politics 115

The data I presented in previous chapters suggests that the content of trade rules and the political mechanism through which they were established constituted interconnected areas of political and social contestation in West Africa. The data I analyze in this chapter shows that participatory trade politics also triggered deeper struggles over political authority itself and put underlying social and political power relations in West African societies into question. Conflict had not openly erupted between the actors in 2009, nor has it, to my knowledge, at the time of writing. Instead, it played out within the framework of the competing meanings that different sets of actors attached to the terms of the debate. Below, I highlight added "capacity," "inclusiveness," and altered "balance of power" in highly asymmetrical EPA negotiations as positive achievements that my interviewees stressed. Debates about the perceived shortcomings of participatory trade politics arose around the notions of "civil society," "representation," and "legitimacy."

Overall, West African participatory trade politics was not only marked by interlinked contestations over political substance and political authority, but constituted a learning process in its own right. When debating the merits and challenges of West African participatory trade politics, my interviewees wrestled with some of the most important problems in political theory. I cannot give full credit to the vast literature on the various theoretical debates in one chapter. Observing participatory trade politics in action, however, carries the benefit of providing empirical evidence on which the literature can subsequently build.

Merits of participation

My interviewees felt that transformative participation broadened the discourse on trade and made debates richer than they would otherwise have been. They confirmed Esty's view that engaging more broadly with civil society organizations and social movements introduces ideas and views that would not otherwise be present to the benefit of the policy outcome.[2] West African actors experienced civil society participation as positive because it boosted West Africa's negotiating capacity and improved their trade policy goals. Transformative participation also helped to correct power asymmetries between ECOWAS and the EU, because it provided the West African side with leverage for political pressure. At the same time, engaging a bigger variety of opinions also introduced otherwise absent controversies into trade decision-making. Thus, the various accounts of what was positive about transformative participation also contained potential for conflict.

116 *Assessments of participatory trade politics*

Capacity

Civil society input enriched trade policy-making in West Africa because it added substance to ECOWAS' understanding of the negotiating agenda, and it provided access to information that would otherwise not have been available. One West African trade official explained that civil society participation was useful, because "there are things that escape us ... [the Platform] provide their input ... for example the contentious issues [that is to say the third party Most Favored Nation (MFN) clause[3] and the non-execution clause[4]] ... We had not thought of that" (West African public official 10). The official added: "To see how they analyze questions is different from our approach ... I pick up things, I repeat in meetings, I take inspiration." One Platform representative confirmed: "the issue of capacity is crucial. ECOWAS needs people who have technical expertise" (Platform representative 3).

Through their transnational networks, Platform members had at times better access to European documents than ECOWAS negotiators (Platform representative 1). One of the pronounced goals of European organizations supporting the Platform campaign was to provide West African organizations with information from the EU policy-making context (European civil society representative 4). The insight that transformative actors could access information from the global North through their transnational networks was one lesson learnt from previous experiences with trade advocacy. The person who had run the Cotton Initiative for ENDA remembered: "I was the expert on cotton in West Africa at the time. Sometimes I got information quicker than the ambassador in Geneva" (European civil society representative 2).

In addition, the Platform's financial independence helped to address ECOWAS' capacity constraints. One West African official explained: "NGOs have more means than the administration ... the administration has more staff, but it cannot always finance all the traveling ... Also, civil society can commission studies" (West African public official 9). The European Commission had also commissioned studies during the EPA process, notably the so-called Sustainability Impact Assessments, carried out by a consortium of international consultancy companies, research groups, and think tanks.[5] As noted in Chapter 1, there were concerns in West Africa that relying on studies commissioned by the negotiating partner would not be a politically wise strategy in trade talks. One Platform representative confirmed: "civil society organizations are flexible and can respond to different needs within government institutions" (Platform representative 3). Another Platform representative added: "We are about to launch a study for 30 million

Assessments of participatory trade politics 117

Francs CFA [approximately €500,000], which ECOWAS would not be able to do" (Platform representative 1).

Exchanging information also improved communication and thus relations between public officials and transformative actors. The exchange on negotiating substance that ensued further minimized the potential for tension among the different actors. One West African trade official explained: "If today I need information, I don't hesitate to call [the Platform] ... civil society [also] approaches the government to verify information before they position themselves publicly" (West African public official 9). The statement suggests that a level of trust had developed between the Platform and public officials that had not been previously present, and that participatory practices helped to create this trust.

Despite successful cooperation, some interviewees doubted that transformative agency had changed the nature of trade policy-making in West Africa in a fundamental way. One representative of a European organization that supported the Platform campaign questioned whether the Platform could continue to participate once West African states gained enough capacity to engage in trade negotiations without support. "It is an interesting model," the representative admitted, "but is it sustainable in the long term? ... The space won't be the same with the state getting stronger" (European civil society representative 2). Similarly, one Platform representative was hesitant on the question of whether trade policy-making was substantially becoming more democratic in West Africa. The representative stated: "Trade negotiators only listen when we supply them with information that is in their interest. I am not sure that we have managed to make them on the whole more aware of our concerns" (Platform representative 2). Another representative confirmed: "Technical aspects are important but there is a political dimension one has to master and I am not sure that we are mastering it" (Platform representative 1).

Some Platform members thus suspected that trade officials had an instrumentalist approach to the Platform and included them in EPA negotiations as long as they perceived the network as useful. The suspicions build on the implicit assumption that public officials' attitudes are static and that participatory trade politics had not altered their view on transformative actors as such. While some statements from trade officials that I cite throughout suggest that such concerns were not entirely unfounded, trade officials also highlighted other positive dimensions, such as a belief in the legitimacy of inclusive policy-making and a conviction that civil society should participate in trade policy-making because trade policy affected the people. Overall, my

118 *Assessments of participatory trade politics*

data support the view that public officials' perceptions of transformative groups did change over time. In fact, many were of the opinion that inclusiveness was a beneficial aspect of participatory trade policy-making mechanisms in and of itself.

Inclusiveness

While public officials and Platform members unanimously valued the inclusiveness of West African participatory trade politics, they stressed different aspects of inclusiveness as essential. For negotiators, the main benefit lay in adding another voice to the debate, which facilitated the formulation of the region's trade political interests and provided inspiration for policy alternatives. For civil society, inclusiveness opened up the opportunity to reclaim autonomy over trade policy-making from the realm of technocracy. European negotiators in principle welcomed West Africa's participatory approach and felt that it was up to ECOWAS to decide how to configure the negotiating team. One European Commission official explained: "negotiating is about trust and if it makes your partner more comfortable to include in their team a wide range of opinions, then it makes a better basis to start off with the whole negotiations" (European public official 1).

When commenting on the inclusive nature of participatory trade policy-making, many public officials stressed their belief that the state's role was to balance many, sometimes diverging interests in society. One West African trade official explained: "Civil society can channel a certain number of preoccupations and bring them to the attention of negotiators, which was not always the case before. It comes with reflections and analyses that allow negotiators to nuance their positions in order to consider the interests of those actors that the negotiating process will have an impact on" (West African public official 6). Another official argued that it was useful for the state to hear as many voices as possible in order to make sure that "decisions will not constitute a monologue ... that it won't be decisions taken within secrets of cabinet which run the risk of not reflecting a reality" (West African public official 4). As becomes apparent throughout my book, the politics in trade politics arises exactly over the question of which reality to reflect, although none of my interviewees directly addressed this issue.

Mirroring insights from the literature,[6] one West African public official felt that adding previously absent voices to trade negotiations would lead to better outcomes. Since overall welfare depended on the behavior of the government, the business community, and the broader public, the official argued, all parties should be heard in trade

Assessments of participatory trade politics 119

policy-making (West African public official 1). Platform organizations shared the view that trade policy directly affected the citizenry in its entirety, as opposed to primarily affecting select groups of special interests, as the standard political economy literature assumes. One Platform representative explained that participation was essential, because "citizens that contribute to the elaboration of the rules of the game, that contribute to the definition of laws, etc., have a better chance to see these laws and rules reflect their interests and therefore have a better chance to have opportunities that help them to escape poverty" (Platform representative 2).

The fact that by 2009, EPAs were framed as "trade and development" agreements, rather than "trade only" agreements, encouraged this view. A European Commission official declared: "I think that that balance is a positive force because ultimately the EPAs are not just trade agreements, they are trade and development partnerships ... so it is important that we get the points of view from civil society and also the private sector to make sure that we get the best deal possible" (European public official 2). European officials testified that seen from the other side of the negotiating table, "there is good communication between ECOWAS, [WAEMU], civil society and the private sector, they normally share a common position."

West African and European trade officials further favored participation on the basis of the expectation that involved groups would communicate results to the population once agreements were signed (West African public officials 1, 2, 3, 5, 6, 7, 8). A European Commission official asserted: "Politically it is positive because we can expect that they [civil society and the private sector] will after that explain where we are and take advice from the different parts of their membership" (European public official 1). At the same time, public officials were critical of how transformative organizations performed in this task. One West African public official noted that the Platform did not always fulfill the role of communicating public trade policy choices well. The issue relates to the obligations that participatory rights entailed for civil society organizations. It connects to broader debates on the notions of "civil society," "representation," and "legitimacy," that I discuss below.

For most Platform interviewees, inclusiveness was related to questions of democratization. One Platform representative identified participatory trade politics as "a system that contributes to democracy in that it provides credibility in society for negotiations that concern its future" (Platform representative 2). From the point of view of Platform representatives, the necessity of democratizing West African trade

120 *Assessments of participatory trade politics*

policy-making arose from the negative impacts of past trade policy decisions highlighted in Chapter 3. They argued that poor trade policy-making in the region had typically been foreign-imposed, notably through Bretton Woods institutions. While the state held trade political authority in West Africa, Platform members felt that in reality, political authority over West African trade regulation predominantly lay in the hands of international technocracy. Democracy, which meant inclusiveness, was a tool to fight this reality.

One Platform representative defined democracy as "the ability of the citizen to get his government to act on behalf of his interest ... and not to act on behalf of other interests" (Platform representative 7). The representative explained: "The problem that I have is that over the past 20 or so years, the primary responsibility of a [West African] government to do this [i.e. to act on behalf of citizens' interests] ... has been taken away. The governments have abdicated to structural adjustment conditionality, to WTO law ... and now to the EPAs ... so part of the fight for democracy is for the right for the governments to formulate policies for its citizens" (Platform representative 7). While they felt that participatory trade politics was a positive step in this direction, some Platform representatives expressed the desire to go further and provide civil society actors with decision-making powers (Platform representative 2). By driving the double strategy of the insider-outsider approach (see Chapter 3), the Platform tried to resolve the inherent tension in their campaign between their desire to reclaim political autonomy from technocracy and their need to speak the language of technocracy to maintain their influential role in trade politics.

Added transparency presented another double-edged benefit of participatory trade politics. One civil society representative commended the fact that Platform involvement made the content and course of negotiations considerably more transparent than was usually the case in trade talks (European civil society representative 1). However, Platform representatives explained that the transparency they provided also endangered their position in the negotiating team, although not leading to the break-down of negotiations, as is sometimes predicted in broader trade governance debates. For example, the regional civil society representative reported back to the Platform on negotiators' behavior and publicly denounced instances where negotiators overstepped the West African negotiating mandate in their view, occasionally using very strong language. In a 2009 declaration, for example, the Platform described European negotiators as "condescending" and "paternalistic" and West African negotiators as "passive," "defeatist," and "insensitive to the long-term stakes of the negotiation."[7]

Unsurprisingly, it was at times politically difficult for Platform representatives to combine the roles of negotiating partner and trade policy watchdog in West Africa.

European officials also judged transparency as a potential obstacle to negotiations. One official explained:

> Normally between the [WAEMU] and ECOWAS Commission and ourselves there is full trust and we know that we work in close meetings and there is very good, positive atmosphere to make progress. But sometimes, also, it's negotiations and we have to defend our line. We don't express openly always our divergences, even if it happens that ... we converge on this, we diverge on that, but if we need to make progress, it is not politicized. But with the representative of civil society we know that we might read in the newspaper the following day about the positioning of the [European] Commission in the negotiations, which is not always very fair.
>
> (European public official 1)

The divergences in actors' assessments of the benefits of inclusiveness suggest that in West Africa, merits and challenges of participatory trade politics were not always neatly separable. The third positive aspect of transformative participation, namely balancing power relations, confirmed this basic tension.

Balance of power

One Platform representative noted during my interview: "the political weight of the EU is such that African countries in general, and the West Africans in particular, are not able to resist its force" (Public representative 2). West African public officials perceived participatory trade politics as positive when Platform organizations innovated on negotiating strategies or provided policy alternatives that they had not considered. In this case, they argued that participation helped to tilt the balance of power between ECOWAS and the EU, even in the absence of economic weight, which is generally perceived as the foundation of negotiating power in trade talks. As indicated in Part I and Appendix II, extreme economic and political asymmetries marked ECOWAS-EU EPA negotiations. The fact that a WTO ruling seemed to back the EU's negotiating strategy exacerbated power asymmetries. Former colonial relationships further created a negotiating atmosphere marked by an air of alleged European technical and political superiority. Highlighting the context-dependent nature of trade policy-making, one

122   *Assessments of participatory trade politics*

West African trade official testified that West African negotiators "realized that civil society had to help the region to upset the balance of power" (West African public official 7).

West African trade officials appreciated the fact that Platform positions often echoed their own concerns in the negotiating process. When listing the advantages of participatory trade politics, almost all West African trade officials used the expression: "they [i.e. the Platform] can say things that we can't say." The perceived freedom to speak their minds not only related to trade policy content, but also to the wording and tone employed at the negotiating table. One West African official testified: "We neither have the negotiating power nor the capacity of developed countries ... civil society is a means that suits us ... it's a pressure group ... One personal opinion: developed countries often draw back on certain questions because civil society stood up to say no ... If they would have left it to us and the big countries, this would be very difficult ... It facilitates our task ... sometimes, they say things that we can't say" (West African public official 9).

In the context of sensitive post-colonial ECOWAS-EU relations and economic dependency, the civil society representative appeared as a person who could openly voice criticisms and present views that would otherwise not have been heard at the negotiating table. Platform representatives, for example, generally did not shy away from applying the imagery of colonial exploitation in order to discredit EPAs.[8] One West African public official explained:

> The European Union is the second wealthiest region in the world, West Africa is the poorest region. Civil society is there to say that the big should not crush the small ... They can say things that we can't say. After 50 years of partnership with the European Union and 2 billion Franc CFA [approximately €3 million] of current financing, you can't tell each other everything anymore. Civil society plays a compensational role.
>
> (West African public official 3)

European Commission officials confirmed that the regional civil society representative on the West African negotiating team made use of his political autonomy. "Even if they [i.e. the Platform] have been nominated by the West African side, they are not entirely bound by the common decisions or common opinions and they do behave independently," one European official explained; "they have their degree of independence and at least in West Africa, you can see that they make use of their independence" (European public official 1).

Assessments of participatory trade politics 123

Transformative organizations balanced power relations in more nuanced ways than public officials highlighted in interviews. Overall, West African trade officials did not share the Platform's transformative EPA stance. Four principal reasons were put forward for this in my interviews. First, public officials were generally not as critical towards the global trade agenda as Platform organizations. Second, officials had a mandate to negotiate a trade agreement with the EU and felt that it was their task to fulfill the mandate. Third, one Platform representative explained that West African political and economic elites, contrary to the majority of West African populations, benefited from European trade deals and thus had an incentive to pursue the EPA (Platform representative 2). Fourth, another Platform representative felt that the difficulty was psychological and rooted in historical relations. The Platform member declared: "All our decision-makers suffer from the complex of the colonized when facing their [European] interlocutor" (Platform representative 1). The representative felt that while public officials might have understood that the EU was not negotiating EPA out of altruism or to comply with WTO rules, but had a hidden agenda in negotiations, the administration lacked the courage to challenge the EU's official discourse (Platform representative 1). The statement implies that past experiences are relevant for present economic policy-making. I discuss this point in detail in the next chapter.

Platform representatives not only confronted the European Commission in EPA negotiations. They could also produce counter-pressure at the domestic level due to the fact that the Platform not only operated at the regional level, but at the same time was a network made up of national organizations. One representative recalled that when resistance to signing the EPA on the 31 December 2007 deadline was mounting in the region, the European Commission "bypassed the minister of trade ... and went directly to the president" in order to put political pressure on individual countries to sign (Platform representative 7). The episode shows that Platform organizations were not the only actors that used a multi-level strategy. It suggests that public officials can behave quite similarly to the way in which transnational actors behave in world politics, thus validating the application of the relational approach to studying the interaction between trade officials and transformative groups.

Thus, Platform members worked against those forces within the West African team that favored the European approach. One Platform member explained: "Civil society acted to counter the influence of [WAEMU] which is extremely commercially and economically dependent on the EU" (Platform representative 3). This led to tension

124 *Assessments of participatory trade politics*

between West African trade negotiators and Platform representatives. Nonetheless, according to Platform members, trade officials' appreciation of transformative actors depended on the policy level at which they met. One Platform representative recalled: "When I approach trade decision-makers at the national level, they say: 'you are a noise-maker.' When I meet them during WTO Rounds, they say: 'oh, nice to see you'." The representative explained: "we provide leverage in negotiations … I don't mind anymore" (Platform representative 7).

While thus welcoming the Platform's outspokenness when it suited their policy goals, West African public officials disapproved of the Platform's behavior in instances where the civil society representatives angered the negotiating partner or openly criticized the negotiating process. In this case, transformative agency presented a challenge to West African officials' monopoly over political authority in trade policy-making and was perceived as problematic. One West African official explained: "The clear-cut position of civil society helped us when facing the Europeans. It allowed negotiators to say that they have to stop emphasizing the trade component. Civil society has no obligation to be diplomatic in its expressions … sometimes, this is an aggression for the negotiating partner. Sometimes it helps, sometimes it creates tension in negotiations" (West African public official 8). Another West African public official declared: "In negotiations, at least the officials have to be more diplomatic and an aspect of civil society is that they are free to speak their minds. Bearing in mind, they should also have some restraint in the sense that we create an atmosphere for negotiations that is conducive." The official added:

> civil society … are also from our side of the table and if by speaking their minds they create an atmosphere which does not assist or facilitate negotiations, that has a knock-on effect on what we do … it is a balance between freedom of speech and ensuring that we are collectively as West Africa … speaking with one voice to the European Union and its Member States.
>
> (West African public official 2)

The ambivalent view on civil society's outspokenness in negotiations exposed a fundamental difference between public- and private-sector agents on the one hand, and transformative actors on the other hand. Public officials were bound by the negotiating mandate. Private-sector representatives usually defended the economic interests of their specific economic constituencies and benefited from a presumption that their behavior is, if not predictable, at least rational within the framework of trade economism. Because civil society was perceived as a more heterogeneous body, trade officials felt that its integration in trade policy formulation introduced a level of uncertainty and unpredictability to the process that they would not have expected to be present otherwise.

Over time, the West African EPA team seemed to start making explicit use of the perceived freedom of the civil society representative in certain instances as one of their negotiating tactics. This point had not been raised when I collected my data in 2009, but became apparent during a trade policy workshop in Dakar in December 2010. It suggests not only that learning continued occurring in West African participatory politics, but that relations among trade officials and Platform actors also continued evolving through its application.

As this section shows, tensions transpired through actors' understandings of inclusiveness and their views on how the regional civil society representative should behave in negotiations. Struggles over political authority became even more visible in actors' discussions of the problems that they experienced with participatory trade politics.

Challenges of participation

The problems with West African participatory trade politics that my interviewees discussed mirror conceptual and theoretical problems in the literature on global governance and democracy. In this section, I highlight three themes to which they referred, namely "civil society," "representation," and "legitimacy." Variations in meanings of these concepts provided the discursive framework for struggles over political authority among the various sets of actors in the EPA policy process. Thus, different types of actors not only defended competing notions of the respective concepts, but also used notions strategically in order to support their own perspective of what appropriate trade policy for West Africa should contain, who should formulate it, and how. Although I treat the three concepts separately, the question of the legitimacy of the policy process underlay disputes over the nature of civil society and the representativity of so-called civil society representatives.

Civil society

Like the Cotonou Agreement, ECOWAS' Negotiating Roadmap referred to civil society without defining what it was. Because the Roadmap provided one chair for regional civil society in the negotiating team, West African trade officials were confronted with a considerable

126 *Assessments of participatory trade politics*

practical problem: "We didn't really know which civil society structure to associate" (West African public official 5). Similarly to the literature which has not produced a unified understanding of civil society's nature and function, political struggles over authority in West African trade decision-making played out in the general confusion over the term.

In the West African EPA debate, the meaning of civil society moved between a narrow, specific and a broad, all-encompassing understanding. The narrow notion referred to organized forms of civil society that either assembled around various defined interests present in the population and/or provided policy expertise on specific issue areas. One West African negotiator explained: "When we are in negotiations with the EC party, regional civil society is supposed to represent the entirety of the different national civil societies that work directly on the negotiations with the EC party" (West African public official 7). While the Platform fitted this description, its members recognized that it was not the only network that could, or did claim the status of civil society under this category (Platform representative 2). By encouraging other organizations to get involved in trade debates, Platform organizations rejected a homogeneous view and highlighted the heterogeneity of civil society, which can never be represented in its entirety.

A broad notion referred to spontaneous or non-institutionalized expressions of civil society, either in the form of popular movements or public demonstrations that had specifically emerged around the EPA process, or as a vague and all-encompassing term for the citizenry, or the population, or the community, or society at large. Officials referred to the all-encompassing notion of civil society to critique the Platform. One West African official explained: "A good part of civil society complained about the fact that they were not in the know ... civil society did not fulfill its task of providing feedback until 2007 ... now we are trying to bring other people along" (West African public official 7). In the first sentence, the official used the term in its all-encompassing meaning to refer to all aspects and iterations of civil society that were not part of the Platform network and hence did not enjoy privileged access to the EPA policy process. In the second sentence, the term denoted the Platform, that is to say the organized group occupying the seat of regional civil society representative in the negotiating structure. Because the failure to communicate with wider civil society was seen as a default of the particular structure that had been associated with negotiations, the official suggested integrating different structures, presumably in the hope that they would fare better at the exercise. The assumption that an organized civil society group was capable of communicating effectively with the entirety of civil society in its broad sense implicitly informed the suggestion. However, the assumption underestimates the heterogeneous character of civil society as a social sphere and at least implicitly requires its unification and organization to a point that would undermine this character.

Platform members in their discourses denied that they were representative of West African civil society in its broad sense and emphasized the Platform's grassroots connections at the same time. Since regional civil society representatives depended on public officials' approval of their right to participation, presenting the Platform as firmly embedded in broader civil society strengthened its position in the policy process for two reasons. First, trade officials' normative preference for inclusiveness, outlined in section one, gave Platform organizations an incentive to highlight their roots in West African society. Second, stressing its embeddedness in civil society enabled the Platform to claim campaign successes of broader networks and movements in which it participated directly or indirectly.

However, discursive imprecision catered to confusion over the problem of representation that I treat below. Claims to a large membership base reinforced public officials' idea that the Platform needed to be representative of certain parts of society. At the same time, Platform members insisted that they were not representatives, but West African citizens who had a democratic right to participation. As I discuss below, this may have caused the Platform legitimacy problems in the long run. On this point, Steve Charnovitz asserts: "If NGOs were more careful not to make absurdly broad claims about themselves, their activist role might be less controversial."[9]

The fact that individual Platform members had diverging views of the role of civil society in negotiations, as explained in Chapter 1, exacerbated these tensions. While some Platform members saw civil society participation as providing inclusiveness, others emphasized the confrontational aspects of their work. In line with Jean Cohen and Andrew Arato's notion of civil society,[10] some Platform members saw their task as interfering with the policy process in order to make sure that their voices as citizens were heard (Platform representative 7).

The lack of clarity of the character of civil society had repercussions for assumptions about participatory politics as a decision-making mechanism. Trade officials argued that participation engaged civil society politically beyond the negotiating process. One West African official identified transformative participation in negotiations as useful, because it meant that "they cannot protest against the agreements later, because they were part of it" (West African public official 1). The question of to what or whom the term civil society referred was thus

128 *Assessments of participatory trade politics*

both crucial and unresolved in the West African EPA process. The idea that the political participation of one organization, or network of organizations, in trade negotiations could bind entire populations is problematic. Since the state reserved the role of final arbiter, it is further questionable to what extent transformative organizations could be responsible for policy outcomes or why society would forfeit its right to criticize policies for which certain civic organizations provide input, but had no power to decide.

Overall, my interviewees had difficulty in disassociating the term civil society from the questions of representation and legitimacy in the EPA process. I therefore turn to the question of representation as a second challenge of participatory trade politics.

Representation

One West African trade official declared in my interview: "It's not all roses ... there is a problem that civil society actors need to solve ... it's the problem of representation" (West African public official 7). In opposition to this concern, a Platform member asserted: "Civil society is not about representation, we don't represent anybody" (Platform representative 7). Debates on representation ultimately pose the questions of how power over policy outcomes is delegated and how the delegation is controlled. Under representative democracy, it is understood that electoral mechanisms instill political actors with representativity. Because this social convention is imperfect in its practical application, citizen participation is generally seen as a necessary corollary for the delegation of political authority to state agents in democratic systems. The terms "representation" and "election" nonetheless hover in proximity in political practice. This makes the terms prone to (not necessarily warranted) interchangeable use, as evidenced by the question: "who elects the NGOs?"[11]

Returning to the underlying question of delegating and controlling power over policy outcomes, Charnovitz explains that the main concern about the rising role of NGOs in world politics comes as their level of influence increases, or, in other words, stems from their "role as a political actor."[12] Instead of counting numbers, he recommends looking at "how useful the ideas are that emanate from an NGO."[13] West African participatory trade politics shows that this begs the next question: who determines, through which mechanism, what constitutes a useful idea?

As with the term "civil society," actors in the West African EPA process conflated different notions of representation and reproduced the conundrum in the theoretical debate in this way. Public officials referred to representation as an agency of all trade interests in society. They demanded representativity from the Platform in order to satisfy their idea that participatory trade politics would enable the state to hear the voices of all citizens that trade policy choices affect. West African trade officials routinely raised the question of representativity in connection with their desire to include grassroots viewpoints in EPA policy-making. One official asked: "What is their level of consultation with the grassroots? Are they not only coming with things that represent their own viewpoint?" The official explained: "This problem is often raised, but not only for civil society, also for the private sector ... they need to show us that they have a good communicational system that allows them to communicate with the grassroots ... otherwise many will continue to think that they simply say what they think themselves" (West African public official 5). The official's statement is in line with the literature's observation that NGOs are not the only actors in global governance that are vulnerable to accusations of poor accountability and representativity.[14]

Platform members tended to understand representation as a delegation of political authority. They saw representativity as a quality that elections or representative selection among a given *demos* or political constituency provide. Based on the argument that citizen participation in decision-making is never representative in this way, they rejected the notion that civil society organizations needed to be representative. They rather saw themselves as citizens, and thus members of civil society in its all-encompassing sense, who brought a specific set of considerations and knowledge to the EPA policy-making process. One Platform representative explained:

> As the people we represent ourselves ... If we have reason to think that your policy direction doesn't better our lives, we have the right to speak up ... if the arguments are right, who we represent doesn't really matter ... So when the question came up ... we said we represent ourselves. We have the right as citizens to air our feelings about the issue ... so you look at the merit of what we say rather than who we represent. We're not a political party.
>
> (Platform representative 3)

One representative of a European transformative organization posed a rhetorical question in my interview: "Does citizen action need to be representative?" Responding in the negative, the representative denounced "the classification of arguments based on their origin" as a "fake problem" (European civil society representative 1). Both

130 *Assessments of participatory trade politics*

representatives confirmed the theoretical view that civil society should be judged in terms of their input into the policy process rather than their representativity of a specific membership. As the re-framing of the trade and development linkage in Part I shows, however, the classification of arguments, including the confirmation or disqualification of specific sets of ideas and world views, was precisely what was at stake in the EPA political process.

In this sense, debates about representation were inseparable from debates about trade political content and masked deeper struggles over political authority in EPA talks. As in the case of the term "civil society," both public officials and Platform actors defended a view on representation that strengthened their standing in the policy process and their own perspective on the merits of participatory trade politics. Highlighting inclusiveness, trade officials deemed representativity as crucial. They neglected the fact that participatory decision-making mechanisms are a supplement to representational practices. Highlighting the direct insertion of otherwise sidelined policy demands and perspectives, Platform representatives felt that direct representativity was a non-issue. They downplayed concerns about the reproduction of existing social asymmetries through participatory trade politics.

Either side catered to the other's view on the importance of representation where this was strategically positive from their perspective. Despite questioning the representativity of the Platform and searching for alternative, more representative networks, trade officials routinely relied on the capacity and political leverage that Platform organizations could provide and perceived this input as positive. In similar fashion, albeit insisting that representation was not relevant, Platform representatives claimed that the Platform was also representative of a large constituency, thus catering to public officials' prerogatives.

At the same time, public officials and civil society actors challenged the other's representativity, albeit in different ways. Public officials doubted that the Platform represented all trade interests voiced among the population and suspected the network of "simply" airing its own opinions. The Platform felt that its opinions were well-founded in technical expertise and that past negative experiences with trade agreements would be repeated if West African public officials were left to negotiate EPAs without citizen control. In this sense, one Platform representative explained: "This is not a platform of participation [in the sense of providing representativity]. Some of us are here to make certain policy demands" (Platform representative 7).

As demonstrated in Chapter 3, Platform members saw citizen action as crucial since they perceived trade officials as unreliable agents for

Assessments of participatory trade politics 131

West African citizens' interests in trade politics. One Platform member explained: "Our campaign organizations are not working on the basis of representation ... we are not working as representatives ... representation is a matter for governments, because they claim to be representative ... The issue is more participation but participation then means: on what terms are you participating?" The representative argued: "We are posing the question as issues of representation and participation when in fact what we are doing is a phenomenon of its effectiveness ... the issue is ... how to better protect West African governments against the intransigence of the European Commission" (Platform representative 7).

My evidence suggests that the Platform's representativity became a controversial issue when the network became effective in this political task it had set itself. In concrete political controversies among state and non-state actors in current world politics, the representation question often becomes a yardstick for measuring the legitimacy of political claims. According to Lisa Jordan and Peter van Tuijl, "one of the most succinct and powerful expressions levied against NGOs is 'who do you represent?'" The authors explain: "Unfortunately, these questions and the suspicion of NGOs are supported by people whose political views or interests are threatened by particular NGOs or the rise of NGOs as a political force."[15] Similarly to Jordan and van Tuijl's insight, the often-posed question "what is their mandate?" (West African public official 5) appeared as particularly relevant because West African trade officials took the Platform stance into account. One West African trade negotiator explained:

> Sometimes there is a gap between the management of an organization and the actual stakeholders it represents ... even within civil society there are different opposing fractions. We have to be careful that we don't adopt a ... position without considering the implications for every other stakeholder. I said that as a preamble for saying that even when anybody, be it civil society, the private sector, or even government, proposes a certain approach, we need to ensure that it has been well thought through and that we believe it carries a lot of the majority of the stakeholders that that particular representative represents.
>
> (West African public official 2)

Public officials' concerns about the representativity of the Platform related to the fact that the regional civil society representative had influence over the negotiating process. A European Commission official noted: "you might sometimes ask who is negotiating. Is it ECOWAS

132 *Assessments of participatory trade politics*

based on a mandate coming from the state, or is it civil society, or the private sector?" The official added: "It is maybe quite difficult to understand for us in Europe that there is a representative of civil society and the private sector but no Member State is there, so he [i.e. the regional civil society representative] has a higher stake in negotiations than the [ECOWAS] Member States themselves" (European public official 1). It was most bluntly expressed in the words of one West African official: "we only ask them [i.e. the Platform] 'who do you represent' when we disagree with what they're saying" (West African public official 2).

European Commission officials declared that the composition of the West African negotiating team lay within the sovereignty of West Africa. One negotiator explained: "I am not aware of how he [the regional civil society representative] has been, *entre guillemets*, elected to go and represent civil society in negotiations and how he is preparing and defending the position of civil society ... we are not informed. But this is for the other party to ask the question, it's their team and we fully respect that" (European public official 1). On the other hand, the official acknowledged that the perceived lack of transparency had repercussions for negotiations. "You do not necessarily know about their mandate or where they are coming from," the official held, "so yes it does change the dynamics of negotiations" (European public official 1). The official added: "It would be beneficial for the process in West Africa if they communicate better on how the civil society representative arrives at his positions, this is not visible from Brussels" (European public official 1).

The fact that the Platform constituted a network of organizations rather than one single group nuanced conflicts over representation to a certain extent. This was visible during preparatory stages of negotiations. One West African official explained: "The ECOWAS approach has been to have representatives—even if it is the Commission that negotiates agreements, we have government representatives and then we negotiate according to a given mandate ... so ... at the level of the MMC which gives us the mandate from the members that we represent ... there are a lot more civil society representatives physically in the room" (West African public official 2). A Platform representative confirmed: "Reality is so large and there is so much work to do that one organization working on its own could not manage" (Platform representative 1).

Nonetheless, the question of representation was asked as a proxy for the substantial questions of which viewpoints and interests were taken into account in the policy process, and whether and how they were balanced. My evidence thus suggests that in political practice,

Assessments of participatory trade politics 133

questions of substance cannot be as easily dissociated from questions of agency as much of the literature on issues of representation and participation seems to assume. Instead, in West Africa, all of these struggles were connected to the deeper question of the legitimacy of participatory trade politics as a decision-making mechanism.

Legitimacy

My interviewees implicitly or explicitly agreed with the Weberian insight that legitimacy beliefs matter for systems of domination.[16] They saw civil society participation as a practice that made EPA negotiations more legitimate. One trade negotiator explained: "including civil society in negotiations provides the final outcome with legitimacy" (West African public official 4), and all interviewees broadly shared this view. Differences emerged on questions of the legitimacy of specific actors as they gained influence over the course of negotiations. West African participatory trade politics in principle confirms the view that standards of legitimacy impact on opportunities for participation.[17] It further shows that legitimacy is neither a universal, nor a static quality. Instead, as Bernstein asserts, governance practices "become institutionalized (or accepted) as 'appropriate' by the community in an ongoing process of legitimization and delegitimization."[18]

Legitimization occurs through discursive justification, while delegitimization occurs through discursive challenge to the norms underlying a policy process.[19] However, the societal consensus on normative reasoning is not exogenous to the process, but rooted in society and culture.[20] In order to be found legitimate during debate, "rules and institutions must be compatible or institutionally adaptable to existing institutionalized rules and norms already accepted by a society."[21] In addition, "there is a constant interaction of rules with the social purposes and goals of relevant audiences."[22] Sigrid Quack adds that "processes of legitimacy-building have to be understood as unfolding in tandem with ... the rule-setting activities."[23] In 2009, the various West African EPA actors were engaged in a joint process of constructing the legitimacy of participatory trade politics through interconnected legitimization and delegitimization attempts that targeted not only their role in the process, but also the content of trade policy, and ultimately the exercise of political authority itself.

As highlighted above, trade officials perceived representativity as a key source of legitimacy of the actors involved in EPA negotiations and had doubts about the Platform's legitimacy in this regard. The Platform, on the other hand, rejected the view that representativity was

134 *Assessments of participatory trade politics*

an appropriate yardstick by which to judge its legitimacy in EPA talks. In order to validate their involvement in the EPA process, Platform members relied on two discursive practices that confirm insights from the literature about the political and ultimately open-ended nature of legitimacy debates. On the one hand, they confirmed Bernstein's argument that "legitimacy must be examined not only from the common perspective of democratic theory, but also from legal and sociological perspectives that may diverge from the democratic normative ideal. Whereas these different conceptions of legitimacy can sometimes push in contradictory directions, the key to legitimate governance is in their convergence."[24] On the other hand, Platform members evoked norms related to good governance, and democratic and civil rights discourse in order to strengthen their view that representativity was not an important factor of their legitimacy.

Pointing to the existence of different types of legitimacy, Platform members defined their legitimacy predominantly as "technical" and "democratic." They argued that they held technical legitimacy because they produced trade policy expertise and had extensive trade advocacy experience. One Platform representative argued: "It is easy to know who works on what, legitimacy comes from what we do" (Platform representative 8). Their view finds support in the literature.[25] As Ann Florini highlights, it is typical for transnational civil society organizations to base their legitimacy claims on the knowledge that they produce.[26]

Emphasizing the importance of combining various forms of legitimacy, the Platform explicitly made reference to human and civil rights discourse, as well as the importance of expertise. One Platform representative declared:

> Citizen participation is a natural right. Constitutions guarantee the right of freedom of association and of participation. Citizen participation provides legitimacy. But there is a debate because there has for a long time been a democratic deficit. There is an ideology which perceives special interests as more legitimate. Then there is also another kind of legitimacy that we don't have, which is representative legitimacy. For a long time, there has been confrontation between the groups about the various types of understanding legitimacy which took place within an overall context of democratic deficit and an ideological bias towards certain types of organizations, notably producers' movements. But it is important to combine the various types of legitimacy instead of continuing to fragment them. This is the importance of political alliances.
>
> (Platform representative 2)

Assessments of participatory trade politics 135

Another Platform interviewee explained:

> I have always refused to enter into legitimacy debates [with nego-
> tiators] ... my response ... was to tell them that there cannot be a
> legitimacy debate because essentially all West African constitutions
> today include the right of citizens to organize in associations.
> Legitimacy also comes from the technical capacity of associations
> that have specialized on a specific topic. They have the right to tell
> the state what they think.
>
> (Platform representative 1)

At the same time, the Platform engaged in attempts to delegitimize public officials in their performance as representatives of West African populations. Platform members implicitly questioned the legitimacy of West African trade officials by suspecting them of signing off a European trade deal without any consideration for the economic consequences for the West African people, unless a strong regional civil society that had the technical and financial resources countered such a deal. Because external institutions traditionally influenced West African trade policy-making heavily, the Platform argued that citizens' attempts to shield West African negotiators from this intransigence were legitimate.

For this reason, Platform actors saw effectiveness in reclaiming political authority from technocratic trade policy prescriptions as one important factor for legitimate civil society participation in trade politics. One Platform member asserted:

> If today another organization claimed ... the right to talk about EPAs,
> I would say: "go ahead, talk. We don't hold the monopoly to talk,
> the main thing is that you talk about it appropriately, it's a tech-
> nical question." Everybody has the right to say what they think. In
> fact, we encourage organizations to speak up. But in terms of going
> to the negotiation table and speaking for civil society ... we reject
> that anybody but us does that. And when ECOWAS was starting to
> create problems ... I told them "we've been working on EPAs ...
> long before ... most negotiators, we know very well what is hap-
> pening at the WTO, we know very well what is going on in EPAs.
> We will not renounce in the benefit of somebody who knows
> nothing." Our legitimacy is technical and political and social,
> because the Platform has thousands of people behind it ... the one
> who represents civil society has to be capable of saying to the
> Europeans: "You are wrong. Here is the proof."
>
> (Platform representative 1)

136 Assessments of participatory trade politics

The fact that Platform members did not see their capacity to provide technical expertise in an apolitical light, as highlighted in Chapter 3, undergirded their legitimacy claims in participatory trade politics.

They felt that the reason for their resilience in the EPA process lay in the fact that they combined several types of legitimacy. Recalling the episode when ECOWAS officials tried to replace the Platform with a different civil society structure in the negotiating process, the Platform representative explained:

> I told [the officials]: "Legitimacy is of two orders, there is political and popular legitimacy, if you like, but there is also technical legitimacy. We claim popular legitimacy. But others can also claim it, because there are many organizations that have come together. But the others do not have technical legitimacy. And we will not accept that someone sits at the table to say that they represent civil society—which may be true—but that they are incapable of understanding what you are talking about. And that all your decisions go through, and that people claim civil society was there, but that civil society didn't understand anything. I do not accept that" ... And this issue is solved ... Nobody could attack us on technical legitimacy. This is the reason why we have a comfortable position in EPA talks.
>
> (Platform representative 1)

Trade officials also went further than questioning the representativity of the civil society representative. One public official expressed concerns that West African civil society might have been co-opted by the negotiating partner. The interviewee explained: "Being too close to Europe, you lose credibility. For example if you critique an institution and then take on consultancy work from them—I don't take that seriously" (West African public official 1). Some sources insisting on anonymity expressed the view that the Platform representative could not have been as vocal in negotiations without being "politically protected." Another anonymous source testified that some members of the West African negotiating team were private consultants paid by the EU, which raised doubts about their credibility. While I could not verify the truth content of the statements, the allegations presented clear attempts at delegitimizing the various actors involved in West African participatory trade politics. Such attempts are not specific to the West African EPA context but represent a common strategy of delegitimization in policy process involving civil society actors and state officials.[27]

Due to the political tensions outlined in this chapter it is not entirely inconceivable that the participatory mechanism in West Africa could break down. The evidence nonetheless suggests that this is unlikely. My data shows that both sides also tried to alleviate the other's concerns about their legitimacy. The fact that Platform representatives had a tendency to highlight the popular legitimacy of the network implied that the Platform acknowledged the validity of the argument that it had to echo the concerns of the people. Trade officials acknowledged that the Platform's legitimacy derived from technical and political sources also and not only from representation. One public official testified: "According to the topic, we look for the appropriate partner ... our cooperation works via consultation," thus at least implicitly admitting that technical legitimacy was an important aspect in creating political alliances (West African public official 5).

Interestingly, Platform members deliberately focused their delegitimization attacks against public officials on trade policy-making and did not question the latter's legitimacy on other grounds. One representative explained that this was a strategic decision which served the purpose of safeguarding solidarity among West Africans. The representative highlighted the importance of constructing relationships and of understanding negotiators and governments "at different moments and at different times ... If you do that there is a lot more solidarity in society ... If you listen carefully, you never hear [the Platform] or ATN attacking corruption ... We don't because we know that's not the issue ... if the organizations want to nuance, they can't confront the government the same way" (Platform representative 7). The statement shows that although challenging each other discursively, West African EPA actors were involved in a common process of legitimization in which they avoided arguments that could potentially break up the process.

From this perspective, ongoing struggles over legitimacy are not a weakness of a given policy process, but rather a characteristic feature of the democratic ideal, which institutionalizes political conflict instead of suppressing it. The process depends on existing rules that "define authority relationships and empower actors and institutions that participate in those relationships and construct governing institutions through their interactions."[28] The Cotonou Agreement, the Negotiating Roadmap and normative preferences for participatory policy-making mechanisms that I analyzed above can be identified as such pre-existing rules that defined authority relationships in a way that enabled transformative actors to break into trade policy-making processes against initial resistance in West Africa.

138 Assessments of participatory trade politics

In addition, all interviewees in principle agreed that transformative participation was a new approach in which learning was occurring. One West African negotiator explained: "The EPA has allowed us to better organize ourselves. I can envisage in the future perhaps having such a similar mandate at the WTO level ... some cooperation role to ensure that we are speaking as a region" (West African public official 2). Another West African negotiator argued that problems with the participatory process were "start-up problems" and should not be overstated (West African public official 8).

At this point, the question arises: why did West African actors engage in a common process of legitimization through a confrontational policy process and continue to do so to date? When asked how fundamental differences in both trade policy preferences and trade policy mechanisms between the two sides were overcome, one Platform representative said: "We overcame it by talking ... the stakes were so high that we kept working" (Platform representative 8). West African trade officials nuanced their negative views of the Platform on the basis of personal contact. One official argued: "They [the Platform] can be extremist and make false statements." The official went on to explain: "Maybe it's part of their technique. I take it as part of their own inherent strategy, it's part of them, it's not an offense. You learn to appreciate people" (West African public official 1). Together, the statements support von Bülow's argument that we must pay analytical attention to the ways in which trade political actors succeed or fail to devise common purpose.[29]

Partly, the benefits of participatory trade politics analyzed in this chapter provide an answer to the question of how public officials and Platform members learned to accept each other's role in trade policy-making. In addition, several interviewees invoked the role of culture and identity in order to explain why public officials and transformative actors "kept talking" and began to "appreciate people" in West African trade policy formation. One Platform representative explained: "West Africa has a strong culture of consultation ... you don't take decisions because of ideology. You take decisions because of public opinion" (Platform representative 3). A representative of a Platform partner organization pointed out that all sides "noted that there was solidarity around common issues" (West African civil society representative 1). A West African journalist equally stressed this point. Since the journalist highlighted both the transformations that public official/Platform relations underwent over time in West Africa and the role of culture in this transformation, I reproduce the relevant section of my interview, in full:

Q: How do negotiators perceive civil society?

A: People saw them as the kind of people who had come to stop things from taking their ordinary course. Negotiators did not accept the role of civil society very well.

Q: Has this changed?

A: Many things have changed ... At the official level, civil society is accepted as a partner, as a stakeholder of negotiations ... but fundamentally, in some sense, there is still this reservation [on the part of public officials], there are a lot of reservations, after all.

Q: This is a bit the same everywhere in the world.

A: As you say, I have seen the same thing in Brussels with European Union officials, between the European Commission and civil society members, it's exactly the same thing.

Q: That is precisely why I would like to know how West African civil society has reached this level of inclusion.

A: Yes, but you know, you have to also take Senegalese specificities into consideration ... Much may be due, I believe, to the fact that in Senegal, at a certain level, people are capable of putting conflicts of an ideological nature aside in order to establish personal relationships that are positively affectionate, positively human. This has helped a lot, because even when discussions were extremely confrontational during meetings, when people afterwards left the meeting room and met in the corridors, they spoke with each other, they exchanged views, they saw that fundamentally, they were maybe looking for the same thing, just in a different way.

(West African journalist)

Conclusion

All EPA actors saw certain aspects, such as heightened negotiating capacity, inclusiveness, and adjustments to balances of power, as positive aspects of participatory trade politics and public officials contemplated transposing the mechanisms to WTO negotiations on the basis of these perceived benefits. However, they emphasized different dimensions of these aspects as beneficial and their assessments were intermingled with their own normative preferences for trade policy. This became ever more evident when my interviewees discussed the problems inherent in participatory trade politics around the notions of "civil society," "representation," and "legitimacy." They exposed considerable levels of disagreement over how trade policy decisions should be made, who should judge the effects, and ultimately, how political authority in trade decision-making should be delegated and controlled.

140 *Assessments of participatory trade politics*

Such disagreements characterize trade policy-making beyond the West African region. Demands for the democratization of trade politics as well as justifications of exclusive trade policy-making practices rely on differing normative answers to the question of what the goal of trade policy is, who should determine its goals, and how it should be achieved. Martha Finnemore reminds us that:

> contestation processes for normative dominance are political. In fact, normative contestation is in large part what politics is all about; it is about competing values and understandings of what is good, desirable, and appropriate in our collective communal life. Debates about civil rights, affirmative action, social safety nets, regulation and deregulation, and the appropriate degree of government intrusion into the lives of citizens are all debates precisely because there is no clear stable normative solution.[30]

In this sense, legitimacy struggles such as the ones observed in West African EPA negotiations are inherent to democratic policy-making, which allows citizens to challenge and potentially redress existing biases through institutionalized political conflict.

The question remains why West African trade institutions institutionalized political conflict. In the next chapter, I argue that to gain a complete picture, we need to look at the mechanisms that West African EPA actors used to overcome their normative differences and continued to engage in a conflictual process of legitimacy building. The immediate structural context of ECOWAS-EU EPA talks and the trade political agency it provoked only provide a partial answer to this question. How distinct discursive challenges played out to alter perceptions of the political environment and its various types of agency cannot be understood without taking the broader historical and social contexts of the region into account. This broad historical and social background provided additional resources that enabled West African EPA actors to put up with the politics in trade politics.

Notes

1 Richard Higgott, "Contested Globalisation: The Changing Context and Normative Challenges," *Review of International Studies* 26, no. 5 (2000): 131–54; James Brassett and Eleni Tsingou, "The Politics of Legitimate Global Governance," *Review of International Political Economy* 18, no. 1 (2011): 1–16.
2 Daniel Esty, "Environmental Governance at the WTO: Outreach to Civil Society," in *Trade, Environment and the Millennium*, ed. Gary P. Sampson and W. Bradnee Chambers (Tokyo: United Nations Press, 1999), 119–44.

Assessments of participatory trade politics   141

3 The third party MFN clause is a policy invention. The EU insists on the inclusion of a clause that requires EPA parties to extend to each other any more beneficial treatment that the parties may accord to any third trading partner after entry into force of the EPA. The Platform considers the clause to be unjust because it interferes with West Africa's policy options for South-South trade agreements once the EPA is signed. See Cheikh Tidiane Dièye and Victoria Hanson, "MFN Provisions in EPAs: A Threat to South-South Trade?" *Trade Negotiations Insights* 7, no. 2 (2008): 1–3.

4 The non-execution clause would give the EU power to impose trade restrictions in cases where EPA partner countries violate human rights, democracy and good governance principles. The Platform argued that the clause was unacceptable because it was not reciprocal and did not give West Africa the power "to take steps against the EU if Senegalese immigrants in France are put in jail in violation of basic human rights principles, for example." See Siolda Agazzi, "African NGOs Oppose Human Rights Clause in EPAs," *IPS News Agency*, 22 March 2011, ipsnews.net/news.asp?idnews=54955.

5 PWC 2004, *Sustainability Impact Assessment (SIA) of the EU-ACP Economic Partnership Agreements. Regional SIA: West African ACP Countries*, trade.ec.europa.eu/doclib/docs/2005/january/tradoc_121200.pdf.

6 Sally Bullen and Brennan van Dyke, *In Search of Sound Environment and Trade Policy: A Critique of Public Participation at the WTO* (Geneva: Centre for International Environmental Law, 1996).

7 Platform, *Declaration on the Conclusion of Negotiations at the Chief Negotiators Level in Dakar, July 22–23* (Dakar: ENDA, 2009).

8 Cheikh Tidiane Dièye 2008, *Cheikh Tidiane Dièye on Trade*, www.youtube.com/watch?v=Xhr2aleGj0Q.

9 Steve Charnovitz, "Accountability of Nongovernmental Organizations (NGOs) in Global Governance," paper prepared for the Conference on Global Administrative Law, New York University Law School, 22–23 April 2005: 27.

10 Jean L. Cohen and Andrew Arato, *Civil Society and Political Theory* (Cambridge, MA: MIT Press, 1994).

11 See Kenneth Anderson, "The Limits of Pragmatism in American Foreign Policy: Unsolicited Advice to the Bush Administration on Relations with International Nongovernmental Organisations," *Chicago Journal of International Law* 2 (2001): 371–88. Anderson cites Rieff asking at a panel on landmines and international civil society at the Washington College of Law of the American University in 1998: "So who elects the NGOs?" Much of the debate has also been triggered through the global media. *The Economist* thus published an influential article on 18 September 2003 titled "Who Guards the Guardians?"

12 Charnovitz, "Accountability of Nongovernmental Organizations (NGOs) in Global Governance," 33.

13 Charnovitz, "Accountability of Nongovernmental Organizations (NGOs) in Global Governance," 35.

14 Peter J. Spiro, "Accounting for NGOs," *Chicago Journal of International Law* 3 (2002): 161–70; Thirukodikaval N. Srinivasan, *Developing Countries and the Multilateral Trading System: From the GATT to the Uruguay Round and the Future* (Boulder, CO: Westview Press, 1998); Paul Wapner, "Defending Accountability in NGOs," *Chicago Journal of International*

142 *Assessments of participatory trade politics*

Law 3 (2002): 197–206; Ruth W. Grant and Robert O. Keohane, "Accountability and Abuses in World Politics," *American Political Science Review* 99 no. 1 (2005): 29–43; and Charnovitz, "Accountability of Nongovernmental Organizations (NGOs) in Global Governance."

15 Lisa Jordan and Peter van Tuijl, *NGO Accountability: Politics, Principles & Innovations* (London: Earthscan, 2006), 4.

16 Max Weber, *Economy and Society* (Berkeley, CA: University of California Press, [1921] 1978).

17 Allen Buchanan and Robert O. Keohane, "The Legitimacy of Global Governance Institutions," *Ethics and International Affairs* 20, no. 4 (2006): 405–37.

18 Steven Bernstein, "Legitimacy in Global Environmental Governance," *Journal of International Law & International Relations* 1, no. 1–2 (2005): 157.

19 Jens Steffek, "The Legitimation of International Governance: A Discourse Approach," *European Journal of International Relations* 9, no. 2 (2003): 249–75.

20 Robert Cox, "Social Forces, States and World Orders: Beyond International Relations Theory," in *Neorealism and Its Critics*, ed. Robert O. Keohane (New York: Columbia University Press, 1986), 204–54.

21 Bernstein, "Legitimacy in Global Environmental Governance," 156.

22 Bernstein, "Legitimacy in Global Environmental Governance," 157.

23 Sigrid Quack, "Law, Expertise and Legitimacy in Transnational Economic Governance: An Introduction," *Socio-Economic Review* 8, no. 1 (2010): 8.

24 Bernstein, "Legitimacy in Global Environmental Governance," 141.

25 Charnovitz, "Accountability of Nongovernmental Organizations (NGOs) in Global Governance."

26 Ann M. Florini, ed., *The Third Force: The Rise of Transnational Civil Society* (Washington: Carnegie Endowment for International Peace, 2000).

27 See Jordan and van Tuijl, *NGO Accountability: Politics, Principles & Innovations.*

28 Bernstein, "Legitimacy in Global Environmental Governance," 157.

29 Marisa von Bülow, *Building Transnational Networks: Civil Society and the Politics of Trade in the Americas* (Cambridge: Cambridge University Press, 2010).

30 Martha Finnemore, "Norms, Culture, and World Politics: Insights from Sociology's Institutionalism," *International Organization* 50, no. 2 (1996): 342.

5 The social dimensions of trade policy formation

- **Trade in West African history**
- **Trade in West African state-society relations**
- **Conclusion**

In addition to the immediate economic, normative and discursive environments of the EPA process, the way in which commercial activities have interacted with social and political organization in the region across time helped West African public officials and transformative organizations to recognize each other as legitimate trade political actors and develop common trade political positions, irrespective of their diverging stances towards the global trade agenda. Several interviewees felt that a sense of solidarity among the West African negotiating team allowed its members to "put considerations of an ideological nature aside" (West African journalist) and "keep talking" (Platform representative 8), instead of "fighting over a theoretical issue" (West African trade official 2), although they perceived their policy perspectives and preferences as conflicting. Despite internal power struggles over trade political authority, West African trade officials and transformative civil society organizations shared a common identity and sense of unity against the European negotiating partner that they consciously created and nurtured.

As the data presented in previous chapters show, the Platform depicted the EU, and thus implicitly European trade negotiators, as the other throughout its campaign in order to support its own role in the negotiating process. In this chapter, I argue that West African historical experiences with trade, and specifically with European trade, and the role that trade plays in West African state-society relations provided further resources for creating common purpose. I present historical experience and state-society relations as two separate categories. To the extent that historical and social dimensions are intertwined, the

144 *Social dimensions of trade policy formation*

opportunities that both dimensions provided for creating common purpose overlapped in real life.

While my analysis leaves the immediate political environment of West African EPA talks far behind, the mechanisms of constructing common purpose cannot be understood without deeper knowledge of the region's wider historical and social background. This supports two general arguments I have made throughout the book. On the one hand, the social dimensions of trade, that is to say the perceived role of the trading activity in shaping social order across space and time, have to be taken seriously in studies on the political economy of trade. On the other hand, by discarding the significance of social, economic and political experiences outside of Eurocentric contexts for theory-building, we are not only destined to misread the world we intend to study—we also risk missing important lessons about its real and potential transformations.

Trade in West African history

West African economic history has created mixed collective experiences with trade that are particularly ambivalent towards trade with Europe. While intra-community barter and exchange have helped to provide society's material basis in the region since time immemorial, novel external commercial influences tended to be disruptive to West African economic, political and social organization across more than 1,000 years of its history. At the same time, parts of West African societies often benefited from commercial engagements with new trading partners in the immediate term and even during their entire lifetime, although the structural adjustments that these engagements engendered affected social organization negatively in the long run.

In Chapter 1, I cited a TWN spokesperson declaring on Ghanaian radio: "Africa and Europe have traded for 500 years and every time we have lost. Why is it that we, the continent that produces everything that people want to survive, are the poorest?"[1] In Chapter 4, I showed how the Platform used historical experience with colonialism in order to discredit EPAs. While European public officials found references to colonialism to be unfair and unfounded, mobilization against EPAs could refer to historical events, specifically the transatlantic slave trade, in order to provoke broad popular resistance.

Although the recent past is arguably more crucial for collective memory, the implications of economic history for current West African state-society relations that I analyze in the next section cannot be understood without describing some dynamics that were set off in the

Social dimensions of trade policy formation 145

pre-colonial era. In this section, I therefore focus on the role of trade in West African economic, political and social organization following two important junctures in the region's history. They are the arrival of Islam in the eighth century and the arrival of Europeans in the fifteenth century. Islamization and the expansion of Muslim trade during the first era set the operational basis for the emergence of two distinct but interconnected economic spheres under the expansion of European trade in the second era.

I use the term "Muslim trade" to capture the historical observation that the spread of Islam and the evolution of a specific trading system across the region were connected in West Africa. The social groups that built and controlled West Africa's regional trading system from the eighth until the nineteenth century and connected it with the Arab world were not from Northern Africa or the Arab Peninsula. Both the individuals who organized the trade and their organizing principles were inspired by the religious practices, rules, and values that emerged as West Africa developed its own strand of Islam.

The arrival of Islam

Islamization and the expansion of Muslim trade that accompanied it provoked two important movements, namely the rise to wealth and power of specific social groups amidst general political and social destabilization, and the spread of forms of economic organization that later came to be perceived as inferior to capitalist mechanisms of production and accumulation. Geographically, West Africa is to the North limited by the Sahara desert, to the West by the Atlantic Ocean and to the South by the Gulf of Guinea. The region is divided into three general vegetation zones, namely desert, savannah and forest. The diversity founds the basis of a long historical tradition of intra-community trade. According to Paul Zeleza, the common assertion that pre-colonial West African societies mainly traded in luxury items is not based on historical reality, but results directly from the under-researched nature of internal production systems.[2] In fact, production and exchange in metallurgy,[3] handcrafts and agriculture predated the arrival of Islam and Muslim trade.[4]

Islam came to North Africa in the mid-seventh century, shortly after Mohammed's death in 632. It spread to West Africa in the eighth century through the creation of trading posts and the integration of African cities and kingdoms in the Sahel region into North African trading networks, thus giving an impulse to urbanization.[5] Flourishing regional and trans-Saharan trade characterized the period from the eighth to the fifteenth centuries.[6] Internally, exchange systems for various products

146   *Social dimensions of trade policy formation*

often operated through one specific good, which connected elaborate networks of market places. The regional kola[7] trade, for example, integrated the trade of products such as gold, cotton, copper and salt.[8] Local and regional markets came together at varying intervals and over time developed a currency system under the leadership of cowries that founded the second pillar of regional economic integration.[9]

West Africa was also integrated into global trade flows of the era. The Mali Empire, for example, traded with the Maghreb and Egypt from at least the thirteenth century.[10] The list of items traded across the Sahara included mining products, textiles, food products, salt, kola, animals, and slaves.[11] Globally, Arab trade connected both continents, with Europe importing gold from the upper Senegal and Ashanti until the European exploration and colonization of the Americas.[12]

Islam provided a cultural and operational framework in which so-called trading diasporas, such as the Dioula[13] or the Hausa, consolidated their social standing and came to control both regional and trans-Saharan trade. Abner Cohen initially developed the notion of "trading diaspora" in the particular context of West African anthropological studies. He defines trading diaspora as "a nation of socially interdependent, but spatially dispersed, communities."[14] Such trading communities typically live in a foreign community where they accustom themselves with local language, customs, and commercial practice. Their interconnected networks are instrumental for overcoming many problems of long-distance and cross-cultural trade and trading diasporas are one of the most long-standing and wide-spread social institutions across human history.

In West Africa, the Dioula became the preferred trading partners for agents from the Sahara, Northern Africa, and the Middle East during the period of Islamization.[15] They also came to monopolize trade relations among communities in the region.[16] Common religious practices under Islam played an important role in consolidating the group and in animating its trade network across and beyond West Africa. They provided crucial skills and norms for cross-cultural commercial interaction, such as literacy and moral codes permitting effective exchange of information, a uniform legal structure, a credit system, and authority structures.

The underlying rationale of pre-colonial West African trade resulted from lineage- and faith-based social organization.[17] Commercial exchange was a social activity which had implications for several social groups extending beyond the trading individual.[18] In order successfully to conduct their activities, traders relied on a vast network of partners and allies, chiefly from family and religious circles, whose values they needed to respect, and into which they were expected to reinvest in order to assure continued support. In doing so, merchants reproduced specific social values and practices and at the same time helped to provide the material basis for their exercise. While individual traders certainly looked for a profit, their activities were inscribed into a set of social values from which they benefited, and to which they contributed at the same time.[19]

Pierre Kipre[20] cites West African merchants, arguing that the obligation of social assistance founded the basis of their authority in society. He explains that wealth had no value in itself but was conceived as a means by which the wealthy catered to the needs of society. From the perspective of accumulation, such practices presented an obstacle to participation in the capitalist system, because the social logic of wealth slowed down capitalist accumulation.[21] While Catherine Coquery-Vidrovitch and Paul Lovejoy[22] argue that the logic led to a destruction of surplus, Leonhard Harding[23] points out that the judgment is premature in view of a social system that does not define wealth through the concept of private property.

The expansion of Islam and of Muslim trade left a double impression on West Africa. While it contributed to growth and benefited specific groups in society, including but not limited to trading diasporas, it also had disruptive effects and was accompanied by political turmoil, displacement, and war. Due to the social and political reorganization that it provoked among the local populations, the new commerce constituted a source of war and conflict.[24] It weakened, for example, the Wagadou Empire by limiting its role as the principle link in North–South trade routes, by displacing exchange routes towards the Senegal and the Niger valleys, by accentuating social cleavages and by the gradual conversion of the population to Islam, which engendered an ideological crisis of the Empire. The several states that emerged from its disintegration subsequently militarized through Muslim trade.[25] The gradual arrival of European merchants since the sixteenth century reinforced the ambivalent historical experience with novel commercial influences and triggered the evolution of the distinct political and economic structures that characterize West African social-economic realities today.

The arrival of Europeans

The Portuguese first arrived on the coast of West Africa in the Guinea area in 1444. The Dutch, English and French replicated attempts to set foot in the region from the seventeenth century onward. As John Fage highlights, upon arrival in West Africa, Europeans "found there

148 *Social dimensions of trade policy formation*

organized kingdoms in which the idea of foreign trade, carried out under royal control and in accordance with state policy by established merchant classes or guilds, was already well established."[26] This was one of the reasons why European merchants found it virtually impossible to expand their operations into the hinterland from the sixteenth to the late nineteenth centuries. Products that were directly traded with Europe since the sixteenth century include palm oil, gold, textiles, metals, spirits, and arms.[27] Until the end of the nineteenth century, Europeans only controlled a few enclaves along the West African coast, from which trading houses operated. They depended on West African trading communities and their regional networks to obtain local goods and to spread European produce in the region. Thus, regional trade remained by and large in the hands of the local trading diasporas. Until the end of the eighteenth century, West African trade did not bring significant economic profit for European trading houses.[28]

The arrival of the Europeans on the coast gradually shifted trans-Saharan trade operated through the Savannah zones to maritime trade along the coasts of Senegambia and the Gulf of Guinea.[29] The resulting reorientation of trading networks, along with the introduction of European products and eventual preponderance of slaves as export items over time led to the marginalization of African trading communities and the regression of material conditions across the region.[30] However, marginalization and regression unfolded as part of a long historical process. The outcome of this process was probably not evident for contemporaries for two reasons. First, since European trade came with an increase in economic activity, it benefited the parts of the West African population that were involved with that trade. Second, both trans-Saharan and European trade remained of marginal economic significance to the region until the end of the nineteenth century.[31]

Instead, regional trade flourished. West African salt trade alone was more valuable than trade across the Sahara.[32] In the eighteenth century, 92 percent of West African imports from Europe were made up of four products, namely textiles, metals, arms, and spirits.[33] For traders of Côte d'Ivoire, for example, dependence on European trade before colonization was limited to guns, ammunition, tobacco, and textiles.[34] Furthermore, in sectors such as textile production and gold-mining, European attempts to displace local production failed.[35] Zeleza concludes: "There can be little doubt ... that until the end of the nineteenth century, regional demands and the regional economy, rather than links with the outside world, were the driving force in West Africa."[36]

In order to insert themselves into local trading systems, Europeans depended on the help of West African intermediaries. Local trading

Social dimensions of trade policy formation 149

diasporas typically fulfilled this role. Until well into the nineteenth century, there was strong interdependence between West African and European traders as local networks connected Atlantic trade along the coast with trade in the hinterland.[37] Both the nature of this partnership and its consequences were ambivalent. Some West African merchants followed the advances of European troops to expand their operational zones, although these advances disrupted their traditional trade circuits at the same time.[38]

Competition among merchants was also fierce. The Dioula tried to use a double strategy of limiting the expansion of European trade and at the same time consolidating their position of prime intermediary.[39] European traders attempted to break into local markets and to challenge the monopoly of the trading communities on which they depended, for example in the case of the Dioula-controlled horse trade in the Senegal and Niger deltas. Europeans used local intermediaries to undermine their European competitors, while local traders played European agents against one another in order to maintain their economic position. Furthermore, European trading houses paid minimal wages to local and European auxiliaries, which therefore often launched informal and illegal operations.[40]

Overall, the nineteenth century saw not only an enormous increase of trade volumes with Europe, but also economic decline, environmental degradation, health degradation, and demographic down-slide. As European trading houses supported local coalitions during war time, their establishment in West Africa modified power relations between the ruling classes and upset alliances among the groups that had previously controlled the region.[41] Europeans further interfered with local politics systematically to favor their economic interests and to control export trade. French traders, for example, came to dominate the peanut trade out of Senegal, Sierra Leone and Portuguese Guinea in the nineteenth century with the help of French government intervention.[42] During the nineteenth century, African merchants suffered from colonial policies that were severely biased against them. Africans were, for example, denied access to the credit system as well as to overseas trade and could not invest in the industrial sector. Attempts by local commercial agents to break into this circuit led to tensions which ultimately reinforced the push towards colonization.[43]

By the mid-nineteenth century, West Africa, along with North Africa, was the most deeply integrated African region in the world economy, making it vulnerable to external shocks. The global economic recession of the late nineteenth century hit at an historical moment when the number of traders engaged in West Africa's international trade had

150 *Social dimensions of trade policy formation*

risen sharply, partly as a result of the abolition of slave trade. Economic depression and the severe degradation of West Africa's terms of trade led to rising competition, which negatively affected profit margins. The volatility of the credit system in West Africa further destabilized the region from the point of view of European merchants.

Competition among traders toughened, which affected both the economic and the political climate in the region negatively. The recession exacerbated existing conflicts and undermined production, for example in West African peanut-growing regions.[44] In the mid-nineteenth century, rivalries among English palm oil traders in Nigeria "spilled over into assaults on African middle-men" and ultimately "began the move to British political control."[45] The sharp rise in the number of traders, the plummeting of West African commodity prices on the European markets, and the demonetization of local currencies culminated in a crisis in the commercial system that reinforced the move towards colonization.[46] By the end of the nineteenth century, Britain and France were engaged in the scramble for West Africa.

The increasing fragmentation of West African economic systems not only reinforced the push to colonization, but also provided opportunities to make a personal profit for specific groups and individuals, although the overall socio-economic consequences of what Zeleza calls "West African trade imperialism" were profoundly disruptive.[47] The Atlantic slave trade is a particularly strong symbol for both trends. Originating in the fifteenth century, it reached its peak in the eighteenth and nineteenth centuries. The number of victims is estimated to range between 9.6 million[48] and 15.4 million.[49] According to some studies, approximately half of all enslaved people originated from West Africa.[50] Western scholarship has long nurtured a sad tradition of downplaying the negative impacts of the slave trade on West African societies.[51] Instead, both the massive expansion of slave trading during the eighteenth century and its abolition in the early nineteenth century created economic strain, political tension, and social hardship in West Africa.[52]

The West African slave trade was a competitive exercise from which not only European but also African merchants drew a profit.[53] At the same time, its broader negative consequences not only affected the coastal areas, but also had repercussions for social and political formations of the hinterland. Thus, the rise of external demand for slave labor fueled internal conflict.[54] It also led to the militarization of the region.[55] Boubacar Barry's study of the Senegalese kingdom of Waalo shows that the European practice of buying slaves for weapons overthrew the balance of power between local groups which eventually

Social dimensions of trade policy formation 151

engaged in civil war. As Muslim spiritual leaders organized to oppose slave trade, Islam turned from a minority religion associated with specific kingdoms and trading diasporas to a popular movement of resistance, bringing with it further violent conflict during its consolidation.[56] Economically, the slave trade not only took a heavy toll on the domestic economies' labor force. Significantly, it also rerouted regional trading systems in food stuffs due to the provisioning that was necessary to transport slaves across the region and on to the Americas. This encouraged speculation among local traders and contributed to pauperization and famine.[57]

The abolition of slave trade further deepened economic crisis. It created revenue losses for those West African merchants and states which had cooperated in the trade, thus weakening West African state structures.[58] Furthermore, it interacted with the global recessions of the nineteenth century to make the economic climate in the region more competitive. As a result of the abolition of slave trade, the number of merchants grew. Zeleza describes:

> a new African merchant class composed primarily of ex-slaves, liberated Africans and the mission-educated elite who began to challenge the commercial and political hegemony of the ruling class ... the struggle between the old and new commercial classes was taking part in the context of growing rivalries between African merchants as a whole and European merchants ... Its ascendancy over the former exacerbated the disintegration of coastal societies, while its effective challenge against the latter ensured that European commercial hegemony could only be attained through colonization.[59]

Competition arose between Marseilles and Bordeaux merchants in the Senegambian gum trade, for example, once slave trade had been abolished. Much of the competition played out on the back of local brokers, which consequently incurred losses and became "increasingly indebted to the resident Frenchmen who had extended them credit. By 1841, their aggregate indebtedness had reached proportions that also touched the solvency of the French merchants to whom they were indebted. Under these conditions, using the economic crisis as justification, Bordeaux merchants were able to persuade the colonial administration to intervene to their competitive advantage."[60] Similarly, Fage notes: "the steps taken by the Europeans against the slave trade and slavery ... hastened the day when, in their own economic interest, they thought it necessary first to conquer the African

152 *Social dimensions of trade policy formation*

kingdoms, and then to continue the process, initiated by African kings and entrepreneurs, of conquering the segmentary societies and absorbing them into unitary political structures."[61]

Case studies of nineteenth-century Côte d'Ivoire and Senegal show that West African traders did not disappear in the face of European competition, but rather adapted their activities gradually in reaction to changing circumstances. Factually, the period saw the progressive exclusion of local traders from both trade with Europe and the modern economy.[62] Crucially, European trade split West African societies into those strands that benefited from the colonial economy and which had a vested interest in its continuation, and the broader masses which saw their living conditions degenerate under the colonial economic arrangement. While some merchants left the commercial profession to enter public office or engage in the production of primary products, others shifted their activity either to the margins of the economy or established a parallel economy to the unfolding colonial system, thus setting the groundwork for what later came to be known as the informal sector. This shift gradually operated over the entire nineteenth century and several West African individuals or groups accumulated considerable amounts of wealth during the process.[63] From an historical perspective, Zeleza argues that these West Africans "were products of the changing old world and a struggling new one."[64]

Taken together, the arrival of Islam and European trade created an ambivalent collective experience with trade, which provided ample material that West African trade political actors could refer to in order to create common purpose and a sense of solidarity in trade negotiations with Europe. The Atlantic slave trade is arguably not only the strongest political symbol for European exploitation. The economic and social impacts of both its imposition and its abrogation feed into the above-quoted perception that West Africans cannot win when they trade with Europe. In addition, history provides the roots of West African state-society relations today.

Trade in West African state-society relations

The post-colonial state's perceived lack of trade political autonomy and society's economic self-organization in response to the formal economy's failure to provide the means of subsistence were relevant characteristics of West African state-society relations in the evolution of participatory trade politics. As shown in previous chapters, the expansion of international institutions' influence over trade policy-making along with the ongoing experience of socio-economic decline

Social dimensions of trade policy formation 153

undermined the legitimacy of the post-colonial states' domestic monopoly over trade policy. It also weakened West African states institutionally and hence provided opportunities to create trade political space for participation.

In Chapter 1, I cited Platform organizations claiming during the EPA campaign that "regional institutions ... need to face up to the failures and shortcomings of economic liberalist free market theory. The engine of sustainable development is not to be found in a one-size-fits-all model imposed by the most powerful countries; new balances must be found in the share-out of responsibilities between state, market and CSOs."[65] In Chapter 3, I highlighted the role of socio-economic hardship for creating a sense among West African state and non-state actors that they fundamentally shared the same policy goal in EPA negotiations. In Chapter 4, I quoted a Platform member explaining that the Platform avoided attacking public officials on problems that did not immediately concern trade policy-making, such as corruption.

The influence of international institutions

The creation of international institutions implies a restriction of sovereignty at the domestic level. The experience of limited sovereignty over trade policy-making in recent decades is therefore not specific to West Africa. However, in the multilateral arena, the historical conditions of accession together with the decision-making mechanisms of the GATT, and later the WTO, meant that West African governments had little to no impact on the system's design. Current West African state structures were inherited from British, French and Portuguese colonial empires after the region gradually gained independence between 1957 and 1975. Table 5.1 shows the years of West African dates of independence with the former colonial power indicated in parentheses.

The colonial legacy strained the relationship between newly independent states and their newly independent citizens.[66] Crucially, as shown above, Europeans also controlled the colonial economy, with West African societies partly assuring their subsistence on its margins or outside of the state's political authority.

When the majority of West African countries gained independence in the early 1960s, the GATT was in its fifth round of trade negotiations. From its inception, the organization was tilted towards the economic interests of the global North.[67] As "a club that was primarily of relevance to [Organisation for Economic Co-operation and Development—OECD] countries,"[68] the GATT regime initially dealt mainly

154 *Social dimensions of trade policy formation*

Table 5.1 West African dates of independence

1957	1958	1960	1961	1965	1974	1975
Ghana (UK)	Guinea (F)	Benin (F)	Sierra Leone (UK)	The Gambia (UK)	Guinea-Bissau (P)	Cape Verde (P)
		Burkina-Faso (F)				
		Côte d'Ivoire (F)				
		Mali (F)				
		Mauritania (F)				
		Niger (F)				
		Nigeria (UK)				
		Senegal (F)				
		Togo (F)				

Notes: Freed American slaves founded and colonized Liberia in the 1820s; F: France; P: Portugal, UK: United Kingdom.

with industrial goods and adopted procedural arrangements that suited the dominant economies in these markets, such as the "principal supplier rule" under which liberalization commitments are made on the basis of bilateral negotiations among the principle suppliers of that good. As Paul Collier notes, it "was not a *global* institution. It was basically a marketplace for OECD countries to strike deals for reciprocal trade liberalization."[69] Despite the clear bias, the integration of West African countries into the multilateral trading system predated their political independence.

It is an often-overlooked fact that the adhesion of many industrialized countries brought vast colonial empires under the umbrella of the multilateral system, in line with Article XXVI:5(a) GATT: "each government accepting this Agreement does so in respect of its metropolitan territory and of the other territories for which it has international responsibility, except such separate customs territories as it shall notify to the Executive Secretary to the Contracting Parties at the time of its own acceptance."

The entire West African region except Liberia joined the GATT system in this way.[70] At independence, governments faced three legal options in terms of future relationships with the multilateral trading system. They could withdraw from the organization, join according to Article XXVI:5(c) GATT on the terms and conditions that their metropolis had previously negotiated on their behalf, or join under

Social dimensions of trade policy formation 155

Article XXXIII GATT as a new contracting party through the ordinary accession procedure. GATT contracting parties had further established a fourth political option at the start of the decolonization process. In 1958, they recommended that contracting parties "should continue to apply de facto the General Agreement in their relations with any territory which has acquired full autonomy in the conduct of its external commercial relations and of other matters provided for in the General Agreement, provided that the territory continues to apply de facto the General Agreement to them."[71]

While former British colonies all joined GATT at independence under the Article XXVI:5(c) procedure, former French and Portuguese colonies typically went through a period of de facto application after which they also joined on the basis of the provision. Table 5.2 indicates de facto application periods and GATT accession for West African countries.

As a GATT Panel clarified in 1971, a contracting party that had acceded under Article XXVI:5(c) assumed all rights and obligations which had previously been accepted on its behalf.[72] Under de facto application, the territory was expected to follow the substantive provisions of the GATT, although procedural and organizational rules were not applied.[73] By the time the Uruguay Round started, only six West African countries had established schedules of tariff concessions under Article II GATT. All six applied the section that France had previously negotiated for them under its own GATT schedule.[74]

Both the fundamental mechanisms of the multilateral trading system and the conditions of (West) African countries' interaction with the system were thus set out during the colonial period. After observers had reported failure of the GATT to generate benefits for developing countries in 1958,[75] African countries began to mount trade barriers under import-substitution development strategies in the 1960s and 1970s.[76] To the extent that West African states also attempted to improve their position in the global trading system following independence, they were relatively unsuccessful.

Nigeria and Ghana, for example, were among the group of 21 global South countries that took an initiative in the GATT to draw contracting parties' attention to their trade concerns in 1963.[77] The initiative led to the adoption of a resolution which helped to build the political momentum that culminated in the adoption of a Trade and Development section in the GATT[78] and the creation of the United Nations Conference on Trade and Development (UNCTAD) in 1964. The main remedy for developing country members of the multilateral trading system since the 1960s is anchored in the idea of non-reciprocity. Non-reciprocity implies that developing country members do not have

156 *Social dimensions of trade policy formation*

Table 5.2 GATT de facto application and accession

	De facto application	*Accession*
Benin (Dahomey)	1960–65	1965
Burkina-Faso (Upper Volta)	1960–63	1963
Côte d'Ivoire	1960–63	1963
Cape Verde	1976–94	–
Gambia	–	1965
Ghana	–	1957
Guinea	1960–94	1994
Guinea-Bissau	1974–94	1994
Liberia	–	–
Mali	1960–93	1993
Mauritania	1960–63	1963
Niger	1960–63	1963
Nigeria	–	1960
Senegal	1960–63	1963
Sierra Leone	–	1961
Togo	1960–64	1964

Note: Cape Verde applied the GATT provisionally from 1976 to 1994 and joined the WTO in 2008. Liberia withdrew from the GATT in 1953 and currently holds observer status with the WTO.

Source: GATT, "Withdrawal of the Government of Liberia," G/45, 1953; GATT, "Admission of Ghana and the Federation of Malaya as Contracting Parties pursuant to Article XXVI:4(c)," L/699, 1957; GATT, "Status of Nigeria: Notification by the United Kingdom (Article XXVI:5(c))," L/1303, 1960; GATT, "Admission of Sierra Leone as a Contracting Party: Action under Article XXVI:5(c)," W.18/3, 1961; GATT, "Admission of Upper Volta as a Contracting Party: Notification by the Executive Secretary," L/2005, 1963; GATT, "Admission of Senegal as a Contracting Party: Certification by the Executive Secretary," L/2065, 1963; GATT, "Admission of Ivory Coast as a Contracting Party: Notification by the Executive Secretary," L/2095, 1963; GATT, "Admission of Niger as a Contracting Party: Certification by the Executive Secretary," L/2102, 1963; GATT, "Admission of Togo as a Contracting Party: Certification by the Executive Secretary," L/2194, 1964; GATT, "Admission of the Gambia as a Contracting Party: Certification by the Executive Secretary, L/2359," 1965; GATT, "Admission of Mauritania as a Contracting Party: Certification by the Executive Secretary," L/2067, 1965; GATT, "Admission of Dahomey as a Contracting Party: Certification by the Executive Secretary," L/2035, 1965; GATT, "Admission of Mali as a Contracting Party: Certification by the Director-General," L/7166, 1993; GATT, "Admission of Guinea as a Contracting Party: Certification by the Director-General," L/7606, 1994; GATT, "Guinea-Bissau Becomes 118th Member of the GATT," GATT/1623, 1994; GATT, "Observer Status in GATT: Note by the Secretariat. Supplement," C/173/SUPPL.4, 1994.

Social dimensions of trade policy formation 157

to reciprocate concessions in multilateral trade negotiations and enjoy leeway in the application of multilateral rules under Special and Differential Treatment (SDT). The adjustments made to the multilateral trading system under SDT since the 1960s have not borne fruit.[79] In general, (West) African countries have routinely failed to adjust negotiating outcomes in their favor.[80]

The unilateral trade liberalization carried out as part and parcel of the World Bank- and IMF-designed Structural Adjustment Programs (SAP) presents the second experience of internationally forged trade reform. In response to the 1980s African debt crisis, wide-ranging adjustment programs to promote economic growth consisted of a deregulatory policy mix that essentially relied on the self-adjusting capacity of the market.[81] International institutions regularly identified misguided trade policy choices under import substitution programs as one element that led to poor economic performance in Africa.[82] Trade reform geared at import liberalization as well as the removal of obstacles to export activity was thus a central element of all African SAPs.[83] Under the trade component of SAPs, most African countries focused on tariffication of quantitative restrictions on trade in goods.[84] Aside from trade reform, the SAP package included liberalization of credit and financial markets, decontrol of interest rates, exchange rate deregulation, privatization of public enterprises, deregulation of labor markets, reduction of budget deficits through reduced government spending and improved tax collection, and other policies designed to create growth.[85]

Trade policy reform was also at the center of attempts to integrate the region economically through institutions such as ECOWAS and WAEMU. The region intended to reduce dependence on world markets through the elimination of trade barriers coupled with policy coordination to boost local production. To the extent that SAPs aimed at enhancing integration into the global economy, there was clear policy incoherence between the two approaches and regional integration projects often proceeded slowly, if at all.[86] On the whole, attempts at improving regional integration since the 1990s showed limited success in integrating West African trade and improving economic performance.[87]

At the same time, the expansion of international institutions' influence over trade policy-making correlated with steady economic and social decline in the region. At independence, observers wrongly predicted good prospects for growth across Africa, especially in comparison to Asia.[88] Instead, West African growth rates were negligible or negative throughout the 1960s, 1970s, and 1980s.[89] From 1986 until 1993, a severe recession hit the eight WAEMU countries,[90] while the economic performance of the other countries was mixed.[91] Thus, seven

158 *Social dimensions of trade policy formation*

West African countries featured among the 20 countries worldwide with the lowest average annual growth rates of real per capita GDP between 1960 and 2001, including four of the region's largest economies, namely Côte d'Ivoire, Ghana, Nigeria, and Senegal.[92]

In 1996, UNCTAD reports that the LDCs[93] had not only encountered problems with growth, but that since the 1970s, their share of world imports and exports had also fallen. At the same time, inequalities grew in comparison to the rest of the world. The gap in per capita income with the group of wealthiest countries and with the group of middle-income countries widened considerably between 1960 and 1991.[94] During the 1980s and 1990s, a combination of rapid population growth and slow economic growth depressed per capita incomes and led to declining living standards and intensifying poverty.[95] Throughout the 1990s and the first decade of the new millennium, West African growth rates improved.[96] However, global financial, energy, and food crises disrupted the trend and improvements in growth rates are not sufficient to meet the UN's Millennium Development Goals.[97]

Peter Gibbon finds a "surprising degree of implicit agreement" in the literature that in Africa, "economic reforms ... have failed to live up to the claims originally made for them, and that ... social conditions have probably continued to decline."[98] Despite problems in quantification, many observers agree that social hardship has steadily increased in West Africa since the 1960s.[99] In the period between 1995 and 2000, 10 West African countries fulfilled UNCTAD's definition of generalized poverty as "a situation in which a major part of the population lives at or below income levels sufficient to meet their basic needs and in which the available resources in the economy, even when equally distributed, are rarely sufficient to cater for the basic needs of the population on a sustainable basis."[100]

In addition, Côte d'Ivoire, Guinea-Bissau, Ghana, Liberia, Mali, Mauritania, Nigeria, Senegal, and Sierra Leone have all experienced violent conflict at varying degrees since independence, or have been described as "collapsed states" that fail to govern to the benefit of their populations and see authority structures and legitimacy dissolve.[101] Claude Ake argues that political struggles against the elite in power are an expression of popular frustration with economic exclusion since independence. In his view, the struggles constitute battles for "a second independence ... from the indigenous elite." Among West African countries, he cites Benin, Côte d'Ivoire, Ghana, Guinea, Mali, Niger, Nigeria, Senegal, Sierra Leone, and Togo as examples for countries where economic crisis has led to "agitation for democratization."[102]

Social dimensions of trade policy formation   159

Arguably, West African participatory trade politics supports Ake's assessment. As I highlighted in Chapters 3 and 4, the Platform used the state's weakness in order to justify its intervention in trade policy-making. The interference of international economic institutions with trade decision-making together with chronic socio-economic decline since independence put the capacity and the capability of the state to make trade policy choices that benefit society into question. In its EPA discourse, the Platform presented democratization of trade decision-making as a necessary requirement for making responsible trade policy choices and explicitly included reclaiming trade policy space from external interference in its democratization ambitions. By highlighting that trade policy-making needed to include the people as those who are affected by its impacts, West African trade officials opened common political ground that the Platform could use to express its concerns. As outlined in Chapter 3, economistic trade policy formation theories today expect trade policy primarily to affect corporate interests and to have minimal impacts on consumers. The view goes back to Frank Taussig's methodological choice to assess the benefits of trade policy measures on the basis of their impact on national industries. Seen against the West African experience of foreign-led trade reform together with dramatic socio-economic decline, the assumption that consumers are not affected by trade policy choices is odd. In response to chronic crisis, economic activity across Africa has disengaged from the state and takes place in what is typically called informal or parallel markets.[103]

The emergence of alternative economic spheres

Various definitions of the term "informal economy" exist in the literature. Friedrich Schneider[104] follows Owen Lippert and Michael Walker[105] in classing informal activity according to type of transaction, notably monetary or non-monetary, and relationship with tax law, namely tax evasion or tax avoidance. While public revenue loss is one aspect of economic informalization, the classification fails to account for the social benefits that informal activity entails, for example by creating employment or providing basic services that the state cannot or does not sponsor.

Studying informal economic governance in Nigeria, Kate Meagher notes that "evidence of the positive effects of African informal economic and religious networks on entrepreneurship and accumulation challenges contemporary representations of African informal economies as shadowy forms of governance steeped in patrimonialism, corruption, and superstitious beliefs."[106] I therefore use Funmilayo Oloruntimehin's

160   *Social dimensions of trade policy formation*

broad definition of the informal economy as an "alternative economic system which exists alongside the official economy."[107]

The size of this alternative economic system is difficult to estimate. According to the United Nations Economic Commission for Africa (UNECA), it accounts for 20 to 90 percent of the national economies in West African countries.[108] According to Jacques Charmes, it makes up 60.6 percent of GDP in sub-Saharan Africa.[109] The overview of informally traded goods in West Africa provided in Appendix V gives further indication of the importance of this type of activity in West African economies. According to UNECA, the products in alternative trading networks cover 159 tariff lines of the World Customs Organization's Harmonized System of Tariff Classification (see Appendix V). The organization therefore concludes:

> African informal trade ... cannot continue to be perceived by the national and community institutions of ECOWAS, WAEMU, and COMESA ... as structural anomalies that hinder growth and weaken modern economies. Whether it be cross-border or domestic, informal trade remains the mode of trade best suited, from the social efficiency perspective, to the distribution of goods to meet the diversity of the African consumer's demand.[110]

In West African countries, economic activity outside of the realm of the state typically entails the unregistered organization of, for example, the transport sector or daily commodity markets. Forms of illegal activity involve corruption, tax evasion, or prostitution.[111] Transborder exchanges between countries such as Mali, Burkina-Faso, Nigeria, Senegal, and Côte d'Ivoire are also an important economic sector that hovers between illegality and law-avoidance.[112] In addition, alternative economic activity can occur in the absence of any specific relationship with the law. Remittances, which today surpass official development aid, constitute one significant example.[113]

Georges Kobou notes that "the formal and informal sectors ... overlap in real life, since some economic agents operate simultaneously in both sectors."[114] UNECA acknowledges that:

> the informal sector should not be considered as a virus attacking formal economic activity; rather, it forms a continuum unhampered by strict constraints, a response to formal trade's shortcomings. It breathes life into official trade, even if it sometimes benefits from unfair competition. It is a classic expression of the type of socialization of exchange where accounting rules and the financial

cost/benefit ratios do not always apply. And as a result, it succeeds in using resources somewhat inefficiently but satisfactorily.[115]

Ake interprets the creation of alternative economic sectors as society's "general acceptance of the necessity of self-reliance" in the face of increasing socio-economic hardship.[116] In other words, the African state "lost its relevance except as a nuisance as people resorted to self-help schemes to stem the decay of infrastructures, to pool resources for economic ventures, and to provide some necessary services for the community."[117] Kobou therefore argues: "the relationship between the various segments of the informal economy and the formal economy could reasonably be construed as a mere product of one form of modernity and a particular type of relationship with the state."[118]

In West Africa, alternative economic activity constitutes a mechanism to avoid economic hardship that increased in response to the social cost of structural adjustment. Trans-border exchanges, for example, played a role of social regulation since economic policy reforms carried out under adjustment programs eradicated social services from public spending.[119] In addition, during the 1980s and 1990s, incomes fell to levels where regular employment, including in the public sector, could no longer sustain livelihoods.[120] Alternative economic activity thus arose as a coping strategy to economic distress, often supplying formal economy activities, such as raising startup capital to a small business or supporting household income.

As these activities showed economic pay-off, civil servants started participating through corrupt practices, which reinforced the distance between society and the state as state agents circumvented the common good.[121] In the case of Nigeria, Alex Gboyega identifies three factors that led to a rise in corruption levels, namely: 1 corruption is a survival strategy under conditions of economic hardship; 2 corruption among the ruling elite set an example for others to follow suit; and 3 anti-corruption rules were not effective. He argues: "These factors created the conditions that made most public servants embrace corruption as a means of surviving harsh economic realities induced by SAP."[122] William Reno's case study of Sierra Leone supports the view of corrupt practices as taking place within the complex interaction between state and society in the struggle for subsistence.[123]

The alternative economic systems therefore do not exist independently from the state. Rather, they use structural conditions that have been put into place by the state in order to exercise their activities. This is particularly obvious in regional alternative trading networks. Bruno Stary describes an "integration from below" that has taken place in

162 *Social dimensions of trade policy formation*

West Africa since the 1980s via networks engaging in commercial activity that evades or infringes state regulation. This network covers an extensive range of products (see Appendix V). Some products are transferred across borders to benefit from price difference, as in the case of cocoa along the Ghana–Côte d'Ivoire and the Nigeria–Benin borders. Alternatively, agents engage in re-exportation from low-tax to high-tax countries, as in the case of rice along the Gambia–Guinea or the Senegal–Mali borders. The goal is not only to derive a gain from price differences in different markets, but also to acquire convertible foreign exchange due to the West African Franc's connection formerly to the French Franc and now the Euro.[124]

The first international studies from the International Labor Organization in the early 1970s saw the informal sector as a marginal activity that provided income or safety nets for the poor.[125] Instead, recent studies show that the middle classes pursue informal activity alongside their engagement with the formal economy and the state today.[126] Case studies from Nigeria and Senegal indicate that alternative activities help individuals not only to improve their incomes and thus increase consumption in the formal economy, but crucially, West Africans also engage in informal activity to raise revenue for setting up small businesses or to put themselves or family members through education. Although hard to quantify, alternative activity is thus an important element in generating startup capital, be it financial or intellectual, in order to participate in the formal sector. Individuals associated with the state benefit from alternative activities in the same way as formal sector employees.[127]

The alternative sector, despite being an expression of the inability of the state and the formal economy to assure social reproduction, has thus at the same time become a condition for the reproduction of both, due to the fact that it provides affordable goods and services and the possibility to generate income in the face of steadily dropping purchasing power.[128] Consequentially, public authorities in African countries have gradually accepted the alternative sector as a tool to offset the negative social impacts of job losses and dwindling growth rates in the formal sector.[129]

Although the alternative sector develops and prospers outside of state regulation, it remains an economic institution that is deeply embedded in society. In order to attract and regulate labor and capital outside of state-guaranteed rules, the informal sector relies on social relations.[130] In particular, alternative activity uses social structures such as family, village community, ethnicity, or religion and organizes through networks.[131] As in the pre-colonial and colonial eras, ethnicity and religion provide norms and codes of conduct that help to maintain reliable economic networks that contribute "to processes of accumulation and

Social dimensions of trade policy formation 163

social cohesion in a context of intense hardship and social disruption."[132] The Dioula and the Hausa mentioned in the first section of this chapter, for example, still play a prominent role in West African alternative arrangements.[133]

Laurence Marfaing and Miriam Sow[134] show that the alternative sector constitutes the continuation of marginalized activities in which West African traders engaged when European traders first spread into West African markets and the colonial state imposed its economic regime. In this sense, the tensions in the relations between state-based political authority, state-registered economic activity, and societies' strategies for providing its material basis are not peculiar to the postcolonial era. Instead, these tensions have been an element of West African political, economic, and social organization since at least the nineteenth century.

The analytical categories of economistic, Eurocentric trade theories do not capture these socio-economic configurations. First, West African economies are at odds with the economic indicators that are commonly expected to represent them. As the case studies on informal trans-border activity suggest, even official statistics in external trade do not account for significant amounts of economic activity.[135] Second, informalization has severe repercussions for standard trade policy recommendations. West African socio-economic realities cannot be factored into the trade theoretical approaches to which policy recommendations typically refer for the simple reason that informal economies are not supposed to exist in the models underlying these recommendations. The typical response from trade and development circles remains the assumption that the informal economy will melt away if and when economic development unfolds. Instead, it has flourished in temporal correlation with the experience of socio-economic decline following trade policy reform.[136]

Economic models concerned with the effects of trade liberalization on domestic market structures distinguish whether the state does or does not interfere with international trade flows.[137] Some scholars highlight the importance of effective domestic institutions for successful trade liberalization.[138] However, in West Africa, the roots of problems with trade policy recommendations are deeper than trade facilitation or market access in the global economy. Even if problems of quantification of informal activity and of enforceability of state regulations could be solved, the unresolved question, as Charmes highlights,[139] is how public policies can interfere with activities that fundamentally rely on state-based political authority's inability to reach all aspects of communal life.

164   *Social dimensions of trade policy formation*

The Platform was well aware of the ways in which theory and practice differed in the trade and development approaches that the EU supported during negotiations, as well as the role that history played in forging the specific political and economic context of the West African region. In the opening paragraph of an edited volume on the future of West African regional trade that ENDA published in 2010, Cheikh Tidiane Dièye writes:

> in West Africa, integration and commercial exchanges have a profound history that is well documented. Many old and recent studies show that trade flows in goods and services between its people have always passed through West Africa. These trade flows and the cultural mix that they provoked throughout the centuries have partly crafted the current image of West Africa and have contributed to drawing the spaces and territories beyond existing borders, the aspiration of the people of moving towards integration, as well as their ideas of the future of the integration. This historical dimension is a fundamental basis for West African integration. In fact, it is the matrix or the foundation on which the institutional and material frameworks that give life to regional integration are destined to be built.[140]

The extent to which realities differ between EPA negotiating parties became apparent when the EU offered to provide technical assistance for fiscal adjustment so that West African governments could offset public revenue losses due to lowering duties on European trade. There clearly is considerable untaxed economic activity in West Africa. However, even if enforceability problems could be overcome, there are evident difficulties in creating state interference with an economic sector that is thriving on the basis of absent or poorly enforced state regulation, without slowing down economic activity in that sector. The fact that the state apparatus is intermingled with the informal economy exacerbates these problems.

Although none of my interviewees mentioned this aspect explicitly, in such a complex context, the statement cited in Chapter 3—"What unites us here is much more important than our little quarrels, we want to defend the interests of our regions. You should not look at me as your opponent and I should not look at you as my opponent. Our opponent is the European Union" (Platform representative 1)—gains specific meaning. Irrespective of personal attitudes towards the global trade agenda, West African citizens live in socio-economic conditions that arose not only alongside previous externally led trade policy

Social dimensions of trade policy formation 165

choices, but which theories underlying the global trade agenda also do not capture. Even if actors disagreed on whether reality or theory had to change, the implicit fundamental insecurity about standard trade policy lines helped bring actors to the table that see their trade policy preferences as diametrically opposed. The Platform's silence on the issue of corruption must be seen in this context. To the extent that corruption is an activity that presents a coping strategy for dealing with the results of failed economic policy reform in the region, its persistence was a silent acknowledgment of the fact that trade policy-making in West Africa needed to change.

Conclusion

In the context of ECOWAS-EU EPA talks, the social dimensions of the trading activity, that is to say the perceived role of the trading activity in shaping social order across space and time, provided resources for the creation of common purpose, and a sense of unity and solidarity among West African trade political actors, despite profoundly diverging normative preferences for trade policy. West Africans shared a collective historical experience with trade where new external commercial influences had benefited specific social groups, but came at the cost of economic, social, and political disruption in the long run. The way in which first European and then colonial trade unfolded in West Africa led to the marginalization of local commercial agents and their traditional forms of economic organization that had assured social reproduction in the region for 1,000 years of its history. One economic sphere under European leadership came to be regulated by the colonial state, while another economic sphere was autonomously organized by West Africans and continued to operate through traditional trading practices. Ultimately, the evolution led to the gradual establishment of a social order in which parts of economic organization function either at the margins or outside of state-based political authority. In this sense, the so-called informal sector was not born in reaction to increasing socio-economic hardship in the post-colonial era, but it resulted from an active process of informalization of the West African economy that went hand in hand with the process of colonization, as the colonial economy was superimposed on traditional economic structures.

The existence of alternative economic spheres, both as a socio-economic reality and as an expression of a particular type of state-society relations, was relevant for the emergence of participatory trade politics in West Africa, because it set a specific socio-political context. As a form

166 *Social dimensions of trade policy formation*

of societal economic self-organization, informal West African sectors are in a conceptually messy, yet factually symbiotic relationship with the state. This specific relationship creates three partly incoherent political realities in West Africa. The state's legal and administrative structures not only provide the niches in which informal activity takes place. The informal sector has also become indispensable in order to maintain the involvement of the middle classes, including state officials, with the formal economy and the state and thus helps to prevent the latter's collapse. At the same time, the alternative economy is not an abnormality in West African social organization, as external observers often expect. It is animated through the traditional trading diasporas that have organized economic exchanges across the region since the eighth century and arguably remains its most successful tool of social reproduction. This reality, however, poses a puzzle for public policy-making, since it escapes the hypothetical state-market-civil society triangle on which trade policy recommendations are implicitly based.[141] In this context, the Platform's claim that trade policy cannot follow a one-size-fits-all model resounded particularly forcefully.

Historical and social experiences shape trade policy in other parts of the global economy. References to protectionism during the economic recession in the 1930s are, for example, a common discursive device to create political pressure for driving trade negotiations forward.[142] Equally, in a study of the political ideas, values and discourses that shaped the free trade debate in late Victorian and Edwardian Britain, Trentmann finds that "the power of free trade ... depended on the ideological construction of 'the consumer,' on national identity, and on moral and civic virtues."[143] He argues that instead of "the market" and "economic self-interest," national history, collective identities, and ideas of political legitimacy and civil society were driving trade policy formation. On the basis of the insights provided in West Africa, I summarize my findings and present reflections on the democratization of trade politics in the concluding chapter.

Notes

1 TWN 2004, *STOP EPA Launched at Africa Social Forum*, www.twnafrica.org/index.php?option=com_content&view=article&id=89:stop-epa-launched-at-africa-social-forum&catid=43:press-releases&Itemid=101.
2 Paul T. Zeleza, *A Modern Economic History of Africa* (Dakar: CODESRIA, 1993).
3 Iron, copper, mercury.
4 Susan K. McIntosh and Roderick J. McIntosh, "Prehistoric Investigations in the Region of Jenne, Mali," *Cambridge Monographs in African Archaeology*

Social dimensions of trade policy formation 167

Number 2 (Oxford: British Archaeological Reports, 1980); and Abdoulaye Bathily, *Les portes de l'or: Le royaume de Galam (Sénégal) de l'ère musulmane au temps de négriers (VIIIe–XVIIIe siècle)* (Paris: Editions L'Harmattan, 1980).

5 Bathily, *Les portes de l'or: Le royaume de Galam (Sénégal) de l'ère musulmane au temps de négriers (VIIIe–XVIIIe siècle)*.

6 Bathily, *Les portes de l'or: Le royaume de Galam (Sénégal) de l'ère musulmane au temps de négriers (VIIIe–XVIIIe siècle)*; and Zeleza, *A Modern Economic History of Africa*.

7 The kola is the nut of the kola tree. It contains caffeine and is traditionally consumed in West African cultures for its perceived stimulating and health-beneficial qualities.

8 Nagnin Ouattara, "Commerçants dyula en Côte d'Ivoire: Permanences et ruptures dans un milieu socioprofessionnel (XIXe–XXe siècles)," in *Commerce et Commerçants en Afrique de l'Ouest: La Côte d'Ivoire*, ed. Leonhard Harding and Pierre Kipre (Paris: Edition L'Harmattan, 1992), 75–117.

9 Zeleza, *A Modern Economic History of Africa*.

10 Ouattara, "Commerçants dyula en Côte d'Ivoire: Permanences et ruptures dans un milieu socioprofessionnel (XIXe–XXe siècles)."

11 Zeleza, *A Modern Economic History of Africa*.

12 Samir Amin, "Underdevelopment and Dependence in Black Africa—Origins and Contemporary Forms," *Journal of Modern African Studies* 10, no. 4 (1972): 503–24.

13 Also spelt dyula or juula.

14 Abner Cohen, "Cultural Strategies in the Organisation of Trading Diasporas," in *The Development of Indigenous Trade and Markets in West Africa*, ed. Claude Meillassoux (London: Oxford University Press, 1971), 267.

15 According to Bathily, historical sources indicate the presence of Dioula communities in the Niger and Senegal deltas from the ninth century onwards. Their genealogy is not entirely certain. Bathily argues that the Dioula emerged from the fusion of several ethno-linguistic elements. Zeleza maintains that common commercial interest, religion and language were the basis of Dioula identity. In any case, it is clear that peaceful Islamization and the spread of the Dioula trading networks proceeded together in West Africa. Zeleza argues that like the Hausa, the Dioula were "held together by common material interests and the ideological pulls of shared language, the invented tradition of ethnic homogeneity, and adherence to one religion, Islam." See Bathily, *Les portes de l'or: Le royaume de Galam (Sénégal) de l'ère musulmane au temps de négriers (VIIIe–XVIIIe siècle)*; and Zeleza, *A Modern Economic History of Africa*, 280.

16 Leonhard Harding and Pierre Kipre, *Commerce et Commerçants en Afrique de l'Ouest: La Côte d'Ivoire* (Paris: Edition L'Harmattan, 1992).

17 Boubacar Barry and Leonhard Harding, *Commerce et commerçants en Afrique de l'Ouest: Le Sénégal* (Paris: Edition L'Harmattan, 1992); and Harding and Kipre, *Commerce et Commerçants en Afrique de l'Ouest: La Côte d'Ivoire*.

18 Leonhard Harding, "Les grands commerçants africains en Afrique de l'Ouest: Le cas du Sénégal et de la Côte d'Ivoire. Essai de synthèse," in *Commerce et Commerçants en Afrique de l'Ouest: La Côte d'Ivoire*, ed. Leonhard Harding and Pierre Kipre (Paris: Edition L'Harmattan, 1992), 5–27.

168 *Social dimensions of trade policy formation*

19 Laurence Marfaing, *Evolution du commerce au Sénégal, 1820–1930* (Paris: Edition L'Harmattan, 1991); and Harding, "Les grands commerçants africains en Afrique de l'Ouest: Le cas du Sénégal et de la Côte d'Ivoire. Essai de synthèse."

20 Pierre Kipre, "Commerce et Commerçants en Côte d'Ivoire du XVIIe au XXe siècle," in *Commerce et Commerçants en Afrique de l'Ouest: La Côte d'Ivoire*, ed. Leonhard Harding and Pierre Kipre (Paris: Edition L'Harmattan, 1992), 35–73.

21 Kipre, "Commerce et Commerçants en Côte d'Ivoire du XVIIe au XXe siècle."

22 Catherine Coquery-Vidrovitch and Paul E. Lovejoy, *The Workers of African Trade* (London: Sage Publications, 1985).

23 Harding, "Les grands commerçants africains en Afrique de l'Ouest: Le cas du Sénégal et de la Côte d'Ivoire. Essai de synthèse."

24 Bathily, *Les portes de l'or: Le royaume de Galam (Sénégal) de l'ère musulmane au temps de négriers (VIIIe–XVIIIe siècle)*, 148.

25 Bathily, *Les portes de l'or: Le royaume de Galam (Sénégal) de l'ère musulmane au temps de négriers (VIIIe–XVIIIe siècle)*.

26 John D. Fage, "Slavery and Slave Trade in the Context of West African History," *Journal of African History* 10, no. 3 (1969): 397.

27 A.J.H. Latham, "Currency, Credit and Capitalism on the Cross River in the Pre-colonial Era," *Journal of African History* 12, no. 4 (1971): 599–605; and Joseph E. Inikori, "West Africa's Seaborne Trade, 1750–1850," in *Figuring African Trade: Proceedings of the Symposium on the Quantification and Structure of the Import and Export and Long Distance Trade in Africa 1800–1913*, ed. Gehard Liesegang, Helma Pasch and Adam Jones (Berlin: Dietrich Reimer Verlag, 1986), 50–88.

28 Bathily, *Les portes de l'or: Le royaume de Galam (Sénégal) de l'ère musulmane au temps de négriers (VIIIe–XVIIIe siècle)*.

29 Amin, "Underdevelopment and Dependence in Black Africa—Origins and Contemporary Forms."

30 Bathily, *Les portes de l'or: Le royaume de Galam (Sénégal) de l'ère musulmane au temps de négriers (VIIIe–XVIIIe siècle)*.

31 P.F. de Moraes Farias, "Silent Trade: Myth and Historical Evidence," *History in Africa* 1 (1974): 9–24; Ralph A. Austen, *African Economic History* (London: James Currey, 1987).

32 Paul E. Lovejoy, "Commercial Sectors in the Economy of the Nineteenth-Century Central Sudan: The Trans-Saharan Trade and Desert-Side Salt Trade," *African Economic History* 13 (1984): 85–116.

33 Inikori, "West Africa's Seaborne Trade, 1750–1850."

34 Kipre, "Commerce et Commerçants en Côte d'Ivoire du XVIIe au XXe siècle."

35 Antony G. Hopkins, *An Economic History of West Africa* (London: Longman, 1973); Jim Silver, "The Failing of the European Mining Companies in the Nineteenth Century Gold Coast," *Journal of African History* 22, no. 4 (1981): 511–29.

36 Zeleza, *A Modern Economic History of Africa*, 294.

37 Harding, "Les grands commerçants africains en Afrique de l'Ouest: Le cas du Sénégal et de la Côte d'Ivoire. Essai de synthèse."

38 Ouattara, "Commerçants dyula en Côte d'Ivoire: Permanences et ruptures dans un milieu socioprofessionnel (XIXe–XXe siècles)."

39 Bathily, *Les portes de l'or: Le royaume de Galam (Sénégal) de l'ère musulmane au temps de négriers (VIIIe–XVIIIe siècle)*.

Social dimensions of trade policy formation 169

40 Bathily, *Les portes de l'or: Le royaume de Galam (Sénégal) de l'ère musulmane au temps de négriers (VIIIe–XVIIIe siècle)*.

41 Bathily, *Les portes de l'or: Le royaume de Galam (Sénégal) de l'ère musulmane au temps de négriers (VIIIe–XVIIIe siècle)*.

42 George E. Brooks, "Peanuts and Colonialism: Consequences of the Commercialisation of Peanuts in West Africa, 1830–70," *Journal of African History* 16, no. 1 (1975): 29–54.

43 Harding, "Les grands commerçants africains en Afrique de l'Ouest: Le cas du Sénégal et de la Côte d'Ivoire. Essai de synthèse."

44 Joye L. Bowman, "Legitimate Commerce and Peanut Production in Portuguese Guinea, 1840s–1880s," *Journal of African History* 28, no. 1 (1987): 87–106.

45 Martin Lynn, "Change and Continuity in British Palm Oil Trade with West Africa, 1830–55," *Journal of African History* 22, no. 3 (1981): 348.

46 Zeleza, *A Modern Economic History of Africa*.

47 Zeleza, *A Modern Economic History of Africa*.

48 Philip D. Curtin, *The Atlantic Slave Trade: A Census* (Madison, WI: University of Wisconsin Press, 1969).

49 Joseph E. Inikori, "Under-Population in Nineteenth Century West Africa: The Role of the Export Slave Trade," *African Historical Demography* II (1981): 283–313.

50 Fage, "Slavery and Slave Trade in the Context of West African History"; and Inikori, "Under-Population in Nineteenth Century West Africa: The Role of the Export Slave Trade."

51 See Fage, "Slavery and Slave Trade in the Context of West African History."

52 Mamadou Fall, "Marchés locaux et groupes marchands dans la longue durée: des marchés du Cayor aux marchés du fleuve Sénégal XVIIIe–début XXe siècle," in *Commerce et Commerçants en Afrique de l'Ouest: Le Sénégal*, ed. Leonhard Harding and Boubacar Barry (Paris: Edition L'Harmattan, 1992), 59–105; and Zeleza, *A Modern Economic History of Africa*.

53 Richard Bean, "A Note on the Relative Importance of Slaves and Gold in West African Exports," *Journal of African History* 15, no. 3 (1974): 351–56; and Inikori, "West Africa's Seaborne Trade, 1750–1850."

54 Bathily, *Les portes de l'or: Le royaume de Galam (Sénégal) de l'ère musulmane au temps de négriers (VIIIe–XVIIIe siècle)*.

55 Iris Berger and E. Frances White, *Women in Sub-Saharan Africa: Restoring Women to History* (Bloomington: Indiana University Press, 1999).

56 Boubacar Barry, *Le royaume du Waalo, 1659–1859* (Paris: Mimeo, 1971).

57 Bathily, *Les portes de l'or: Le royaume de Galam (Sénégal) de l'ère musulmane au temps de négriers (VIIIe–XVIIIe siècle)*.

58 Fage, "Slavery and Slave Trade in the Context of West African History."

59 Zeleza, *A Modern Economic History of Africa*, 383.

60 Margaret O. McLane, "Commercial Rivalries and French Policy on the Senegal River, 1831–58," *African Economic History* 15 (1986): 46.

61 Fage, "Slavery and Slave Trade in the Context of West African History," 403.

62 Harding, "Les grands commerçants africains en Afrique de l'Ouest: Le cas du Sénégal et de la Côte d'Ivoire. Essai de synthèse."

63 Harding and Kipre, *Commerce et Commerçants en Afrique de l'Ouest: La Côte d'Ivoire*; and Barry and Harding, *Commerce et commerçants en Afrique de l'Ouest: Le Sénégal*.

170   *Social dimensions of trade policy formation*

64 Zeleza, *A Modern Economic History of Africa*, 388.
65 Bibiane Mbaye Gahamanyi, *West Africa in the EPA Negotiations with the European Community* (Dakar: ENDA, 2004), 4.
66 Mahmood Mamdani, *Citizen and Subject: Contemporary Africa and the Legacy of Late Colonialism* (Princeton: Princeton University Press, 1996); and Claude Ake, *The Feasibility of Democracy in Africa* (Dakar: CODESRIA, 2000). For an analysis of how colonialism shaped the public sphere in African countries, see Peter Ekeh, "Colonialism and the Two Publics in Africa: A Theoretical Statement," *Comparative Studies in Society and History* 17, no. 1 (1975): 91–112.
67 Klaus Knorr, "The Bretton Woods Institutions in Transition," *International Organization* 2, no. 1 (1948): 19–38; Robert E. Hudec, *The GATT Legal System and World Trade Diplomacy* (Salem: Buttworth Legal Publishers, 1990); John G. Ikenberry, "A World Economy Restored: Expert Consensus and the Anglo-American Postwar Settlement," *International Organization* 46, no. 1 (1992): 289–321; J.L.P. Gabilondo, "Developing Countries in the WTO Dispute Settlement Procedures: Improving their Participation," *Journal of World Trade* 35, no. 4 (2001): 483–88; Linda Weiss, "Global Governance, National Strategies: How Industrialized States Make Room to Move Under the WTO," *Review of International Political Economy* 12, no. 5 (2005): 723–49; and Rorden Wilkinson, *The WTO: Crisis and the Governance of Global Trade* (London: Routledge, 2006).
68 Bernard Hoekman and Michel Kostecki, *The Political Economy of the World Trading System* (Oxford: Oxford University Press, 2001), 385.
69 Paul Collier, "Why the WTO is Deadlocked: And What Can be Done About it," *The World Economy* 29, no. 10 (2006): 1425, italics in original.
70 See GATT documents GATT/CP/22, L/1809 and BISD 11th Supplement. See Michael Tomz, Judith L. Goldstein and Douglas Rivers, "Do We Really Know that the WTO Increases Trade? Comment," *American Economic Review* 97, no. 5 (2007): 2005–18 for an analysis of how this misjudgment of the geographical applicability of the GATT impacts on studies of the effects of multilateral trade policies. Many studies diagnose a spike in developing country GATT membership in the 1960s. While it is true that full membership came with procedural and organizational rights that lifted the quality of participation in the GATT system, the substantial rules of the organization had already applied to these countries since 1947. Thus, decolonialization together with subsequent formal accession of former colonial territories to the GATT raised the number of official contracting parties during the 1960s without expanding the geographical scope of GATT application.
71 GATT, *Trends in International Trade: A Report by a Panel of Experts* (Geneva: GATT, 1958), cited in GATT, "De Facto Application of the General Agreement: Note by the Secretariat," C/130, 1984, 2.
72 GATT, "Jamaica—Margins of Preferences, Report of the Panel adopted on 2 February 1971," L/3485-18S/183, para. 13.
73 GATT, "Article XXVI:5(c) Note by Secretariat," MTN.GNG/NG7/W/31, 1987, 6.
74 See GATT, "Admission of Upper Volta as a Contracting Party: Notification by the Executive Secretary," L/2005, 1963; GATT, "Admission of Ivory Coast as a Contracting Party: Notification by the Executive Secretary," L/2095, 1963; GATT, "Admission of Niger as a Contracting Party:

Social dimensions of trade policy formation 171

Certification by the Executive Secretary," L/2102, 1963; GATT, "Admission of Senegal as a Contracting Party: Certification by the Executive Secretary," L/2065, 1963; GATT, "Admission of Dahomey as a Contracting Party: Certification by the Executive Secretary," L/2035, 1965; GATT, "Admission of Mauritania as a Contracting Party: Certification by the Executive Secretary," L/2067, 1965.

75 GATT, *Trends in International Trade: A Report by a Panel of Experts.*

76 T. Ademola Oyejide, "Trade Liberalisation, Regional Integration, and African Development in the Context of Structural Adjustment," in *African Voices on Structural Adjustment: A Companion To: Our Continent Our Future*, ed. Thandika Mkandawire and Charles C. Soluda (Dakar and Ottawa: CODESRIA and IDRC, 2003), 73–102.

77 GATT, *Basic Instruments and Selected Documents Eleventh Supplement: Decisions, Reports, etc. of the Twentieth Session* (Geneva: GATT, 1963).

78 Namely Part IV on Trade and Development.

79 Robert E. Hudec, *Developing Countries in the GATT/WTO Legal System* (Aldershot: Gower Publishing, 1987); Bernard Hoekman, "Preference Erosion and the Doha Development Agenda," presented at the conference *Trade for Development: the Future of Special and Differential Treatment of Developing Countries*, IFRI, Paris, 28 October 2005.

80 Michael J. Finger, *The Doha Agenda and Development: A View from the Uruguay Round* (Manila: Asian Development Bank, 2002); Bernard Hoekman, Constantine Michalopolous and L. Alan Winters, "Special and Differential Treatment of Developing Countries in the WTO: Moving Forward After Cancún," *The World Economy* 27, no. 4 (2004): 481–506.

81 Alan Roe and Hartmut Schneider, *Adjustment and Equity in Ghana* (Paris: OECD, 1992).

82 World Bank, *Accelerated Development in Sub-Saharan Africa: An Agenda for Action* (Washington: World Bank, 1981); and World Bank, *Adjustment in Africa: Reforms, Results and the Road Ahead* (New York: Oxford University Press published for the World Bank, 1994).

83 Oyejide, "Trade Liberalisation, Regional Integration, and African Development in the Context of Structural Adjustment."

84 IMF, *International Trade Policies: The Uruguay Round and Beyond. Volume II. Background Papers* (Washington, DC: International Monetary Fund, 1994); and Oyejide, "Trade Liberalisation, Regional Integration, and African Development in the Context of Structural Adjustment."

85 Tshikala B. Tshibaka, *Structural Adjustment and Agriculture in West Africa* (Dakar: CODESRIA, 1998); and Kowadwo Konadu-Agyemang, "The Best of Times and the Worst of Times: Structural Adjustment Programs and Uneven Development in Africa: The Case of Ghana," *The Professional Geographer* 52, no. 3 (2000): 469–83.

86 Oyejide, "Trade Liberalisation, Regional Integration, and African Development in the Context of Structural Adjustment."

87 Jaime de Melo and Arvind Panagariya, *New Dimensions in Regional Integration* (Cambridge: Press Syndicate of the University of Cambridge, 1993); Jeffrey Fine and Stephen Yeo, "Regional Integration in Sub-Saharan Africa: Dead End or A Fresh Start?" in *Regional Integration and Trade Liberalisation in Sub-Saharan Africa: Framework, Issues and Methodological Perspectives*, ed. T. Ademola Oyejide, Ebrahim Ebadawi and Paul

172 *Social dimensions of trade policy formation*

Collier (London: Macmillan, 1997), 429–74; and World Bank, *Trade Blocs. A World Bank Policy Research Report* (New York: Oxford University Press published for the World Bank, 2000).

88 World Bank, *Economic Growth in the 1990s: Learning from a Decade of Reform* (Washington: World Bank, 2005).

89 ECOWAS, *Ten Years of ECOWAS* (Lagos: ECOWAS, 1985); and Victor A.O. Adetula, *The Role of the Economic Community of West African States (ECOWAS) in the Industrialisation of West Africa*, PhD thesis, Department of Political Science, Faculty of Social Sciences, University of Jos, 1986.

90 They are: Benin, Burkina-Faso, Côte d'Ivoire, Guinea-Bissau, Mali, Niger, Senegal and Togo.

91 Paul R. Masson and Catherine Pattillo, "Monetary Union in West Africa (ECOWAS): Is it Desirable and How Could it be Achieved?" *IMF Occasional Paper*, no. 204 (Washington, DC: International Monetary Fund, 2001).

92 World Bank, *Economic Growth in the 1990s: Learning from a Decade of Reform*. The three other countries are Liberia, Niger and Sierra Leone.

93 In 1996, this included 12 West African countries: Benin, Burkina-Faso, Côte d'Ivoire, The Gambia, Guinea, Guinea-Bissau, Liberia, Mali, Mauritania, Niger, Sierra Leone and Togo.

94 UNCTAD, *The Least Developed Countries: 1996 Report* (New York: United Nations Publications, 1996).

95 UNCTAD, *The Least Developed Countries: 1996 Report*.

96 Abena D. Oduro and Ivy Aryee, "Investigating Chronic Poverty in West Africa," *CPRC Working Paper* 28 (Accra: Chronic Poverty Research Centre, 2003); and UNECA, *Recent Economic and Social Developments in West Africa and Prospects for 2010* (Addis Ababa: United Nations Economic Commission for Africa, 2010).

97 UNECA, *Recent Economic and Social Developments in West Africa and Prospects for 2010*.

98 Peter Gibbon, "Introduction: Economic Reform and Social Change in Africa," in *Social Change and Economic Reform in Africa*, ed. Peter Gibbon (Uppsala: Nordiska Afrikainstitutet, 1993), 11–12.

99 Adebayo Adedeji, "Foreword," in *The Human Dimension of Africa's Persistent Economic Crisis*, ed. Adebayo Adedeji, Sadiq Rasheed and Melody Morrison (London: Hans Zell Publishers for the United Nations Economic Commission for Africa, 1990), vii–x; UNCTAD, *The Least Developed Countries: 1996 Report*; and Konadu-Agyemang, "The Best of Times and the Worst of Times: Structural Adjustment Programs and Uneven Development in Africa: The Case of Ghana."

100 They are: Benin, Burkina-Faso, The Gambia, Guinea, Guinea-Bissau, Liberia, Mali, Niger, Sierra Leone, and Togo. UNCTAD, *The Least Developed Countries Report 2002: Escaping the Poverty Trap* (New York: United Nations Publications, 2002), 39; Abena D. Oduro and Ivy Aryee, "Investigating Chronic Poverty in West Africa."

101 I. William Zartman, *Collapsed States: The Disintegration and Restoration of Legitimate Authority* (Boulder, CO: Lynne Rienner Publishers, 1995); and Transnational Institute, African Studies Centre (Leiden), The Centre of Social Studies (Coimbra University) and The Peace Research Centre CIP-FUHEM Madrid 2003, *Failed and Collapsed States in the International System*, www.tni.org/archives/reports/failedstates.pdf.

Social dimensions of trade policy formation 173

102 Ake, *The Feasibility of Democracy in Africa*, 47–48.
103 Naomi Chazan, "Patterns of State-Society Incorporation and Disengagement in Africa," in *The Precarious Balance: State and Society in Africa*, ed. Donald Rothchild and Naomi Chazan (Boulder, CO: Westview Press, 1988), 121–48; Adebayo Olukoshi, "Associational Life," in *Transition without End: Nigerian Politics and Civil Society Under Babangida*, ed. Larry Diamond, Anthony Kirk-Green and Oyeleye Oyediran (Ibadan: Vantage Press, 1997), 564–78; and Georges Kobou, *Les économies réelles en Afrique: études de cas/Real Economies in Africa: Case Studies* (Dakar: CODESRIA, 2003).
104 Friedrich Schneider, "Size and Measurement of the Informal Economy in 110 Countries around the World," paper presented at Workshop of Australian National Tax Centre, Canberra, 17 July 2002.
105 Owen Lippert and Michael Walker, *The Underground Economy: Global Evidences of its Size and Impact* (Vancouver: The Frazer Institute, 1997).
106 Kate Meagher, "Trading on Faith: Religious Movements and Informal Economic Governance in Nigeria," *Journal of Modern African Studies* 47, no. 3 (2009): 401.
107 Funmilayo Oloruntimehin, "Women and Prostitution," in *Les économies réelles en Afrique: études de cas/Real Economies in Africa: Case Studies*, ed. Georges Kobou (Dakar: CODESRIA, 2003), 237.
108 UNECA, *Assessing Regional Integration in Africa IV: Enhancing Intra-African Trade* (Addis Ababa: United Nations Economic Commission for Africa, 2010).
109 Jacques Charmes 2000, *Export Group on Informal Sector Statistics*, www.unescap.org/stat/isie/reference-materials/National-Accounts/Measurement-Contribution-GDP-Concept-Delhi-Group.pdf.
110 UNECA, *Assessing Regional Integration in Africa IV: Enhancing Intra-African Trade*, 178.
111 Ousseynou Faye, "Les pratiques des tablibés de la transaction au marché de Sandaga (Dakar)," in *Les économies réelles en Afrique. Real Economies in Africa*, ed. Georges Kobou (Dakar: CODESRIA, 2003), 270–80; Cheikh Guèye, "Café et Pain Touba: Entreprenariat individuel, méthodologie collective et croyances," in *Les économies réelles en Afrique. Real Economies in Africa*, ed. Georges Kobou (Dakar: CODESRIA, 2003), 281–92; and Alex Gboyega, "Economic Distress and Corruption in Local Government Councils and the Police Services," in *Les économies réelles en Afrique. Real Economies in Africa*, ed. Georges Kobou (Dakar: CODESRIA, 2003), 203–16.
112 Emmanuel Grégoire and Pascal Labazée, *Grands commerçants de l'Afrique de l'Ouest: logiques et pratiques d'un groupe d'hommes d'affaires contemporains* (Paris: Karthala, 1993).
113 Meagher, "Trading on Faith: Religious Movements and Informal Economic Governance in Nigeria." According to the World Bank, the overall value of remittances surpasses the amount of development aid three times. In West Africa, top remittance receivers in 2010 are Nigeria (US$10 billion), Senegal ($1.2 billion), Mali ($400 million), and Togo ($300 million). They are also among the top 10 in sub-Saharan Africa. See World Bank, *Migration and Remittances Factbook 2011* (Washington, DC: World Bank, 2011).

174 *Social dimensions of trade policy formation*

114 Kobou, *Les économies réelles en Afrique: études de cas/Real Economies in Africa: Case Studies*, 26.
115 UNECA, *Assessing Regional Integration in Africa IV: Enhancing Intra-African Trade*, 178–79.
116 Ake, *The Feasibility of Democracy in Africa*.
117 Ake, *The Feasibility of Democracy in Africa*, 46–47.
118 Kobou, *Les économies réelles en Afrique: études de cas/Real Economies in Africa: Case Studies*, 26.
119 Daniel Bach, "Afrique de l'Ouest: organisations régionales, espaces nationaux et régionalismes transétatiques: les leçons d'un mythe," in *L'Afrique politique 1994*, Centre d'Etudes d'Afrique Noire (Institut d'Etudes Politiques de Bordeaux) (Paris: Karthala, 1994), 93–115.
120 Jacques Charmes, "Le secteur informel, nouvel enjeu des politiques de développement?" in *Vers quel désordre mondial?L'Homme et la Société* 105–6 (1992): 63–77; Yusuf Bangura, "Economic Restructuring, Coping Strategies and Social Change: Implications for Institutional Development in Africa," *Development and Change* 25, no. 4 (1994): 785–827; and Gboyega, "Economic Distress and Corruption in Local Government Councils and the Police Services."
121 Gboyega, "Economic Distress and Corruption in Local Government Councils and the Police Services"; Isaac O. Albert, "Smuggling Second-hand Cars through the Benin-Nigeria Borders," in *Les économies réelles en Afrique. Real Economies in Africa*, ed. Georges Kobou (Dakar: CODESRIA, 2003), 217–33; Oloruntimehin, "Women and Prostitution."
122 Gboyega, "Economic Distress and Corruption in Local Government Councils and the Police Services," 204.
123 William Reno, *Corruption and State Politics in Sierra Leone* (Cambridge: Cambridge University Press, 1995).
124 Bruno Stary, "Réseaux marchands et espaces transfrontaliers en Afrique de l'Ouest," *Afrique Contemporaine* 177, no. 1 (1996): 45–53.
125 ILO, *Employment, Incomes and Equality: A Strategy for Increasing Productive Employment in Kenya* (Geneva: ILO, 1972).
126 UNECA, *Assessing Regional Integration in Africa IV: Enhancing Intra-African Trade*.
127 Kobou, *Les économies réelles en Afrique: études de cas/Real Economies in Africa: Case Studies*.
128 Charmes, "Le secteur informel, nouvel enjeu des politiques de développement?"
129 Charmes, "Le secteur informel, nouvel enjeu des politiques de développement?"; Laurence Marfaing and Miriam Sow, *Les opérateurs économiques au Sénégal: Entre le formel et l'informel (1930–1996)* (Paris: Karthala, 1999).
130 Linda Weiss, "Explaining the Underground Economy: State and Social Structure," *British Journal of Sociology* 38, no. 2 (1987): 216–34.
131 Stary, "Réseaux marchands et espaces transfrontaliers en Afrique de l'Ouest"; Marfaing and Sow, *Les opérateurs économiques au Sénégal: Entre le formel et l'informel*; Kobou, *Les économies réelles en Afrique: études de cas/Real Economies in Africa: Case Studies*; Meagher, "Trading on Faith: Religious Movements and Informal Economic Governance in Nigeria."

Social dimensions of trade policy formation 175

132 Meagher, "Trading on Faith: Religious Movements and Informal Economic Governance in Nigeria," 402.

133 Victoria Ebin, "Les commerçants mourides à Marseille et à New York: regards sur les stratégies d'implantation," in *Grands commerçants de l'Afrique de l'Ouest: logiques et pratiques d'un groupe d'hommes d'affaires contemporains* (Paris: Karthala, 1993), 101–24; Cheikh A. Babou, "Brotherhood, Solidarity, Education and Migration: The Role of the *Dahiras* Among the Murid Muslim Community of New York," *African Affairs* 101, no. 403 (2002): 151–70; and Meagher, "Trading on Faith: Religious Movements and Informal Economic Governance in Nigeria."

134 Marfaing and Sow, *Les opérateurs économiques au Sénégal: Entre le formel et l'informel.*

135 Michel Norro, *Economies africaines: analyse économique de l'Afrique subsaharienne* (Brussels: De Boek & Larcier, 1994); and Kobou, *Les économies réelles en Afrique: études de cas/Real Economies in Africa: Case Studies.*

136 Olukoshi, "Associational Life"; and Kobou, *Les économies réelles en Afrique: études de cas/Real Economies in Africa: Case Studies.*

137 See Jacob Viner, *Studies in the Theory of International Trade* (New York: Harper and Brothers, 1937); Elhanan Helpman and Paul R. Krugman, *Market Structure and Foreign Trade: Increasing Returns, Imperfect Competition and the International Economy* (Cambridge, MA: MIT Press, 1987); Dani Rodrik, "Imperfect Competition, Scale Economies, and Trade Policy in Developing Countries," in *Trade Policy Issues and Empirical Analysis*, ed. Robert E. Baldwin (Chicago, IL: University of Chicago Press, 1988), 109–43; and David Evans, "Alternative Perspectives on Trade and Development," in *Handbook of Development Economics*, ed. Hollis Chenery and Thirukodikaval N. Srinivasan (Amsterdam: North-Holland, 1989), 1241–304.

138 L. Alan Winters, "Trade Liberalisation and Economic Performance: An Overview," *The Economic Journal* 114, no. 493 (2004): 4–21.

139 Charmes, "Le secteur informel, nouvel enjeu des politiques de développement?"

140 Cheikh Tidiane Dièye, "Introduction: Quel futur pour l'intégration et le commerce intra-régional en Afrique de l'Ouest?" in *Le Futur du Commerce Intra-Régional en Afrique de l'Ouest*, ed. Cheikh Tidiane Dièye (Dakar: ENDA, 2010), 13.

141 TWN, *STOP EPA Launched at Africa Social Forum.*

142 Rorden Wilkinson, *The WTO: Crisis and the Governance of Global Trade* (London: Routledge, 2006).

143 Frank Trentmann, "Political Culture and Political Economy: Interests, Ideology and Free Trade," *Review of International Political Economy* 5, no. 2 (1998): 218–19.

6 Conclusion

- **Practical lessons for participatory trade politics from West Africa**
- **Adjusting trade policy formation theory**
- **Trade and democracy**

In Part I of this book, I provided empirical evidence indicating that trade policy formation can institutionally incorporate political contestation from a variety of social groups with diverging attitudes towards the global trade agenda. In West Africa, a civil society network called "the Platform" was integrated in the region's negotiating team towards a trade agreement with the EU. The network was highly critical of the EU's suggestions for trade policy reform, openly confronted trade decision-makers on their policy lines, and provided unparalleled levels of transparency in ECOWAS-EU EPA negotiations. Although the practice introduced previously absent political contestations into the trade policy-making process, neither the trade talks, nor cooperation between trade officials and civil society's critical branches on the West African side of the negotiating table broke down. Instead, participatory trade politics influenced the course of negotiations, as trade officials from both sides acknowledged in my interviews.

Based on this observation, I argued that current theoretical approaches to trade policy formation cannot account for the participatory practice, especially as West African trade negotiators initially shared their Northern colleagues' skepticism about the merits of debating trade policy-making with transformative organizations that criticize the global trade agenda. Most theoretical approaches today project a particular reading of the economic on the trade policy-making processes that they analyze. This reading includes a predefinition of wealth and/or welfare in terms of capital endowment and access to goods and services, the assumption that the impact of trade policy on economic operators is the appropriate proxy for assessing the impacts of trade

Conclusion 177

policy on society, a peculiar view of politics as abnormal or disturbing in the field of economic policy-making, and a disregard for how perceptions of economic interests are embedded in society and culture. While parts of the literature see this as an expression of dominant ideologies, they implicitly accept the depiction of trade policy formation as occurring in a potentially contested from the outside, yet factually narrow economic sphere that operates by and large along the lines of a neoclassical market mechanism.

This may go some way in accounting for the trade political status quo. Two theoretical and practical problems, however, haunt such a conceptualization of trade politics and make trade political theory unsuitable for resolving the efficiency/legitimacy deadlock in trade debates. On the one hand, the view neglects the nature of the trading activity as not only an economic, but also a social activity. Any challenges to trade policy-making that emanate from the social realm therefore by definition fall outside of the analytical framework of trade policy formation theory. On the other hand, because theory presents its economism as naturally flowing from the policy field, it has become an obstacle to imagining transformations in trade politics away from exclusive decision-making styles. In other words, the economistic bias inherent in dominant trade policy formation theories justifies opaque trade policy-making practices at domestic and global policy levels.

In political economy and global governance debates, non-state, non-corporate social agents face a legitimacy bias, despite the fact that social and political considerations continue to mark trade policy-making in real life. The gap is remarkable, since we understand why trade policy-making is contested: with the ongoing expansion of the global trade agenda, trade policy impacts noticeably on several other policy areas, including labor and environmental standards, public health, education, and so forth. Reflections on the necessary balancing exercise resulting from this fact have occupied the minds of international legal scholars since the creation of the GATT. Yet, the reading of the economic underlying political economy theories of trade juxtaposes societal and economic concerns, not because the latter are factually incommensurable, but because economistic foundations, contested in trade theory since the nineteenth century, expect them to be.

As pointed out in Chapter 2, trade policy formation theories lag behind the discipline of economics in this regard, which supports my argument that the link between economics and trade policy formation theory is predominantly methodological. It results from the distinct historical evolution of trade theory as an academic field of inquiry, and can and should be reviewed. The foundations on which such a review

178 *Conclusion*

is possible are already laid in parts of the literature. In Part II of the book, I thus studied the transformations in West African trade policy-making mechanisms during EPA negotiations with the aim of answering the research question that currently dominant trade policy formation theories cannot ask: why did trade politics become participatory in West Africa? I suggested adjustments to the analytical framework of trade policy formation on the basis of the conceptual advances made in parts of the trade literature and the empirical data that I gathered on ECOWAS-EU EPA talks.

The work of scholars such as Ford, Eagleton-Pierce, and Wilkinson confirms that perceptions and world views play a role in global trade institutions.[1] As opposed to deriving (static) assumptions about social agents' trade preferences from political or economic structure, Trentmann points to the importance of social and political context for the ways in which trade political interests are defined across space and time.[2] Building on these arguments, I applied von Bülow's relational approach for studying transnational trade networks which emphasizes the double embeddedness of political actors in social networks and in political environments to the interactions between trade officials and their critics.[3] I argued that the approach can help to make visible the interactions of ideas and interests in the way in which society governs itself and thus respects Curtin's observation that commercial interaction has been one of the most important external stimuli to social transformation in human history.[4]

Based on this larger perspective that acknowledges that the economic and social dimensions of the trading activity cannot be conceptualized in isolation from each other, I drew a picture of West African participatory trade politics emerging in the following way: strong asymmetries in terms of economic weight and negotiating capacity, but also adherence to specific norms and principles, including WTO regulation, the Cotonou Agreement and general good governance criteria, such as inclusiveness and transparency, as well as past and present collective experiences with (European) trade structured the political environment of ECOWAS-EU EPA negotiations. Their integration into broader North-South and South-South transnational networks enabled West African transformative actors to mount the resources that allowed them to recognize and to use the political opportunity that the structures provided. In addition, they also framed the West African EPA debate in ways that were conducive to transformative participation and by spawning solidarity that helped to overcome heated debates over diverging normative preferences for trade policy.

West African public officials changed their view on transformative actors, because they proved to be beneficial allies in trade negotiations. Added technical capacity and unexpected influence in highly asymmetrical trade talks strengthened West African officials' existing beliefs in the legitimate character of inclusive trade policy-making mechanisms. While West African trade political actors struggled with many aspects of participatory trade politics, such as issues connected to representation and legitimacy, they continued to engage in a joint process of legitimization based on the above-mentioned perceived benefits and a sense of unity and solidarity among the members of their negotiating team. This sense was not initially present in the EPA context. West African trade political actors created common purpose by drawing on the historical and social experiences that are specific to the region (and the negotiating partner in question).

Participatory trade politics in West Africa remains contested. Because democratic policy-making incorporates political conflict and does not suppress it, West Africa provides many lessons for thinking through possibilities for democratizing trade policy-making. My analysis thus opens avenues for future research that would help us to adjust our theoretical framework and enable us better to conceptualize real and potential transformations in trade politics. It also implies that the debate over possibilities for trade policy's democratization must be relocated.

Practical lessons for participatory trade politics from West Africa

West African participatory trade politics fits with Scholte's recommendations for opening trade policy-making. Scholte invites participants in trade debates to clarify their trade policy objectives, to institutionalize their relations, to improve staff capacity, to coordinate their activities, and to "consciously nurture attitudinal change that promotes more constructive dialogue."[5] Institutional relations, capacity, and coordination clearly all helped to put West African participatory trade politics into practice and to create a climate that was conducive to constructive dialogue. The example accentuates the usefulness of institutionalized rights. The legal rights to participation deducted from the Cotonou Agreement and inscribed in ECOWAS' Negotiating Roadmap guaranteed access to the decision-making process, including access to information and internal documentation, as well as physical access to trade institutions and the negotiating room. Such institutionalized relations made the question of who assumes these rights a central political issue in the participatory practice.

180 *Conclusion*

From the perspective of trade officials, the question of which civil society structure to associate with was a practical problem that, in 2009, they were unsure had been conclusively resolved. From the point of view of transformative organizations for whom the civil society label presented an opportunity for taking a role in the policy process, the West African experience highlighted the importance of networking. On the one hand, networks enhanced the Platform's legitimacy from the perspective of public officials. On the other hand, participatory trade politics improved the Platform's capacity to foster relations with other groups, suggesting that participatory trade politics was an ongoing process, in which learning continued occurring. Ultimately, there cannot be one universal answer for the question of who trade officials must consult and not consult in policy-making, or how to go about approaching that question, because the establishment of the appropriate criteria for participation is part of the legitimization process that every decision-making mechanism undergoes to become stable. However, the West African experience shows that including a variety of voices, conformist and transformative, in participatory trade politics is possible and remains a matter of political will.

West African participatory trade politics stresses the importance of staff capacity in trade policy-making. Staff capacity was crucial for dialogue and in West African EPA talks it was a particularly powerful tool for gaining and maintaining access to public officials. Trade constitutes a technocratic policy field. It would currently be very difficult for any actor to enter trade policy-making and contribute to its evolution without mastering the technical knowledge. At the same time, West African EPA actors demonstrated that technical knowledge is not cast in stone, implying that while inserting political claims into highly technical policy fields is a difficult exercise, it is not impossible. Rather, technical language often masks political content and if mastered, can be used to express and introduce alternative political claims. Inspired by transformative input, the West African negotiating team convincingly challenged the EU's legal interpretation of Article XXIV GATT, for example.

Debates in the trade law literature provide guidance on possible alternative interpretations of many other provisions in international trade law[6] and therefore confirm that technical knowledge on the global trading system is not free from social construction. Scrutinizing WTO dispute settlement, Jan Klabbers points to the political opportunity inherent in the law when he highlights "the awkward circumstance that both parties [to a dispute settlement procedure] can present widely diverging interpretations with the help of the same rule," without this being "regarded as an embarrassment."[7] While legal rules may sometimes look unequivocal from the distance of other academic disciplines, the close-up perspective of legal theory defies this view. In his reflection on treaty interpretation and the WTO, Klabbers concludes that even in trade law, "there is fairly little point in taking the politics out of politics."[8]

Coordinating their activities clearly also facilitated cooperation between public officials and transformative actors. In West Africa, capacity problems in public trade institutions made Platform events and information on trade policy attractive from the point of view of public officials. The recognition led one observer to doubt whether the space would be the same if the state got stronger and gained more capacity. While capacity problems facilitated access to decision-makers in West Africa, their experience with participatory trade politics also disclosed the long-term merits of cooperation. Engaging in heated debates over trade policy preferences, rather than avoiding them, was at times a politically frustrating exercise for all EPA actors in the immediate term. In the long run, it raised understanding of the other's trade policy concerns and eventually helped public officials and transformative actors to see that they were fundamentally "looking for the same thing, just in a different way" (West African journalist). This constituted an important learning process that West African actors went through and of which they were self-reflexively aware. It exposes the flawed nature of any assumptions that relations between different sets of trade political actors can be pre-defined and are static.

To facilitate cooperation, it is evidently useful for all participants in trade debates to clarify their objectives. The Platform had a very clear EPA stance, although the shift from "no to EPA" to "EPA only if it is good for development" in 2007 arguably blurred that objective, because policy recommendations for development are a contested policy field. Nonetheless, the fact that trade is currently prominently mainstreamed into development policies suggests that the connection is important, independently of the theoretical question of whether social and economic justice is a trade or a non-trade issue. This point reveals the double-edged nature of recommending clear-cut trade policy positions.

Because challenges to the global trade agenda include essentially political questions of how trade policy should be set, by whom, and to what effect, demanding clear-cut trade policy positions could be, and sometimes is, construed as an argument for sidelining transformative demands. If we judge trade policy outcomes in terms of domestic industries' capital endowment, as parts of the literature do, a narrower range of positions qualifies under the label "clear-cut trade policy

182　*Conclusion*

position," than if we agree that good trade policy outcomes include environmental protection and decent labor conditions. In the first case, the trade policy positions of transformative actors are blurred at best. In the second case, they are very clear. Therefore, "attitudinal change" requires not only admitting that competing normative preferences for trade policy exist, but also recognizing their validity in trade policy-making processes, which are two different things.

West African participatory trade politics provides positive examples for the merits of daring to politicize trade policy debates. Through their interactions, both sets of actors acquired insights that they would not otherwise have had. Furthermore, they developed policy options that previously were not thought to exist. The Platform's position on Côte d'Ivoire and Ghana adhering to interim EPAs provided one example for how far innovation could potentially go.

As highlighted throughout the book, Côte d'Ivoire and Ghana were particularly concerned about losing European market access since they are not on the UN list of LDCs and do not qualify for preferential EBA treatment. At the same time, their adherence to an EPA put West African regional integration at peril. As a remedy, the Platform proposed a regional solidarity fund into which all ECOWAS countries would pay in order to help the two countries come to terms with their anticipated export losses until regional integration would have strengthened regional trade. A Platform representative explained in my interview that the proposal was connected to the Platform's specific vision of economic policy-making. The representative said: "We are not in an economistic logic anymore, we are not talking about economic rationality … even the poor can help the rich, if we are in a different logic that is called solidarity, that is called integration, that is called political will. There cannot be integration without sacrifice and there is no solidarity if there isn't a bit of everybody giving a little of what he has to the collective" (Platform representative 1).

It seems counter-intuitive that a group of countries at the bottom of most global economic indicators should support two countries that are placed somewhat higher on these rankings. The Platform representative explained: "The European Union told us: 'You are crazy'" (Platform representative 1). However, export dependence on the world market is not a sustainable strategy for the region in the long run and the question remains how West Africa can devise economic policy strategies to break out of the dependence. Although the proposal was not adopted, the example shows that including broader perspectives can spur policy innovation and provide alternative visions for trade political problems beyond existing prescriptions.

Conclusion 183

In addition, West African participatory trade politics draws attention to the importance of transparency for all actors. All interviewees underlined the fact that it was crucial to be informed about the internal proceedings of other actors and to understand how they reach the trade policy line that they pursue. Being very clear on whose behalf and for what reasons a social agent speaks out on trade policy supports the legitimization of participatory trade politics. The Platform did not manage to communicate its internal proceedings very successfully to public officials who in turn added concerns about their lacking knowledge on how the regional civil society representative reached his or her positions to their demands for better representativity. However, the fact that Platform members also participated at national levels slightly nuanced the concerns, because it gave the Platform "many faces" and demonstrated that it was more than a one-person operation.

One practical lesson from West African participatory trade politics, therefore, is that entrusting civil society representation to one single individual may be overtaxing and cause political problems that can be avoided. Furthermore, to the extent that civil society is a fuzzy concept, the expectation that any organization or network of organizations can represent it is unrealistic. Therefore, references to non-state actors rather than civil society representatives, as in the Cotonou Agreement, might have alleviated some political (and analytical) problems, although leaving the question largely unresolved as to how representative participants in participatory policy-making mechanisms need to be.

Finally, transparency also concerns the legitimacy of the trade policy-making mechanism itself. According to my data, legitimacy debates in West Africa about participatory trade politics were not entirely resolved in 2009. As I pointed out in Chapter 4, the situation partly arose from the fact that debates over the legitimacy of specific actors were on one level connected to understandings of the terms of the debate over political authority, and at the same time connected to debates over trade political substance. The conundrum recurs in the trade literature. We tend to presume a controversial relationship between public officials and transformative civil society organizations that criticize the global trade agenda. At the same time, we presume that public officials co-operate with corporate non-state actors. One open question is whether the presumption is empirically valid. In her study on the European Commission's stance in intellectual property talks, Hannah has already responded in the negative.[9] The West African evidence further suggests that this is not necessarily the case and that relationships are not static. Practically, to the extent that legitimacy in democratic policy-making cannot be contingent on one

184   *Conclusion*

specific set of normative preferences for the policy outcome, trade policy debates should and could be held more openly between all types of trade political actors everywhere. In addition to these practical lessons, West African participatory trade politics has repercussions for trade policy formation theory.

Adjusting trade policy formation theory

Despite radical transformations in global trade politics, the analytical repercussions of the underlying economism of trade theory and trade policy formation theory have not been subject to open debate in the recent literature on trade policy's legitimacy crisis. This is strange, since we realize that trade policy formation theory has weaknesses, in particular in understanding the ideas/interests nexus in trade policy formation.[10] The lack of scholarly debates on our economistic theoretical foundations impedes scholars not only from envisaging participatory trade politics and from contributing to their evolution. It also hinders theoretical advances on the deeper questions, because interests are assumed to arise mechanically from the structures of the global political economy, and because the possibility that agency might shift the underlying paradigms of interest formation in trade politics is given too limited analytical space.

Economistic accounts that rely on utility maximizing ambitions as explanatory factors for trade political agency lack the sensitivity to historical and socio-economic context without which the evolution of West African participatory trade politics cannot be understood. Under the economistic lens, civil society should not be influential on trade policy. In addition, a major trader like the EU should not have difficulty in forging a trade agreement with a small economy. The ECOWAS-EU EPA negotiating history contradicted these predictions, also to the surprise of the European Commission. It shows that the conditions that generally underlie political action, namely historical and socio-economic contexts, continue to structure trade policy-making and that theorists and practitioners should pay attention to the dynamics that they set off. Analytical attention to these dimensions can also shed new light on questions of why trade institutions resist transformation— which are questions that we would not be able to ask under an economistic framework.

A focus on the historical and socio-economic dimensions of international trade arrangements also helps to understand better how trade interacts with social and economic organization. Under such a focus, Keasbey's statement still holds that "from the standpoint of production

Conclusion   185

commerce has certainly made material civilization possible, but from the point of view of distribution it has undoubtedly accentuated the inequality of wealth."[11] Typically, our analysis of the interaction between trade and so-called trade-related problems takes a bottom-up approach. We ask why and how governments can or cannot use trade rules to improve their countries' economic situation, save turtles in shrimp fishing or protect their citizens from food products that they deem risky, to take the examples of some prominent trade controversies.

Instead, how we currently understand trade policy and the trading activity itself may be one consequence of the way in which we conceptualize, or neglect, the interplays between economic, social, and political organization more broadly. Many assertions that I have quoted in my study, like protectionism being a social right, obligations of social assistance providing the foundations of the wealthy person's standing in society, or the idea that the poor can help the rich under specific circumstances, appear absurd from the vantage point of our current understanding of economic activity. This highlights the importance of variations in meanings of concepts. If we find it impossible to consolidate social and environmental concerns with economic concerns today, our inability testifies to the way in which we have constructed the world and our understanding of it, rather than describing a universal, a-historical fact of life.

My analysis confirms Trentmann's argument that interests are not pre-social but embedded in society and culture.[12] While material interests are an important motivational factor in trade policy-making, the recognition that there is other wealth that transcends economic wealth that informed trade theory debates in the late nineteenth and early twentieth centuries continues to create momentum for trade political agency. Since public officials and corporate representatives are individuals with multiple identities as state agents, producers, consumers, citizens, family members, etc., it is not clear why it is reasonable to expect theoretically that they are immune to broader notions of welfare and political claims based on such categories, or why they would necessarily be and remain oblivious to the social implications of trade policy choices. The economistic presumption that the relationship between these actors and transformers is necessarily confrontational, which gives trade an air of a special policy field outside of the realm of political contestation, cannot be maintained.

Instead, real life trade politics increasingly creates opportunities for successful transformative advocacy. During my last field trip to West Africa in 2010/11, I learnt that the Central African EPA region had a very similar negotiating experience with a high involvement of

186   *Conclusion*

transformative organizations in policy-making that mirrored many benefits and challenges of West African participatory mechanisms (Central African civil society representative). In this sense, the West African experience is not the only example that invites us to realign trade policy formation theory with the patterns of real life trade politics. The future of participatory practices like those witnessed in Central and West Africa of course hinges partly on actors' access to financial and human resources. Nonetheless, the examples show us that we need to reconsider our received notions of trade in order to be able to reflect the challenges and struggles that characterize trade policy-making today in our analytical work.

In more immediate trade politics, the West African example shows that variations in meanings of concepts can play a crucial role in transformations of policy mechanisms. On the one hand differences in understanding of concepts can present obstacles to communication and strain cooperation. The term "civil society" presents a good example for the effect. At the same time, actors that are aware of variations in meanings can, under certain conditions, manipulate concepts to change the nature of a debate and make the policy environment more conducive to their goals. This became clear when the Platform along with other actors changed the meaning of the term "EPA negotiations" from "negotiations for a trade agreement" to "negotiations for a trade and development partnership." The shift had knock-on effects, for example by allowing trade political actors to interpret the Cotonou Agreement in a way that made participatory trade politics look like the practice was based on an international legal obligation.

The reflection on concepts in trade politics that could be manipulated in this way has only just begun. In addition, the literature supports the view that negotiations under bilateral agreements and PTAs differ from the multilateral arena.[13] At the same time, PTAs and the multilateral trading system interact as policy venues and will continue to do so even if the WTO should not bring the Doha Round to a successful conclusion. It is currently unclear how the two spheres will evolve. However, it is clear that stalling multilateral talks are not the endpoint of trade political controversy. The fact that the global trade agenda advances through PTAs today suggests that multi-level, multi-issue trade governance is here to stay, which ultimately increases the potential for inserting political contestations at various corners of the complex system.

Von Bülow's contribution on transnational trade activists proved useful for broader reconceptualizations of trade politics, in the sense that her relational approach can help to explain why and how trade

Conclusion 187

political actors across the common state-market-civil society triangle come to engage in common trade policy-making processes, despite the fact that their understandings of, approaches to, and goals for trade policy are everything but homogeneous. The key lies in relaxing assumptions about the nature of trade politics including assumptions about how trade political interests form. Instead, trade politics must be seen as a dynamic process with protagonists that are firmly embedded in and interact with broader constitutions and reconstitutions of global, regional, and local political environments across space and time. In her book, von Bülow concludes:

> The dynamic contours of transnational collective action are the result of the continuous negotiation and reappraisal of choices made by actors, as they become part of new networks and react to changes in political contexts. These processes of negotiation and reappraisal happen within as well as among civil society organizations and inside as well as outside national boundaries. Their outcomes cannot be predetermined from a set of economic and political structures.[14]

Similarly, trade policy formation is a dynamic process of continuous learning, in which actors negotiate and reappraise their choices as they become part of new social configurations and react to changes in political contexts. Crucially, these processes of negotiation and reappraisal can happen among specific trade political groups such as state and non-state actors, or conformers and transformative organizations, and are not limited to the confines of the state. Their outcomes cannot be predetermined from a set of economic and political structures.

My study makes small additions to the transnational studies literature. On the one hand the West African example is compatible with the theoretical view that distinct collective experiences can present political opportunity structures in the same vein as ideas, norms, and discourses. On the other hand, West African participatory trade politics pushes us to explore the links and interconnections between world politics and international law that the international law literature highlights.[15] Through participatory trade politics, the Platform inserted Diouf's 2009 study *Article XXIV of GATT and the EPA: Legal Arguments to Support West Africa's Market Access Offer*[16] into the ECOWAS-EU EPA process, thus reversing negotiating dynamics and slowing down the entire process. The West African evidence indicates that we should pay attention to the limits and possibilities inherent in the law when studying real and potential political opportunity for

188 *Conclusion*

transformation in governance practices. Legal scholars within the pluralist tradition see trade law as creating "a framework for self-directed human interaction rather than coercion of self-interested individuals."[17] Variations in meanings of concepts thus not only affect economic policy-making, but also economic law. For pluralists, this is one feature through which legal frameworks fulfill their role of structuring discourses about social order. "Rather than seeing contracts as enforceable obligations entered into by rational egoists worried about cheating by their partners," Robert Wolfe explains, "pluralists think that contracts and treaties often furnish a kind of framework for an ongoing relationship, not a precise definition of that relationship."[18] Political economy studies should consider these options when thinking about actors' possibilities for creating political opportunity, which can include legal opportunity, in their efforts to impact on economic decision-making.

Taking all these reflections into account, the view that economistic trade policy considerations and principles of democratic decision-making must compete for legitimacy seems odd. The insight that legitimacy is not a universal quality, but is also socially constructed and deconstructed further weakens the claim. The West African example highlights "the relevance of people's perceptions of the rightfulness and appropriateness of authority for their acceptance and support for political and social order."[19] The ultimate question is whether we follow Evans, quoted in the introduction, and deem the choice between a trade and a democratic nirvana in global governance rightful and appropriate.[20]

Trade and democracy

As I have shown in Part I, the view that trade is differently political than other policy fields tilts current theoretical and practical debates towards pessimistic assessments of the possibilities for democratizing trade policy-making. However, the view of "trade as special politics" is a relatively recent attitude in the history of political economy. It originated with the marginalist school's methodological choice to assess the impact of trade policy-making on society on the basis of the impact of trade policy-making on one specific type of social actor, at the time industries. In the real world, this methodological choice translates as a political choice because it affects the distribution of wealth and power in society. The political choice is normalized because it disappears in the fundamental assumptions of economistic trade policy formation theories.

Conclusion 189

Under this lens, the question "is trade policy efficient?" is depicted as the appropriate yardstick for assessing the relationship between trade and democracy. Due to the social embeddedness of all political action that parts of the trade literature highlight and the inherently political nature of the efficiency argument that I uncovered in Chapter 2, it is clear that the question cannot be asked in this abstract way. Instead, it needs to be contextualized. From the perspective of the various economic studies that the Platform and its allies used, including the work of United Nations institutions and scholars such as Joseph Stiglitz, signing the EPA in the form that the EU had initially foreseen was expected to lead to economic downturn in West Africa. Overall, in real life trade politics, trade negotiations are thus never about whether trade politics is efficient. They are always about the question for whom trade policy is efficient.

Put differently, while one may misconstrue my study as evidence for the view that transformative participation in trade politics leads to efficiency loss in trade policy-making, I instead show that the real questions are "efficiency loss for whom?" and "on the basis of which economic theory?" As I show in Chapter 2, the questions are counter-intuitive to today's theory, precisely because trade theorists in the late nineteenth and early twentieth centuries used a context-bound perspective that immediately privileged one social group in relation to others (namely "the particular industries mostly affected by the tariff," see Chapter 2) in order to be able to resolve the long-standing free trade vs. protectionism debate in theory universally (in favor of free trade).

The problem remains that only in theory is trade detached from individual and collective life experience. With the political move in the theoretical foundations of the efficiency argument recognized, the common view that trade politics should not be democratic is of course still possible. What comes under scrutiny, however, is the legitimacy bias in favor of corporate actors that undergirds most trade theories today. My study resituates the trade and democracy debate, because it shows that normative preferences for a supposedly efficient trading system are only one set of possible normative preferences among many. Its appointment to the position of trump-all argument in trade debates was built on the theoretical construct that marked the shift from the historical school of trade theory to the marginalist paradigm that I highlighted in Chapter 2. Interestingly, it does not even necessarily lead to one set of coherent claims towards trade politics, as anybody who spends any time inside global trade institutions will swiftly note. In this sense, a rejection of participation due to the fact that critics of the global trade agenda are not only "self-appointed," but also "fungible ... and divisible,

190 *Conclusion*

frequently combining and dividing according to circumstances or objectives,"[21] which fails to note that the same criticism applies to corporate lobbies, is a reflection of trade economism and its inherent legitimacy bias, rather than a compelling argument in debates about the nature of democratic life.

Accordingly, the result of my study relocates the debate on trade and democracy for at least two reasons. First, it banalizes trade as a policy field, and thus counters the argument that trade *is* a special politics that is different from other politics. Second, it exposes the inherently political nature of the argument that trade *should* be a special politics in the name of efficiency. The difference between trade as an activity and democracy as a principle of political organization becomes evident through the lens of these considerations.

The first assertion is that trade *is* in fact different than other politics, because it is in and of itself a technical matter. Contrary to this view, my analysis of transformations in West African trade politics shows that elements such as material conditions, existing norms and rules, differing normative preferences, and monopolies over interpretations of language structure the policy field and provide the framework for power struggles within it. Trade policy is thus in a very fundamental way a policy field like any other, which means that it is practically open to political contestation from the vantage point of a variety of normative preferences, and theoretically open to alternative interpretation from the vantage point of a variety of academic approaches.

The second assertion is that trade *should be* different than other politics, because otherwise it would not be efficient. However, as I showed in Chapter 2, the efficiency argument is in essence a normative argument that is disguised as a technical reality. West African EPA negotiations provide evidence for my theoretical claim. In this instance, even the European Commission's own Sustainability Impact Assessment was skeptical of the impacts that an EPA would have on living conditions in the region. Efficiency is a political concept that embodies and informs one type of normative preference for how the world should be governed. The question then remains how competition between different normative preferences should play out in trade politics.

As I have highlighted throughout, trade is one of the general activities observable in the vast majority of human societies across recorded history. Despite the quasi-universality of the trading activity as an exchange of human produce (be it material, knowledge-based or cultural), trade is not dependent on a specific value system. It requires a rules-based framework of organization and, as in the case of West African trading diasporas, the rules can be rooted in shared value and

Conclusion 191

belief systems, in this instance provided by Islam. Nonetheless, the trading activity can be successfully organized independently from any specific value system. History specifically defies the view that trade depends on capitalist social relations in order to be organized across long distances or that it is inevitably embedded in a capitalist social order.

Democracy, on the other hand, is a principle of political organization and as such, quite simply, both an idea and an ideal. It is necessarily based on certain values, notably equality and freedom, and cannot tolerate variations in these values without turning into a different idea. Thus, any exclusion of policy fields from the realm of democracy is damaging to democracy. In democratic practice, opening debates on why we pursue specific policy lines, in the name of who or what, and what their impact on society is, has to be allowed. This is in line with Heikki Patomäki and Teivo Teivainen's reminder: "in democratic politics speech and action must be free from any exclusive and restrictive focus, such as that imposed by 'free trade'."[22] Trade and democracy therefore do not warrant direct comparison between a human activity observed across all recorded human history and a principle of political organization that historically emerges in human societies on the basis of a specific set of values.

If we accept that democracy should be the guiding principle of social organization, the pertinent questions are: is trade policy-making democratic? If the answer is negative as current observers concur, can international trade be organized in ways that are more democratic? In relation to the second question, the West African experience provides important empirical evidence and avenues for learning. This is not to say that the West African negotiating set-up fulfilled all conditions of democratic decision-making or remained without its problems. By showing that participatory trade politics is possible, West Africa nonetheless made a step in a direction that evinces practical and theoretical emancipatory potential.

Notes

1 Jane Ford, *A Social Theory of the WTO: Trading Cultures* (Basingstoke: Palgrave Macmillan, 2003); Rorden Wilkinson, "Language, Power and Multilateral Trade Negotiations," *Review of International Political Economy* 16, no. 4 (2009): 597–619; and Matthew Eagleton-Pierce, *Symbolic Power in the World Trade Organization* (Oxford: Oxford University Press, 2012).
2 Philip D. Curtin, *Cross-cultural Trade in World History* (Cambridge: Cambridge University Press, 1984); and Frank Trentmann, "Political Culture and Political Economy: Interests, Ideology and Free Trade," *Review of International Political Economy* 5, no. 2 (1998): 217–51.

192 Conclusion

3 Marisa von Bülow, *Building Transnational Networks: Civil Society and the Politics of Trade in the Americas* (Cambridge: Cambridge University Press, 2010).

4 Curtin, *Cross-cultural Trade in World History.*

5 Jan Aart Scholte, "The WTO and Civil Society," in *Trade Politics*, ed. Brian Hocking and Steven McGuire (London: Routledge, 2004), 158.

6 For an example see the recent debate on so-called SPS Imperialism under the Agreement on Sanitary and Phyto-sanitary Measures that mirrors similar previous discussions on Article XX GATT: Christian Conrad, "PPMs, the EC-Biotech Dispute and Applicability of the SPS Agreement: Are the Panel's Findings Built on Shaky Ground?" *The Hebrew University of Jerusalem Research Paper* No. 8-06 (2006); Jacqueline Peel, "A GMO by Any Other Name ... Might Be an SPS Risk! Implications of Expanding the Scope of the WTO Sanitary and Phytosanitary Measures Agreement," *European Journal of International Law* 17, no. 5 (2006): 1009–31; and Joanne Scott, *The WTO Agreement on Sanitary and Phytosanitary Measures: A Commentary* (Oxford: Oxford University Press, 2007).

7 Jan Klabbers, "On Rationalism in Politics: Interpretation of Treaties and the World Trade Organisation," *Nordic Journal of International Law* 74, no. 3–4 (2005): 414.

8 Klabbers, "On Rationalism in Politics: Interpretation of Treaties and the World Trade Organisation," 426. For a detailed discussion of the theoretical implications of this insight for political economy studies of trade, see Silke Trommer, "Legal Opportunity in Trade Negotiations: International Law, Opportunity Structures and the Political Economy of Trade Agreements," *New Political Economy*, forthcoming.

9 Erin Hannah, "NGOs and the European Union: Examining the Power of Epistemes in the EC's TRIPS and Access to Medicines Negotiations," *Journal of Civil Society* 7, no. 2 (2011): 179–206.

10 Helen V. Milner, "The Political Economy of International Trade," *Annual Review of Political Science* 2 (1999): 91–114; William J. Ethier, "The Theory of Trade Policy and Trade Agreements: A Critique," *European Journal of Political Economy* 23, no. 3 (2007): 605–23; and Ann Capling and Patrick Low, *Governments, Non-State Actors and Trade Policy-Making: Negotiating Preferentially or Multilaterally?* (Cambridge: Cambridge University Press and World Trade Organisation, 2010).

11 Lindley M. Keasbey, "L'Evolution du Commerce dans les Diverses races Humaines by Ch. Letourneau," *Political Science Quarterly* 13, no. 3 (1898): 542.

12 Trentmann, "Political Culture and Political Economy: Interests, Ideology and Free Trade."

13 Capling and Low, *Governments, Non-State Actors and Trade Policy-Making: Negotiating Preferentially or Multilaterally?*; and Edward D. Mansfield and Helen V. Milner, *Votes, Vetoes and the Political Economy of International Trade Agreements* (Princeton, NJ: Princeton University Press, 2012).

14 Marisa von Bülow, *Building Transnational Networks: Civil Society and the Politics of Trade in the Americas* (Cambridge: Cambridge University Press, 2010), 190.

15 Martti Koskenniemi, "The Politics of International Law—20 Years Later," *European Journal of International Law* 20, no. 1 (2009): 7–19.

Conclusion 193

16 El Hadji Diouf, *Article XXIV of GATT and the EPA: Legal Arguments to Support West Africa's Market Access Offer* (Dakar: ENDA, 2009).
17 Robert Wolfe, "See you in Geneva? Legal (Mis)Representations of the Trading System," *European Journal of International Relations* 11, no. 3 (2005): 342.
18 Wolfe, "See you in Geneva? Legal (Mis)Representations of the Trading System," 344.
19 Sigrid Quack, "Law, Expertise and Legitimacy in Transnational Economic Governance: An Introduction," *Socio-Economic Review* 8, no. 1 (2010): 8.
20 Phil Evans, "Is Trade Policy Democratic? And Should it Be?" in *The New Economic Diplomacy: Decision-Making and Negotiation in International Economic Relations*, ed. Nicholas Bayne and Stephen Woolcock (Aldershot: Ashgate, 2003), 147–59.
21 David Robertson, "Civil Society and the WTO," *The World Economy* 23, no. 9 (2000): 1123.
22 Heikki Patomäki and Teivo Teivainen, *A Possible World: Democratic Transformations of Global Institutions* (London: Zed Books, 2004), 86.

Appendices

Appendix I: EPA regional groups in 2003

Table A.1 EPA regional groups in 2003

EPA region	Countries
Caribbean	Antigua and Barbuda, Bahamas, Barbados, Belize, Dominica, Dominican Republic, Grenada, Guyana, Haiti, Jamaica, St Kitts and Nevis, St Lucia, St Vincent and Grenadines, Surinam, Trinidad and Tobago
Central Africa	Cameroon, Central African Republic, Democratic Republic of the Congo, Chad, Equatorial Guinea, Gabon, Republic of the Congo, São Tomé and Príncipe
Eastern/Southern Africa	Burundi, Comoros, Djibouti, Eritrea, Ethiopia, Kenya, Madagascar, Malawi, Mauritius, Rwanda, Seychelles, Somalia, Sudan, Tanzania, Uganda, Zambia, Zimbabwe
Pacific	Cook Islands, East Timor, Fiji, Kiribati, Marshall Islands, Micronesia, Nauru, Niue, Palau, Papua New Guinea, Samoa, Solomon Islands, Tonga, Tuvalu, Vanuatu
South African Development Community	Angola, Botswana, Lesotho, Namibia, Mozambique, Swaziland
West Africa	Benin, Burkina Faso, Cape Verde, Côte d'Ivoire, Gambia, Ghana, Guinea, Guinea Bissau, Liberia, Mali, Mauritania, Niger, Nigeria, Senegal, Sierra Leone, Togo

Appendix II: West Africa-EU trade statistics

Traded goods

Trade with the EU: €43.6bn in 2008

Figure A.1 West Africa: main exports to the EU (2008)

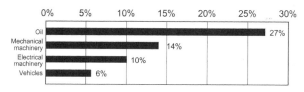

Figure A.2 West Africa: main imports from the EU (2008)

Trade balance

In € billion	WA imports from EU	WA exports to EU	WA trade balance with EU
2002	12.012	11.161	-0.851
2003	12.317	12.444	0.127
2004	12.409	11.081	-1.328
2005	13.700	14.196	0.496
2006	15.652	17.180	1.528
2007	18.499	17.204	-1.295
2008	22.318	22.365	0.047
2009	19.269	16.853	-2.416

196 *Appendices*

Source: (Calculated on the basis of Eurostat data, European Commission 2010, *EuroStat*, epp.eurostat.ec.europa.eu/portal/page/portal/eurostat/home)

Appendix III: EPA state of play

Table A.3 EPA state of play: 1 January 2008

Region	EPA	No EPA
Caribbean	Antigua and Barbuda	
	Bahamas	
	Barbados	
	Belize	
	Dominica	
	Dominican Republic	
	Grenada	
	Guyana	
	Haiti	
	Jamaica	
	St Kitts and Nevis	
	St Lucia	
	St Vincent and the Grenadines	
	Surinam	
	Trinidad andTobago	
Central Africa	Cameroon	Central African Republic
		Democratic Republic of the Congo
		Republic of the Congo
		Chad
		Equatorial Guinea
		Gabon
		São Tome and Príncipe
Eastern/Southern Africa	Burundi	Djibouti
	Comoros	Eritrea
	Madagascar	Ethiopia
	Mauritius	Malawi
	Kenya	Somalia
	Rwanda	Sudan
	Seychelles	Zambia
	Tanzania	
	Uganda	
	Zimbabwe	

Table A.3 (continued)

Region	EPA	No EPA
Pacific	Papua New Guinea Fiji	Cook Islands East Timor Kiribati Marshall Islands Micronesia Nauru Niue Palau Samoa Solomon Islands Tonga Tuvalu Vanuatu
South African Development Community	Botswana Lesotho Namibia Mozambique Swaziland	Angola South Africa
West Africa	Côte d'Ivoire Ghana	Benin Burkina Faso Cape Verde Gambia Guinea Guinea-Bissau Liberia Mali Mauritania Niger Nigeria Senegal Sierra Leone Togo

Source: (European Commission 2007, *ACP Market Access Outlook 1 January 2008*, tradoc_137335)

198　*Appendices*

Table A.4 EPA state of play: 14 November 2008

Region	Current status	Next steps
Caribbean	Comprehensive EPA signed. Main features: Covers trade in services as well as goods. Countries commit to other measures to boost trade, in areas such as investment, competition, public procurement, and intellectual property. Establishes new joint oversight bodies. Provides for ongoing monitoring and review.	Fully implement initial tariff cuts. Complete ratification. Agree on joint monitoring system.
Central Africa	Cameroon signed the interim EPA for the Central African region. European and Central African negotiators met last time in Bangui on 26–30 September 2011 to continue negotiations at technical level. Negotiating groups discussed market access, services, cultural cooperation and accompanying measures. Progress was also made on the text of the agreement.	Regional negotiations are focusing on market access, rules of origin, services and investment, cultural cooperation, accompanying measures (development cooperation) and fiscal impact. Market access and development assistance, in particular, require more progress.
East/Southern Africa	Madagascar, Mauritius, Seychelles and Zimbabwe signed interim agreements. The inaugural EPA Committee under the Interim EPA was held in October 2012 in Brussels. The Customs Cooperation Committee and the Joint Development Committee were also held in the margins of the EPA Committee.	The comprehensive EPA negotiations focus on trade in goods, services, trade-related areas and development cooperation provisions. More talks are needed, in particular, on export taxes, rules of origin and special agricultural safeguards.

Appendices 199

Table A.4 (continued)

Region	Current status	Next steps
Pacific	Papua New Guinea and Fiji signed interim EPAs. EU and Pacific region representatives held talks on 22–24 November 2012 on a comprehensive regional EPA. Discussions were based on a revised draft text and draft market access offers, which were submitted by the region in July 2011. Discussions covered trade in goods, development cooperation, sustainable development, and fisheries (including rules of origin).	Talks continue towards completing negotiations for a regional comprehensive EPA. However, the Commission is ready to explore the possibility of widening the membership and deepening the content of the existing EU-Pacific interim EPA.
South African Development Community	Botswana, Lesotho, Mozambique and Swaziland signed interim EPAs. Last Technical Working Group and Senior Official Meeting in May 2012 in South Africa. It addressed all matters: market access, textual unresolved issues, rules of origin and trade-related issues.	In February 2010, Botswana, Lesotho, Namibia, Mozambique and Swaziland informed the Commission that they did not intend to provisionally apply the Interim EPA initialled in 2007. They proposed to focus on reaching an "inclusive" and comprehensive agreement with the whole SADC EPA Group (these countries plus Angola and South Africa) by the end of 2010. Negotiations are now focusing on market access issues, in particular between the EU and South Africa.

(continued on the next page)

200 *Appendices*

Table A.4 (continued)

Region	Current status	Next steps
West Africa	Côte d'Ivoire and Ghana initialled interim EPAs. EU and West African negotiators met in Brussels at technical and Senior Official level on 17–20 April 2012, to discuss the way ahead in the regional EPA talks. Progress was made in particular on the text of the agreement, work continues on issues including West Africa's market access offer and the EPA Development Programme (PAPED).	The regional agreement currently negotiated will cover goods and development cooperation and include rendezvous clauses for services and rules chapters.

Source: (European Commission 2012, *Overview of EPA: State of Play*, tradoc_144912)

Appendices 201

Appendix IV: List of interviewees (affiliations as at time of interview)

Platform

- Aurélien Atidegla—PASCIB, Benin—5 August 2009, Dakar (interview in French).
- Taoufik Ben Abdallah—ENDA, Senegal—9 and 29 July 2009 and 1 November 2010, Dakar (interviews in French).
- Bathie Ciss—ENDA, Senegal—26 June and 16 July 2009, Dakar (interviews in French).
- Cheikh Tidiane Dièye—ENDA, Senegal—27 April 2009, Geneva; 29 June, 28 July and 6 August 2009, 15 November and 6 December 2010, Dakar (interviews in French).
- Tetteh Hormeku—TWN, Ghana—4 August 2009, Dakar (interview in English).
- Edwin Ikhuoria—NANTS, Nigeria—3 August 2009, Dakar (interview in English).
- Bibiane Mbaye—Action Aid, Kenya; former ENDA, Senegal—4 August 2009, Dakar (interview in French).
- Aniekan Upke—NANTS, Nigeria—15 April 2009, Dakar (interview in English).

Civil society and private sector

- Didier Awadi—Singer, Senegal—25 January 2011, Dakar (interview in French).
- Djibo Bagna—ROPPA, Mali—17 September 2010, Geneva (interview in French).
- El Hadji Diouf—ICTSD, Switzerland—29 April and 30 September 2009, Geneva (interviews in French).
- Elimane Diouf—Trade Union Monitoring Committee of the Cotonou Agreement, Senegal—14 July 2009, Dakar (interview in French).
- Mamadou Mignane Diouf—Senegalese Social Forum, Senegal—6 August 2009, Dakar (interview in French).
- Pape Nalle Fall—National Employers Council, Senegal—14 July 2009, Dakar (interview in French).
- Mohamed Guèye, journalist, Senegal—8 July 2009, Dakar (interview in French).
- Eric Hazard—Oxfam, Senegal—3 December 2009, Helsinki/Dakar (Skype interview in English).

202 *Appendices*

- Arianne Idzenga—national representative Burkina Faso at BD—Broederlijk Delen; former Oxfam International, Burkina-Faso—3 May 2009, Helsinki/Ouagadougou (Skype interview in English), and 29 November 2010, Dakar (interview in English).
- Jacob Kotcho—ACDIC, Cameroon—15 April 2009 and 10 February 2011, Dakar (interviews in French).
- Falou Samb—Centre for Socio-Eco-Nomic Development, Switzerland—25 and 31 March and 28 April 2009, Geneva (interviews in French and English).
- Pascal Sambou—Friedrich Ebert Foundation, Senegal—7 July 2009, Dakar (interview in French and German).

Public officials

- Magdi Farahat—UN Economic Commission for Africa, Switzerland—3 March 2009, Geneva (interview in English).
- Alain Faustin Bocco—WAEMU, Burkina-Faso—21 July 2009, Dakar (interview in French).
- Dominique Fifatin—ECOWAS, Nigeria—20 July 2009, Dakar (interview in French).
- Makhtar Lakh—Trade Ministry, Senegal—15 July 2009, Dakar (interview in French).
- Claude Maerten—European Commission, Belgium—15 September 2009, Brussels (interview in English).
- Cheikh Ndir—WAEMU, Burkina-Faso—22 July 2009, Dakar (interview in French).
- Gbenga Grg. Obideyi—ECOWAS, Nigeria—21 July 2009, Dakar (interview in English).
- Iba Mar Oularé—Economics and Finance Ministry, Senegal—10 July 2009, Dakar (interview in French).
- Aicha Pouye—International Trade Centre, Switzerland—6 April 2009, Geneva (interview in French).
- Sacko Seydou—ECOWAS, Nigeria—22 July 2009, Dakar (interview in French).
- Jean-Luc Senou—WAEMU, Burkina-Faso—23 July 2009, Dakar (interview in French).
- Kola Sofola—ECOWAS, Nigeria—21 July 2009, Dakar (interview in English).
- Aminata Sy—Trade Ministry, Senegal—15 July 2009, Dakar (interview in French).
- Cristophe de Vroey—European Commission, Belgium—30 July 2009, Dakar (interview in French).

Appendices 203

- Marta Zaoralova—European Commission, Belgium—15 September 2009, Brussels (interview in English).

Appendix V: Harmonized system lists of products in informal West African trade

Table A.5 HS4 list of unprocessed products in informal West African trade

HS code	Product
0101	Live horses, asses, mules and hinnies
0102	Live bovine animals
0103	Live swine
0104	Live sheep and goats
0105	Live poultry, "fowls of the species gallus domesticus," ducks, geese, turkeys and guinea fowls
0106	Live animals (excl. horses, asses, mules, hinnies, bovine animals, swine, sheep, goats, poultry, fish, crustaceans, mollusks and other aquatic invertebrates, and micro-organic cultures, etc.)
0201	Meat of bovine animals, fresh or chilled
0203	Meat of swine, fresh, chilled or frozen
0204	Meat of sheep or goats, fresh, chilled or frozen
0205	Meat of horses, asses, mules or hinnies, fresh, chilled or frozen
0206	Edible offal of bovine animals, swine, sheep, goats, horses, asses, mules or hinnies, fresh, chilled or frozen
0302	Fish, fresh or chilled (excl. fish fillets and other fish meat of heading 0304)
0304	Fish fillets and other fish meat, whether or not minced, fresh, chilled or frozen
0305	Fish, fit for human consumption, dried, salted or in brine; smoked fish, fit for human consumption, whether cooked before or during the smoking process; flours, meals and pellets of fish, fit for human consumption
0306	Crustaceans, fit for human consumption, whether in shell or not, live, fresh, chilled, frozen, dried, salted or in brine, incl. crustaceans in shell cooked beforehand by steaming or by boiling in water; flours, meals and pellets of crustaceans, fit for human consumption
0307	Mollusks, fit for human consumption, whether in shell or not, live, fresh, chilled, frozen, dried, salted or in brine, incl. aquatic invertebrates other than crustaceans and mollusks; flours, meals and pellets of aquatic invertebrates other than crustaceans
0701	Potatoes, fresh or chilled
0702	Tomatoes, fresh or chilled
0703	Onions, shallots, garlic, leeks and other alliaceous vegetables, fresh or chilled
0704	Cabbages, cauliflowers, kohlrabi, kale and similar edible brassicas, fresh or chilled

(continued on the next page)

204 *Appendices*

Table A.5 (continued)

HS code	Product
0705	Lettuce "lactuca sativa" and chicory "cichorium spp.," fresh or chilled
0706	Carrots, turnips, salad beetroot, salsify, celeriac, radishes and similar edible roots, fresh or chilled
0707	Cucumbers and gherkins, fresh or chilled
0708	Leguminous vegetables, shelled or unshelled, fresh or chilled
0709	Other vegetables, fresh or chilled (excl. potatoes, tomatoes, alliaceous vegetables, edible brassicas, lettuce "lactuca sativa" and chicory "cichorium spp.," carrots, turnips, salad beetroot, salsify, celeriac, radishes and similar edible roots, cucumbers)
0710	Vegetables, uncooked or cooked by steaming or boiling in water, frozen
0713	Dried leguminous vegetables, shelled, whether skinned or split
0714	Roots and tubers incl. manioc, arrowroot, salep, jerusalem artichokes, sweet potatoes and others with high starch or inulin content, fresh, chilled, frozen or dried, whether sliced or in the form of pellets; sago pith
0801	Coconuts, brazil nuts and cashews, fresh or dried, whether shelled or peeled
0802	Other nuts, fresh or dried, whether shelled or peeled (excl. coconuts, brazil nuts and cashews)
0803	Bananas, plantains, fresh or dried
0804	Dates, figs, pineapples, avocados, guavas, mangoes and mangosteens, fresh or dried
0805	Citrus fruit, fresh or dried
0807	Melons, incl. watermelons, and papaws
0810	Fresh strawberries, raspberries, blackberries, black, white or red currants, gooseberries and other edible fruits (excl. nuts, bananas, dates, figs, pineapples, avocadoes, guavas, mangoes, mangosteens, papaws "papayas," citrus fruit, grapes, melons or apples)
1001	Wheat and meslin
1005	Maize or corn
1006	Rice
1007	Sorghum grain

Source: (United Nations Economic Commission for Africa, *Assessing Regional Integration in Africa IV: Enhancing Intra-African Trade* (Addis Ababa: UNECA, 2010))

Appendices 205

Table A.6 The major artisanal products in West African informal trade

HS code	Product
1401	Vegetable materials used primarily for plaiting, e.g., bamboos, rattans, reeds, rushes, osier, raffia, cleaned, bleached or dyed cereal straw, and lime bark
1402	Vegetable materials used primarily for stuffing or padding, e.g., kapok, vegetable hair and eel-grass, whether put up as a layer, with or without supporting material
1403	Vegetable materials, such as broomcorn, piassava, brush-grass and thistle, used primarily in brooms or in brushes, whether in hanks or bundles
1404	Vegetable products n.e.s. for dyeing or tanning
4101	Raw hides and skins of bovine or equine animals, fresh, or salted, dried, limed, pickled or otherwise preserved, but not tanned, parchment-dressed or further prepared, whether dehaired or split
4102	Raw skins of sheep or lambs, fresh, or salted, dried, limed, pickled or otherwise preserved, but not tanned, parchment-dressed or further prepared, whether dehaired or split (excl. those with wool, fleeces of astrakhan, caracul, persian, broadtail)
4103	Other raw hides and skins, fresh, or salted, dried, limed, pickled or otherwise preserved, but not tanned, parchment-dressed or further prepared, whether dehaired or split (excl. those of bovine animals, equine animals, sheep and lambs)
4104	Bovine or equine leather, dehaired (excl. chamois leather, patent leather, patent laminated leather and metallic leather)
4105	Sheep or lambskin leather, without wool (excl. chamois leather, patent leather, patent laminated leather and metallic leather)
4106	Goat or kidskin leather, dehaired (excl. chamois leather, patent leather, patent laminated leather and metallic leather)
4107	Leather of pigs, reptiles and other animals, dehaired, and leather of hairless animals (excl. leather of bovine and equine animals, sheep and lambs, goats and kids, chamois leather, patent leather and patent laminated leather and metallic leather)
4108	Chamois leather, incl. combination chamois leather (excl. glazed, tanned leather subsequently treated with formaldehyde and leather stuffed with oil only after tanning)
4109	Patent leather and patent laminated leather; metallic leather (excl. lacquered or metallic reconstituted leather)
4112	Leather further prepared after tanning or crusting incl. parchment-dressed leather of sheep or lambs, without wool, whether or not split (excl. chamois leather, patent leather and patent laminated leather and metallic leather)
4113	Leather further prepared after tanning or crusting incl. parchment-dressed leather of goats or kids, pigs, reptiles and other animals, without wool or hair, and leather of hairless animals, whether or not split

(continued on the next page)

206 *Appendices*

Table A.6 (continued)

HS code	Product
4114	Chamois leather, incl. combination chamois leather (excl. glacé-tanned leather subsequently treated with formaldehyde and leather stuffed with oil after tanning); patent leather and patent laminated leather; metallic leather
4115	Composition leather with a basis of leather or leather fiber, in slabs, sheets or strip, whether or not in rolls; parings and other waste of leather or of composition leather, not suitable for the manufacture of leather articles; leather dust, powder
4201	Saddlery and harness for any animal, incl. traces, leads, knee pads, muzzles, saddle cloths, saddlebags, dog coats and the like, of any material (excl. harnesses for children and adults, riding whips and other goods under heading 6602)
4202	Trunks, suitcases, vanity cases, executive bags, briefcases, spectacle cases, binocular bags, camera cases, musical instrument cases, gun cases, holsters and similar; toiletbags, rucksacks, handbags, school satchels, shopping bags, wallets, purses, map case, cigarette cases, tobacco cases
4203	Articles of clothing and accessories, of leather or composition leather (excl. footwear and headgear and parts thereof, and other goods such as shin-guards, fencing masks)
4204	Articles for technical use, of leather or composition leather
4205	Articles of leather or composition leather (excl. saddlery and harness bags; cases and similar containers; apparel and accessories; articles for technical uses; whips, riding crops and similar under heading 6602; furniture; lighting appliances; toys)
4206	Articles of gut, goldbeater's skin, bladders or tendons (excl. silkworm gut, sterile catgut, sterile surgical suture material and strings for musical instruments)
9701	Paintings, e.g., oil paintings, watercolors and pastels and drawings executed entirely by hand (excl. technical drawings and the like under heading 4906, and handpainted or hand-decorated manufactured articles); collages and similarly decorative plaques
9702	Original engravings, prints and lithographs
9703	Original sculptures and statuary, in any material

Source: (United Nations Economic Commission for Africa, *Assessing Regional Integration in Africa IV: Enhancing Intra-African Trade* (Addis Ababa: UNECA, 2010))

Appendices 207

Table A.7 Non-exhaustive HS4 list of major products for re-export in West Africa

HS code	Product
0201	Meat of bovine animals, fresh or chilled
0202	Meat of bovine animals, frozen
0203	Meat of swine, fresh, chilled or frozen
0204	Meat of sheep or goats, fresh, chilled or frozen
0206	Edible offal of bovine animals, swine, sheep, goats, horses, asses, mules or hinnies, fresh, chilled or frozen
0207	Meat and edible offal of fowl of the species gallus domesticus, ducks, geese, turkeys and guinea fowl, fresh chilled or frozen
0302	Fish, fresh or chilled (excl. fish fillets and other fish meat under heading 0304)
0401	Milk and cream, neither concentrated nor containing added sugar or other sweetening matter
0402	Milk and cream, concentrated or containing added sugar or other sweetening matter
0403	Buttermilk, curdled milk and cream, yogurt, kefir and other fermented or acidified milk and cream, whether concentrated or flavored or containing added sugar or other sweetening matter, fruits, nuts or cocoa
0405	Butter, incl. dehydrated butter and ghee, and other fats and oils derived from milk; dairy spreads
0406	Cheese and curd
0807	Melons, including watermelons, and papaws/papayas, fresh
0808	Apples, pears and quinces, fresh
1001	Wheat and meslin
1101	Wheat or meslin flour
1102	Cereal flours (excl. wheat or meslin)
1103	Cereal groats, meal and pellets
1507	Soya-bean oil and its fractions, whether or not refined (excl. chemically modified)
1508	Ground-nut oil and its fractions, whether or not refined, but not chemically modified
1509	Olive oil and its fractions obtained from the fruit of the olive tree solely by mechanical or other physical means under conditions that do not lead to deterioration of the oil, whether or not refined, but not chemically modified
1510	Other oils and their fractions, obtained solely from olives, whether or not refined, but not chemically modified, incl. blends of these oils or fractions with oils or fractions under heading 1509
1511	Palm oil and its fractions, whether or not refined (excl. chemically modified)
1512	Sunflower-seed, safflower or cotton-seed oil and fractions thereof, whether or not refined, but not chemically modified
1513	Coconut "copra," palm kernel or babassu oil and fractions thereof, whether or not refined, but not chemically modified

(continued on the next page)

208 *Appendices*

Table A.7 (continued)

HS code	Product
1516	Animal or vegetable fats and oils and their fractions, partly or wholly hydrogenated, interesterified, re-esterified or elaidinized, whether or not refined, but not further prepared
1517	Margarine, other edible mixtures or preparations of animal or vegetable fats or oils and edible fractions of different fats or oils (excl. fats, oils and their fractions, partly or wholly hydrogenated, inter-esterified, re-esterified or elaidinized)
1604	Prepared or preserved fish; caviar and caviar substitutes prepared from fish eggs
2009	Fruit juices, incl. grape must, and vegetable juices, unfermented, not containing added spirit, whether or not containing added sugar or other sweetening matter
2201	Waters, incl. natural or artificial mineral waters and aerated waters, not containing added sugar, other sweetening matter or flavored; ice and snow
2203	Beer made from malt
2204	Wine of fresh grapes, incl. fortified wines; grape must, partly fermented and of an actual alcoholic strength of > 0.5% vol. or grape must with added alcohol of an actual alcoholic strength of > 0.5% vol.
2205	Vermouth and other wine of fresh grapes, flavored with plants or aromatic substances
2206	Cider, perry, mead and other fermented beverages and mixtures of fermented beverages and non-alcoholic beverages, n.e.s. (excl. beer, wine or fresh grapes, grape must, vermouth and other wine of fresh grapes flavored with plants or aromatic substances)
2207	Undenatured ethyl alcohol of an alcoholic strength by volume of > = 80%; ethyl alcohol and other spirits, denatured, of any strength
2208	Undenatured ethyl alcohol of an alcoholic strength by volume of < 80%; spirits, liqueurs and other spirits (excl. compound alcoholic preparations of a kind used for the manufacture of beverages)
2209	Vinegar, fermented vinegar and substitutes for vinegar obtained from acetic acid
2401	Unmanufactured tobacco; tobacco refuse
2402	Cigars, cheroots, cigarillos and cigarettes of tobacco or of tobacco substitutes
2403	Manufactured tobacco and manufactured tobacco substitutes and "homogenized" or "reconstituted" tobacco, tobacco extracts and tobacco essences (excl. cigars, incl. cheroots, cigarillos and cigarettes)
4012	Retreaded or used pneumatic rubber tyres; solid or cushion tyres, interchangeable tyre treads and tyre flaps of rubber
4013	Rubber inner tubes
5208	Woven fabrics of cotton, containing > = 85% cotton by weight and weighing < = 200 g/mý

Appendices 209

Table A.7 (continued)

HS code	Product
5209	Woven fabrics of cotton, containing > = 85% cotton by weight and weighing > 200g/mý
5210	Woven fabrics of cotton, containing predominantly, but < 85% cotton by weight, mixed principally or solely with man-made fibres and weighing < = 200 g/mý
5211	Woven fabrics of cotton, containing predominantly, but < 85% cotton by weight, mixed principally or solely with man-made fibres and weighing > 200 g/mý
5212	Woven fabrics of cotton, containing predominantly, but < 85% cotton by weight, other than those mixed principally or solely with man-made fibres
6211	Track suits, ski suits, swimwear and other garments n.e.s. (excl. knitted or crocheted)
6212	Brassieres, girdles, corsets, braces, suspenders, garters and similar articles and parts thereof, of all types of textiles, whether or not elasticized, incl. knitted or crocheted (excl. belts and corselets made entirely of rubber)
6213	Handkerchiefs, of which no side exceeds 60 cm (excl. knitted or crocheted)
6214	Shawls, scarves, mufflers, mantillas, veils and similar articles (excl. knitted or crocheted)
6215	Ties, bow ties and cravats of textiles (excl. knitted or crocheted)
6216	Gloves, mittens and mitts, of all types of textile materials (excl. knitted or crocheted and for babies)
6217	Made up clothing accessories and parts of garments or clothing accessories, of all types of textile materials n.e.s. (excl. knitted or crocheted)
6301	Blankets and travelling rugs of all types of textile materials (excl. table covers, bedspreads and articles of bedding and similar furnishing under heading 9404)
6302	Bed linen, table linen, toilet linen and kitchen linen of all types of textile materials (excl. floor-cloths, polishing-cloths, dish-cloths and dusters)
6303	Curtains, including drapes, and interior blinds; curtain or bed valances of all types of textile materials (excl. awnings and sunblinds)
6304	Articles for interior furnishing of all types of textile materials (excl. blankets and travelling rugs, bed linen, table linen, toilet linen, kitchen linen, curtains, incl. drapes, interior blinds, curtain or bed valances, lampshades)
6305	Sacks and bags, of a kind used for the packing of goods, of all types of textile materials
6306	Tarpaulins, awnings and sunblinds; tents; sails for boats, sailboards or landcraft; camping goods of all types of textile materials (excl. flat protective coverings of light woven fabrics; shelter tents; rucksacks, knapsacks and similar containers)

(continued on the next page)

210   *Appendices*

Table A.7 (continued)

HS code	Product
6307	Made up articles of textile materials, incl. dress patterns, n.e.s.
6308	Kits consisting of woven fabric and yarn, whether or not with accessories, for making up into rugs, tapestries, embroidered table cloths or serviettes, or similar textile articles, put up in packings for retail sale
6309	Used clothing and clothing accessories, blankets and travelling rugs, household linen and articles for interior furnishing, of all types of textile materials, including all types of footwear and headgear, showing signs of appreciable wear
8702	Motor vehicles for the transport of > = 10 persons, incl. driver
8703	Motor cars and other motor vehicles principally designed for the transport of persons, incl. station wagons and racing cars (excl. motor vehicles under heading 8702)
8706	Chassis fitted with engines for tractors, motor vehicles for the transport of 10 or more persons, motor cars and other motor vehicles principally designed for the transport of persons, motor vehicles for the transport of goods
8707	Bodies, including cabs, for tractors, motor vehicles for the transport of ten or more persons, motor cars and other motor vehicles principally designed for the transport of persons, motor vehicles for the transport of goods and special purpose motor vehicles

Source: (United Nations Economic Commission for Africa, *Assessing Regional Integration in Africa IV: Enhancing Intra-African Trade* (Addis Ababa: UNECA, 2010))

Appendices 211

Table A.8 List of pharmaceutical products traded in the informal sector

HS code	Product
2935	Sulphonamides
2936	Provitamins and vitamins, natural or reproduced by synthesis, incl. natural concentrates and derivatives thereof used as vitamins, and intermixtures, whether or not in any solvent
2939	Vegetable alkaloids, natural or reproduced by synthesis, and their salts, ethers, esters and other derivatives
2941	Antibiotics
3003	Medicaments consisting of two or more constituents mixed for therapeutic or prophylactic uses, not in measured doses or for retail sale (excl. goods under headings 3002, 3005 or 3006)
3004	Medicaments consisting of mixed or unmixed products for therapeutic or prophylactic uses, in measured doses or for retail sale (excl. goods under headings 3002, 3005 or 3006)
3005	Wadding, gauze and bandages, e.g., dressings, adhesive plasters, poultices, impregnated or covered with pharmaceutical substances or for retail sale for medical, surgical, dental or veterinary purposes
3006	Pharmaceutical preparations and products
3006	Paracetamol tablets
3006	Quotrimo (Bactrim)
3006	Flagyl
3006	Chloranphenicol
3006	Prometadine
3006	Indocide
3006	Ibuprofen
3006	Nivaquine tablets
3006	Chloroquine
3006	Erythromycin
3006	Cypro
3006	Nivaquine syrup
3006	Chloroquine syrup
3006	Bactrim syrup
3006	Gripe water
3006	Paracetamol syrup
3006	Amoxicillin
3006	Quinine
3006	Maloxine
3006	Fansidar
3006	Combimal
3006	Aluminium Hydroxide
3006	Duofem (contraceptive)
3006	Gentamicin
3006	Tetracycline pomade
3006	Plastic wrapping
3006	Diclofen
3006	Bisalax

(continued on the next page)

212 *Appendices*

Table A.8 (continued)

HS code	Product
3006	Novalgin
3006	Chlorpheniramine Maleate
3006	Viagra
3006	Antibiotics not defined elsewhere
3006	Diazepam
3006	Febrilex
3006	CaC1000
3006	Mixagrip
3006	Vitamins
3006	Benzodiazepines
3006	Neuroleptics
3006	Sedatives

Source: (United Nations Economic Commission for Africa, *Assessing Regional Integration in Africa IV: Enhancing Intra-African Trade* (Addis Ababa: UNECA, 2010))

Routledge Global Institutions Series

77 Transformations in Trade Politics (2013)
Participatory trade politics in West Africa
by Silke Trommer (Murdoch University)

76 Rules, Politics, and the International Criminal Court (2013)
Committing to the Court
by Yvonne M. Dutton (Indiana University)

75 Global Institutions of Religion (2013)
Ancient movers, modern shakers
by Katherine Marshall (Georgetown University)

74 Crisis of Global Sustainability (2013)
by Tapio Kanninen

73 The Group of Twenty (G20) (2013)
by Andrew F. Cooper (University of Waterloo) and Ramesh Thakur (Australian National University)

72 Peacebuilding (2013)
From concept to commission
by Rob Jenkins (Hunter College, CUNY)

71 Human Rights and Humanitarian Norms, Strategic Framing, and Intervention (2013)
Lessons for the Responsibility to Protect
by Melissa Labonte (Fordham University)

70 Feminist Strategies in International Governance (2013)
edited by Gülay Caglar (Humboldt University, Berlin), Elisabeth Prügl (the Graduate Institute of International and Development Studies, Geneva), and Susanne Zwingel (the State University of New York, Potsdam)

69 The Migration Industry and the Commercialization of International Migration (2013)
edited by Thomas Gammeltoft-Hansen (Danish Institute for International Studies) and Ninna Nyberg Sørensen (Danish Institute for International Studies)

68 Integrating Africa (2013)
Decolonization's legacies, sovereignty, and the African Union
by Martin Welz (University of Konstanz)

67 Trade, Poverty, Development (2013)
Getting beyond the WTO's Doha deadlock
edited by Rorden Wilkinson (University of Manchester) and James Scott (University of Manchester)

66 The United Nations Industrial Development Organization (UNIDO) (2012)
Industrial solutions for a sustainable future
by Stephen Browne (FUNDS Project)

65 The Millennium Development Goals and Beyond (2012)
Global development after 2015
edited by Rorden Wilkinson (University of Manchester) and David Hulme (University of Manchester)

64 International Organizations as Self-Directed Actors (2012)
A framework for analysis
edited by Joel E. Oestreich (Drexel University)

63 Maritime Piracy (2012)
by Robert Haywood (One Earth Future Foundation) and Roberta Spivak (One Earth Future Foundation)

62 United Nations High Commissioner for Refugees (UNHCR) (2nd edition, 2012)
by Gil Loescher (University of Oxford), Alexander Betts (University of Oxford), and James Milner (University of Toronto)

61 International Law, International Relations, and Global Governance (2012)
by Charlotte Ku (University of Illinois)

60 Global Health Governance (2012)
by Sophie Harman (City University, London)

59 The Council of Europe (2012)
by Martyn Bond (University of London)

58 The Security Governance of Regional Organizations (2011)
edited by Emil J. Kirchner (University of Essex) and
Roberto Domínguez (Suffolk University)

57 The United Nations Development Programme and System (2011)
by Stephen Browne (FUNDS Project)

56 The South Asian Association for Regional Cooperation (2011)
An emerging collaboration architecture
by Lawrence Sáez (University of London)

55 The UN Human Rights Council (2011)
by Bertrand G. Ramcharan (Geneva Graduate Institute of International
and Development Studies)

54 Responsibility to Protect (2011)
Cultural perspectives in the Global South
edited by Rama Mani (University of Oxford) and
Thomas G. Weiss (The CUNY Graduate Center)

53 The International Trade Centre (2011)
Promoting exports for development
by Stephen Browne (FUNDS Project) and
Sam Laird (University of Nottingham)

52 The Idea of World Government (2011)
From ancient times to the twenty-first century
by James A. Yunker (Western Illinois University)

51 Humanitarianism Contested (2011)
Where angels fear to tread
by Michael Barnett (George Washington University) and
Thomas G. Weiss (The CUNY Graduate Center)

50 The Organization of American States (2011)
Global governance away from the media
by Monica Herz (Catholic University, Rio de Janeiro)

49 Non-Governmental Organizations in World Politics (2011)
The construction of global governance
by Peter Willetts (City University, London)

48 The Forum on China-Africa Cooperation (FOCAC) (2011)
by Ian Taylor (University of St. Andrews)

47 Global Think Tanks (2011)
Policy networks and governance
by James G. McGann (University of Pennsylvania) with Richard Sabatini

46 United Nations Educational, Scientific and Cultural Organization (UNESCO) (2011)
Creating norms for a complex world
by J.P. Singh (Georgetown University)

45 The International Labour Organization (2011)
Coming in from the cold
by Steve Hughes (Newcastle University) and
Nigel Haworth (University of Auckland)

44 Global Poverty (2010)
How global governance is failing the poor
by David Hulme (University of Manchester)

43 Global Governance, Poverty, and Inequality (2010)
edited by Jennifer Clapp (University of Waterloo) and
Rorden Wilkinson (University of Manchester)

42 Multilateral Counter-Terrorism (2010)
The global politics of cooperation and contestation
by Peter Romaniuk (John Jay College of Criminal Justice, CUNY)

41 Governing Climate Change (2010)
by Peter Newell (University of East Anglia) and
Harriet A. Bulkeley (Durham University)

40 The UN Secretary-General and Secretariat (2nd edition, 2010)
by Leon Gordenker (Princeton University)

39 Preventive Human Rights Strategies (2010)
by Bertrand G. Ramcharan (Geneva Graduate Institute of International
and Development Studies)

38 African Economic Institutions (2010)
by Kwame Akonor (Seton Hall University)

37 Global Institutions and the HIV/AIDS Epidemic (2010)
Responding to an international crisis
by Franklyn Lisk (University of Warwick)

36 Regional Security (2010)
The capacity of international organizations
by Rodrigo Tavares (United Nations University)

35 The Organisation for Economic Co-operation and Development (2009)
by Richard Woodward (University of Hull)

34 Transnational Organized Crime (2009)
by Frank Madsen (University of Cambridge)

33 The United Nations and Human Rights (2nd edition, 2009)
A guide for a new era
by Julie A. Mertus (American University)

32 The International Organization for Standardization (2009)
Global governance through voluntary consensus
*by Craig N. Murphy (Wellesley College) and
JoAnne Yates (Massachusetts Institute of Technology)*

31 Shaping the Humanitarian World (2009)
*by Peter Walker (Tufts University) and
Daniel G. Maxwell (Tufts University)*

30 Global Food and Agricultural Institutions (2009)
by John Shaw

29 Institutions of the Global South (2009)
by Jacqueline Anne Braveboy-Wagner (City College of New York, CUNY)

28 International Judicial Institutions (2009)
The architecture of international justice at home and abroad
*by Richard J. Goldstone (Retired Justice of the Constitutional Court of
South Africa) and Adam M. Smith (Harvard University)*

27 The International Olympic Committee (2009)
The governance of the Olympic system
*by Jean-Loup Chappelet (IDHEAP Swiss Graduate School of Public
Administration) and Brenda Kübler-Mabbott*

26 The World Health Organization (2009)
by Kelley Lee (London School of Hygiene and Tropical Medicine)

25 Internet Governance (2009)
The new frontier of global institutions
by John Mathiason (Syracuse University)

24 Institutions of the Asia-Pacific (2009)
ASEAN, APEC, and beyond
by Mark Beeson (University of Birmingham)

23 United Nations High Commissioner for Refugees (UNHCR) (2008)
The politics and practice of refugee protection into the twenty-first century
by Gil Loescher (University of Oxford), Alexander Betts (University of Oxford), and James Milner (University of Toronto)

22 Contemporary Human Rights Ideas (2008)
by Bertrand G. Ramcharan (Geneva Graduate Institute of International and Development Studies)

21 The World Bank (2008)
From reconstruction to development to equity
by Katherine Marshall (Georgetown University)

20 The European Union (2008)
by Clive Archer (Manchester Metropolitan University)

19 The African Union (2008)
Challenges of globalization, security, and governance
by Samuel M. Makinda (Murdoch University) and F. Wafula Okumu (McMaster University)

18 Commonwealth (2008)
Inter- and non-state contributions to global governance
by Timothy M. Shaw (Royal Roads University)

17 The World Trade Organization (2007)
Law, economics, and politics
by Bernard M. Hoekman (World Bank) and Petros C. Mavroidis (Columbia University)

16 A Crisis of Global Institutions? (2007)
Multilateralism and international security
by Edward Newman (University of Birmingham)

15 UN Conference on Trade and Development (2007)
by Ian Taylor (University of St. Andrews) and
Karen Smith (University of Stellenbosch)

14 The Organization for Security and Co-operation
in Europe (2007)
by David J. Galbreath (University of Aberdeen)

13 The International Committee of the Red Cross (2007)
A neutral humanitarian actor
by David P. Forsythe (University of Nebraska) and
Barbara Ann Rieffer-Flanagan (Central Washington University)

12 The World Economic Forum (2007)
A multi-stakeholder approach to global governance
by Geoffrey Allen Pigman (Bennington College)

11 The Group of 7/8 (2007)
by Hugo Dobson (University of Sheffield)

10 The International Monetary Fund (2007)
Politics of conditional lending
by James Raymond Vreeland (Georgetown University)

9 The North Atlantic Treaty Organization (2007)
The enduring alliance
by Julian Lindley-French (Center for Applied Policy,
University of Munich)

8 The World Intellectual Property Organization (2006)
Resurgence and the development agenda
by Chris May (University of the West of England)

7 The UN Security Council (2006)
Practice and promise
by Edward C. Luck (Columbia University)

6 Global Environmental Institutions (2006)
by Elizabeth R. DeSombre (Wellesley College)

5 Internal Displacement (2006)
Conceptualization and its consequences
by Thomas G. Weiss (The CUNY Graduate Center) and David A. Korn

4 The UN General Assembly (2005)
by M.J. Peterson (University of Massachusetts, Amherst)

3 United Nations Global Conferences (2005)
by Michael G. Schechter (Michigan State University)

2 The UN Secretary-General and Secretariat (2005)
by Leon Gordenker (Princeton University)

1 The United Nations and Human Rights (2005)
A guide for a new era
by Julie A. Mertus (American University)

Books currently under contract include:

The Regional Development Banks
Lending with a regional flavor
by Jonathan R. Strand (University of Nevada)

Millennium Development Goals (MDGs)
For a people-centered development agenda?
by Sakiko Fukuda-Parr (The New School)

UNICEF
by Richard Jolly (University of Sussex)

The Bank for International Settlements
The politics of global financial supervision in the age
of high finance
by Kevin Ozgercin (SUNY College at Old Westbury)

International Migration
by Khalid Koser (Geneva Centre for Security Policy)

Human Development
by Richard Ponzio

The International Monetary Fund (2nd edition)
Politics of conditional lending
by James Raymond Vreeland (Georgetown University)

The UN Global Compact
by Catia Gregoratti (Lund University)

Institutions for Women's Rights
*by Charlotte Patton (York College, CUNY) and
Carolyn Stephenson (University of Hawaii)*

International Aid
by Paul Mosley (University of Sheffield)

Global Consumer Policy
by Karsten Ronit (University of Copenhagen)

The Changing Political Map of Global Governance
*by Anthony Payne (University of Sheffield) and
Stephen Robert Buzdugan (Manchester Metropolitan University)*

Coping with Nuclear Weapons
by W. Pal Sidhu

Private Foundations and Development Partnerships
by Michael Moran (Swinburne University of Technology)

The International Politics of Human Rights
*edited by Monica Serrano (Colegio de Mexico) and
Thomas G. Weiss (The CUNY Graduate Center)*

Twenty-First-Century Democracy Promotion in the Americas
*by Jorge Heine (The Centre for International Governance Innovation)
and Brigitte Weiffen (University of Konstanz)*

EU Environmental Policy and Climate Change
*by Henrik Selin (Boston University) and
Stacy VanDeveer (University of New Hampshire)*

Making Global Institutions Work
Power, accountability and change
edited by Kate Brennan

The Society for Worldwide Interbank Financial Telecommunication (SWIFT)
*by Susan Scott (London School of Economics and Political Science)
and Markos Zachariadis (University of Cambridge)*

Global Governance and China
The dragon's learning curve
edited by Scott Kennedy (Indiana University)

The Politics of Global Economic Surveillance
by Martin S. Edwards (Seton Hall University)

Mercy and Mercenaries
Humanitarian Agencies and Private Security Companies
by Peter Hoffman

Regional Organizations in the Middle East
James Worrall (University of Leeds)

Reforming the UN Development System
The Politics of Incrementalism
by Silke Weinlich (Duisburg-Essen University)

Corporate Social Responsibility
by Oliver Williams (University of Notre Dame)

Post-2015 UN Development
Making change happen
*Stephen Browne (FUNDS Project) and
Thomas G. Weiss (The CUNY Graduate Center)*

For further information regarding the series, please contact:
Craig Fowlie, Publisher, Politics & International Studies
Taylor & Francis
2 Park Square, Milton Park, Abingdon
Oxford OX14 4RN, UK
+44 (0)207 842 2057 Tel
+44 (0)207 842 2302 Fax
Craig.Fowlie@tandf.co.uk
www.routledge.com

Index

ACP group (African, Caribbean, Pacific countries): aid 93; Cotonou Agreement 8, 93; development 93; EPA 9, 10, 11, 43–44, 48; Marrakesh Agreements 89; *see also* ECOWAS; EPA

actor 18, 19, 180, 187; categorization 24–25 (conformers/reformers/rejectionists 24; corporate/non-corporate groups 24; supportive/challenging the global trade agenda 24); legitimacy 18; perception 18, 19; political environment 18, 19, 114; social embeddedness 18, 19, 114; transformative actor 25, 51, 54, 62, 64, 65, 67, 75, 77, 98, 106–9, 114–42, 180; *see also* civil society; private sector; state

advocacy 185–86; development 5; economistic trade policy formation theories 75; 'insider/outsider' approach 49, 104–5, 120–21; Platform 49; transnational advocacy 38, 41, 60, 96, 98, 100, 116, 178, 186–87; West African participatory trade politics 88, 89, 90, 96–101, 110, 178; *see also* civil society; Cotton Initiative; Platform

aid 10, 58, 93, 160, 173

Ake, Claude 158–59, 161

Arato, Andrew 127

Ashley, Richard 66

ATN (Africa Trade Network) 52, 55, 96, 97, 107; EPA 45, 52; membership 55; Platform 34; *see also* TWN

Baldwin, Robert 75

Barone, Enrico 73

Barry, Boubacar 150

Bastable, Francis 71, 72

Bathily, Abdoulaye 167

Bernstein, Steven 134

Bidwell, Percy 74

Bretton Woods institutions 120

Brock, William 75

Buchanan, James 75

Burkina-Faso 33, 98, 99; Zongo, Tertius 50

capacity 115, 116–18, 139, 179, 180–81

capitalism 27, 69, 145, 147, 191

Cassing, James 75

Caves, Richard 75

CECIDE (Centre du Commerce International pour le Développement) 33, 52

Central African EPA region 185–86

Charmes, Jacques 160, 163

Charnovitz, Steve 127, 128

Christian Aid 34

civil society 3; African context 24; categorization 24–25; contestation 18, 87, 110, 114, 115, 127, 179; Cotonou Agreement 125; definition 23–24, 92–93, 115, 119, 125–28, 139, 183, 186; demonstrations 51, 126; EPA 11, 12, 13; European civil society 43, 54, 109; European context 24; heterogeneity 126–27; individual activism 88, 96, 107–9, 110 (personal merit 108–9); legitimacy 115, 119, 125, 133–39, 177, 179, 183; representativity 115,

224   *Index*

119, 125, 127, 128–33, 134, 139, 179, 183; right to make oral statement 13; roles 127; Senegal 13, 97–98; state/market/civil society triangle 25–26, 37, 110, 119, 124–25, 153, 166; transparency 120–21, 132; West African participatory trade politics 11, 12, 13–14, 25, 28, 96–101 (inclusion 13–14, 17, 42; status 13–14); *see also* actor; advocacy; ATN; civil society/public officials interaction; ENDA; NGO; participation; Platform; TWN; West African participatory trade politics
civil society/public officials interaction 14, 41, 46, 90, 101, 102–7, 110, 123–25, 128–39, 176, 179; confrontation 4, 87, 109, 110, 114, 124, 130, 135–37, 138, 181, 185; hostility 87; mistrust 110, 130–31; skepticism 4, 54, 60, 87, 94, 98, 110; solidarity 94–95, 106, 110, 137, 138, 143, 152, 165, 178–79, 182; trust 117, 121; *see also* civil society; state; West Africa, state/society relations and trade
Clark, John 71, 72
Clow, Frederick 68
Cohen, Abner 146
Cohen, Benjamin 62–63, 67
Cohen, Jean 127
Cold War 30, 74
Cole, Arthur 73
Collier, Paul 154
colonial system 121, 122, 144, 149, 150, 151, 152, 153, 155, 162, 165
constructivism 15
consumer 166; consumer/producer surplus 73; variable trade economism 61–62, 64
contestation 140; civil society 18, 87, 110, 114, 115, 127, 179; development 21; participatory trade politics 17; trade economism 185; trade policy-making 3, 5, 19, 176, 177, 185, 190
Coquery-Vidrovitch, Catherine 147
corruption 137, 153, 159, 160, 161, 165
Côte d'Ivoire 10–11, 101, 158, 182
Cotonou Agreement 4, 8, 47; ACP group 8, 93; Article 2 90; Article 37 47, 48; civil society 96, 97, 125; democracy 34; development/trade separation 8, 42; EDF 8;

networking 38; Platform 32, 34, 91–93; right to participation 90–93, 95, 109, 137, 179; West African participatory trade politics 15, 88, 90–93, 95, 96, 108, 109, 178, 186
Cotton Initiative 98–100, 106, 110, 116; Traoré, François 100
Cummings, John 72
Curtin, Philip D. 6, 178

democracy 27, 120, 191; civil society representativity 125, 127, 128, 134; Cotonou campaign 34; 'democratic nirvana' 3, 5, 188; democratization 27, 158; democratization of trade policy-making 5, 36, 76, 117, 119, 140, 159, 179, 188, 191; erosion of 27; inclusiveness 119–20; legitimacy 137, 140, 188; non-execution clause 116, 141; participatory trade politics 26–27; Platform 27, 36, 38, 120, 125, 128, 134; protectionism 3; trade and democracy 27, 188–91
developing country 8, 56, 89, 99, 170; GSP 10; non-reciprocity 155, 157; SDT 43, 157
development 19–21; ACP group 93; advocacy 5; contestation 21; definition 19, 21; development aid 10, 160, 173; development cooperation 11; development indices 19–21; development/trade separation 8, 42; EPA 11, 43–47, 56, 97, 101, 119, 130, 181 (EPA Development Programme 52, 58); equivocal nature of the term 19; EU 43, 44–45, 46; how can it be achieved? 21, 47, 181; International Centre for Trade and Sustainable Development 52; Platform 42–47, 55, 101, 186; Save the Children 19, 20, 21; sustainable development 27, 37, 44, 113, 153; trade/development relationship 43, 45, 46, 95, 181; UN Human Development Index 19, 20, 21; West African participatory trade politics 21; West African region 20–21; World Bank 19, 20; WTO 89, 99
DG Development (Directorate-General for Development) 13, 56
DG Trade (Directorate-General for Trade) 12, 13, 56
Dièye, Cheikh Tidiane 164

Index 225

Diouf, El Hadji 52–53; *Article XXIV of GATT and the EPA* 53, 187
Doha Round 3, 22, 23, 99, 186

Eagleton-Pierce, Matthew 6, 178
EBA (Everything but Arms) 10, 48
econometrics 74
economics 6, 74–75; economic theory 62–63, 75; economics imperialism 63, 64, 75; economism 5, 19; *see also* neoclassical economics; trade economism; trade policy formation theory
ECOWAS (Economic Community of West African States): common external tariff 52, 58; customs union 10–11, 105; Daramy, Mohammed 53; ECOWAS common external tariff 52, 58; ECOWAS Council of Ministers 11; ECOWAS/EU bilateral relations 9–10; EPA 8, 15, 46–47; EPA deadline 49–50; external trade 8; GDP 9; market opening 53; membership 9; MMC 11–12, 132; Negotiating Roadmap 11, 13, 15, 24, 40 (right to participation 90, 91, 109, 125, 137, 179); RNC 12–13; trade critics 7; trade reform 157; *see also* EPA; West African participatory trade politics
EDF (European Development Fund) 8, 13, 45, 92, 93
Elgström, Ole 46, 56
ENDA (Environment and Development of the Third World) 15, 32, 96, 99, 116, 164; ACP Secretariat 34; EPA 49, 52; European Commission 34; Gahamanyi, Bibiane 36–37, 44; Platform 32, 33, 34, 40, 41, 54, 91–92 (leading role in Platform 41, 54); regional integration 36; Uruguay Round 89
EPA (Economic Partnership Agreement) 4, 7–11, 178, 184; ACP group 9, 10, 11, 43–44, 48; asymmetries 9, 105, 121, 164; the Caribbean 10, 11; Central African EPA region 185–86; civil society 11, 12, 13; consultative trade policy-making 15; criticism 45, 51–52, 122; customs union 10–11, 105; deadline 10, 41, 47, 48–52, 101, 123;

deadlock 51, 53–54; development 43–47, 56, 97, 101, 119, 130, 181 (EPA Development Programme 52, 58); ECOWAS 8, 15, 46–47; ENDA 49, 52; fragmentation 8, 10; free trade 45, 56; goals 35; GSP 10, 48; impact 43–45, 50–51, 190; legitimacy 133; participatory trade policy-making 15, 41–54, 184; regional groups 8, 194; *rendez-vous* clauses 47, 57; rules of origin 11, 48, 198, 199; 'Six Reasons to Oppose the EPA in their Current Form' 43; social dimension of trade 144, 146–47, 165; state of play 11, 196–200; trade-in-goods interim 10–11, 47, 54, 57, 101; trade liberalization 43–44, 46, 49, 53; trade reform 35, 45–46, 176; TWN 43, 44; WAEMU 8; West African dependence on Europe 9–10, 122, 148; West African trade political practice 7, 11, 41–42; *see also* ECOWAS; EU; Platform and EPA; West African participatory trade politics
Esty, Daniel 115
EU (European Union): civil society participation 92–93; development 43, 44–45, 46; EC–Bananas case 8, 47; ECOWAS/EU bilateral relations 9–10; European civil society 43, 54, 109; European Parliament 43; GDP 9; RNC 12–13; trade policy and negotiating capacity 105; *see also* EPA; European Commission
European Commission 42, 47; Ashton, Catherine 46; civil society participation 108; commissioned studies 116; *Global Europe Strategy* 10; Mandelson, Peter 35, 43, 44, 45, 46; Michel, Louis 45, 48; political actors 25; 'pure trade deal' 43; Sustainability Impact Assessment 43, 190; trade reform 45–46
European STOP EPA movement 34, 42
Evans, Phil 3, 188

Fage, John 147, 151–52
Falkenberg, Karl 44
Fine, Ben 71, 73
Finger, Michael 89
Finnemore, Martha 140

226 *Index*

Florini, Ann 134
Ford, Jane 23, 178
free trade 22–23, 70, 74, 80, 153, 166;
benefits 72; definition 21–22; EPA
45, 56; global North 23; government
intervention 80; hegemony 22;
protectionism/free trade controversy
61, 64, 68, 69–76, 76 189;
protectionist/free trade attitudes 34–
35, 61; *see also* trade liberalization
Friedrich Ebert Foundation 34
funding 90, 92, 97; Platform 34, 38, 39, 40

GATS (General Agreement on Trade
in Services) 43
GATT (General Agreement on Tariffs
and Trade) 74, 105, 153–54; Article
XXIV 10, 11, 43, 47, 52–53, 180;
Article XXIV of GATT and the EPA
53, 187; Article XXVI:5 154, 155,
156; Article XXXIII 155;
membership 170; Trade and
Development section 155; trade
liberalization 22, 154; West African
region 153–56
GAWU (General Agricultural
Workers' Union) 33, 49, 52
Gboyega, Alex 161
Ghana 10–11, 101, 155, 158, 182
Gibbon, Peter 158
Global Coalition for Africa 96–97
global North: free trade 23; global
North partner organizations 34, 38,
39–40, 43, 97, 102, 116; North-
South networks 97, 100, 178
global South 27, 89; civil society 99;
North-South networks 97, 100, 178;
protectionism 23
global trade agenda 18, 177; criticism
35, 44, 65–66, 77, 165, 176; definition
23; Platform 35, 44; policy lines 23
global trade governance 6–7; *see also*
trade policy-making; trade politics
Gordon, Margaret S. 74
GRAPAD (Groupe de Recherche et
d'Action pour la Promotion de
l'Agriculture et du Développement)
33, 52
GSP (Generalized System of
Preferences) 9, 10, 48

Hamilton, Alexander 69–70
Hannah, Erin 25, 183

Harbeson, John 25, 26
Harding, Leonhard 147
Hazard, Eric 100
Hill, William 69
Hillman, Arye 75
Hobson, John 22
human rights 35, 55, 141

ICTSD (International Centre for Trade
and Sustainable Development) 113
Imam, Ayesha 25
IMF (International Monetary Fund)
35, 45; SAP 157, 161
informal economy 159–65, 203–12;
alternative economic system 160;
corruption 159, 160, 161; definition
159–60; illegal activity 160; Nigeria
159, 162; participatory trade politics
165–66; products in informal West
African trade 160, 163, 203–12;
remittance 160, 173–74; size of 160;
social embeddedness 162–63; socio-
economic hardship 163; state 161,
162, 166; tax evasion/avoidance159,
160, 164; trade economism theories/
trade policy-making 163, 165, 166;
see also West Africa, state/society
relations and trade
institutionalism 15, 63, 68
intellectual property 10, 22, 23, 47, 53,
75, 183
International Relations 27, 63
international trade 37, 71, 72, 80, 163,
191; global trade governance 6–7;
international trade law 22, 180
International Trade Organization 74

Jones, Kent 75
Jordan, Lisa 131

Kachingwe, Nancy 35
Kautsky, Karl 69
Keasbey, Lindley 69, 184–85
Kipre, Pierre 147
Klabbers, Jan 180–81
Kobou, Georges 160, 161

LDC (least developed country) 10, 11,
99, 158
legitimacy 133, 134, 140, 180, 183–84,
188; actor 18; civil society 115, 119,
125, 133–39, 177, 179, 183;
delegitimization 133, 135, 136;

Index 227

democracy 137, 140, 188; efficiency/
legitimacy deadlock 6, 60–61, 76,
77–78, 177; EPA 133; legitimization
133; Platform 41, 115, 119, 125,
127, 133–39, 180, 183; state, lack of
legitimacy 152; technical legitimacy
134–37; trade policy-making 3, 5,
184; types of 134–36; WTO 3
Levasseur, Émile 69
Lippert, Owen 159
List, Friedrich 69–70
Lomé Conventions 8, 10, 47, 48, 89,
90, 93, 96
Lovejoy, Paul E. 147

Magee, Stephen 75
Mali Empire 146
Malthus, Thomas 68
Mama, Amina 25
Mandelson, Peter 35, 43, 44, 45, 46
Marfaing, Laurence 163
marginalist school 70–74, 188, 189;
see also trade policy formation
theory
Marrakesh Agreements 88–90
Marshall, Alfred 73
Marvel, Howard 75
Marx, Karl 68
Mayer, Wolfgang 75
Meagher, Kate 159
media 15, 39, 141
methodology: economics/political
economy studies of trade link 63,
177; *Methodenstreit* 70;
participatory trade politics 55;
present study 15–17, 201–3; 'trade
as special politics' 188; trade
scholarship 63, 66, 68; trade
theory/trade politics separation
65, 67, 72; *see also* trade
economism; trade policy formation
theory
MFN clause (Most Favored Nation)
116, 141
Mill, John Stuart 68, 70
Milner, Helen 61, 62
Milonakis, Dimitris 71, 73
MMC (Ministerial Monitoring
Committee) 50, 92, 101, 108
multilateral trading system 22, 47, 99,
153, 154, 155, 157, 186

NANTS (National Association of
Nigerian Traders) 33, 34, 35; trade
liberalization 44; Ukaoha, Ken 37,
44–45, 95
neoclassical economics 6, 22, 74, 78,
80, 83; economics imperialism 63,
64, 75; social sciences 80; trade
policy formation theory 62, 64–65,
67, 74–76, 77, 80, 177; *see also* trade
economism
networking 180; Cotonou Agreement
38; North-South networks 97, 100,
178; Platform 38–39, 116, 132, 178;
see also ATN; TWN
NGO (non-governmental
organization) 4, 127, 128, 129, 131;
see also civil society
Niamey Declaration 45, 49
Nigeria 8, 10, 51, 155, 158, 161;
informal economy 159, 162; *see also*
NANTS
non-execution clause 116, 141

OECD (Organisation for Economic
Co-operation and Development)
153, 154
Oloruntimehin, Funmilayo 159–60
Olson, Mancur 75
Ostry, Sylvia 89
Oxfam UK 34

participation 11, 13, 107, 108, 127,
134–35; complimentary/critical
participation 92–93; Cotonou
Agreement 90–93, 95, 109, 137, 179;
ECOWAS Negotiating Roadmap
90, 91, 109, 125, 137, 179; *see also*
civil society
participatory trade politics *see* West
African participatory trade politics
PASCIB (Plateforme des Acteurs de la
Société Civile au Bénin) 33
Patomäki, Heikki 191
perception 6, 7, 15, 18, 19, 23, 98, 178
Platform (Platform of West African
Civil Society Organizations on the
Cotonou Agreement) 4, 23, 32–59,
62; *Article XXIV of GATT and the
EPA* 187; ATN 34; Cotonou
Agreement 32, 34, 91–93; credibility
96, 136; democracy 27, 36, 38, 120,
125, 128, 134; democratization of
trade politics 36, 159; ENDA 32, 33,

228 *Index*

34, 40, 41, 54, 91–92; European STOP EPA movement 34, 42; financial independence 116; global North partner organizations 34, 38, 39–40; global trade agenda 35, 44; grassroots links 40, 127, 129; legitimacy 41, 115, 119, 125, 127, 133–39, 180, 183; membership 33–34, 52, 127, 130; origin 32–33, 54; reformative/rejectionist member 37; regional integration 36; representativity 40, 129–31, 133–34, 183; structuralism 14–15; *see also* Platform and EPA

Platform and EPA 13, 91–93, 98, 164, 176, 186; advocacy 49 ('insider/outsider approach' 49, 104–5, 120–21); EPA stance 34–37, 123, 181 (criticism 35–36, 37, 176); impact on EPA negotiations 41–54, 94 (development 42–47, 55, 101, 186; EPA deadline 48–52, 101; GATT, Article XXIV 52–53); internal proceedings and campaign strategy 35, 38–41, 54, 91, 103–4, 138 (education/technical information 39, 40, 88, 96, 101–7, 110, 113, 116, 117, 134–35, 179, 180; lobbying 38, 48, 98; networking 38–39, 116, 132, 178; public mobilization 48, 49, 51, 91, 101, 104; Regional Dialogues 38, 39, 54); politicization of trade 32, 35, 43, 103–4, 182; transparency 41, 120–21, 132, 176, 178, 183; *see also* West African participatory trade politics

Polanyi, Karl 22, 67

political economy 68; Cold War 74; desocialization and dehistoricization 6, 63, 67, 72, 74; economics/political economy studies of trade link 63, 74, 177; from classical political economy to economics 74–75, 80; interests/ideas interaction in trade politics 6, 7, 184; political economy as science 6, 68, 71, 72–73; trade 6, 68; *see also* trade economism; trade policy formation theory; trade policy-making; trade politics

political environment 18, 19, 98, 105, 114, 178, 187

political opportunity 7, 91, 93, 95, 99, 110, 178, 187–88

poverty 35, 157–58, 162, 182, 185

Powers, Perry 69

private sector: informal/parallel market 159; involvement/voice, high level of 14; right to make oral statement 13; state/market/civil society triangle 25–26, 37, 110, 119, 124–25, 153, 166; West African participatory trade politics 11, 12, 14, 124–25; *see also* actor

protectionism 23, 73, 75, 80, 166, 185; African countries 8; democracy 3; global South 23; government intervention 80; protectionism/free trade controversy 61, 64, 68, 69–76, 76 189; protectionist/free trade attitudes 34–35, 61

PTA (Preferential Trade Agreement) 22, 186

Quack, Sigrid 133

Ray, Edward 75

realism 63

regime theory 63

regional integration 8, 9, 16, 53, 157; civil society 36, 101; EPA 58, 182; integration from below 161–62; West Africa 145–46, 154, 157, 161–62, 164, 182; *see also* ECOWAS; WAEMU

remittance 160, 173–74

Reno, William 161

representation 129; civil society 115, 119, 125, 127, 128–33, 134, 139, 179, 183; democracy 125, 127, 128, 134; NGO 127, 128, 129, 131; Platform 40, 129–31, 133–34, 183; trade policy-making 5

Ricardo, David 22–23, 70, 73, 76

Rist, Gilbert 21

RNC (Regional Negotiating Committee) 12–13

Robertson, David 67

Rodrik, Dani 75

Rogowski, Ronald 64

ROPPA (Réseau des Paysans et des Producteurs Agricoles de l'Afrique de l'Ouest) 50, 52, 99, 107

Ruggie, John 63

rules of origin 11, 48, 198, 199

Sachs, Wolfgang 21

Samuelson, Paul 64, 80

Index 229

Save the Children 19, 20, 21
Schmoller, Gustav 70
Schneider, Friedrich 159
Scholte, Jan Aart 24, 179
Schumpeter, Joseph 73
science: exact science 72–73;
neoclassical economics 74, 80;
political economy as science 6, 68, 71,
72–73; social science 68, 72, 74, 80
SDT (Special and Differential
Treatment) 43, 157
Senegal 139, 158, 162; Awadi, Didier
51–52; Ba, Amadou 50; civil society
13, 97–98; EPA 13, 49; Pouye,
Aicha 98; Wade, Abdoulaye 51
sensitive products 52, 58, 102
services 11, 47, 57
Shaw, Timothy 27–28
Sierra Leone 161
Singapore Issues 47, 52, 58
'Six Reasons to Oppose the EPA in
their Current Form' 43
slave trade 51, 52, 144, 148, 150–52
Smith, Adam 68
social embeddedness 189; actor 18, 19,
114; economic/social interrelation of
trade 6, 63, 67, 72, 144, 146–47,
165, 177, 178; historical and socio-
economic interaction 143–44, 184–
85; informal economy 162–63; trade
political interests 15, 63, 178, 185,
187; trade political practice 6, 178,
184; *see also* West African
participatory trade politics
solidarity 94–95, 106, 110, 137, 138,
143, 152, 165, 178–79, 182
Sow, Miriam 163
Stanwood, Edward 71
Stary, Bruno 161–62
state: 'collapsed states' 158; corruption
161; decline 27–28; informal
economy 161, 162, 166; legitimacy,
lack of 152; regime theory 63;
sovereignty 153; state/market/civil
society triangle 25–26, 37, 110, 119,
124–25, 153, 166; weakness 153,
158, 159, 163; West African
participatory trade politics,
historical evolution 14, 106, 159; *see
also* civil society/public officials
interaction; West Africa, state/
society relations and trade
Stigler, George 75

Stolper, Wolfgang 64, 80
structuralism 14–15

tariff 69–70, 71; ECOWAS, common
external tariff 52, 58; tariff reduction
23; tariff setting 69, 72; United
States 69, 71 (US 1922 Tariff Act
73)
Taussig, Frank William 61, 68–69, 70,
71, 78, 159
Teivainen, Teivo 191
trade 6, 190; advocacy 5, 88, 89, 90,
96–101, 110, 178; desocialization
and dehistoricization 6, 63;
economic/social interrelation of
trade 6, 63, 67, 72, 144, 146–47,
165, 177, 178; historical and socio-
economic interaction 143–44, 184–
85; trade/development relationship
43, 45, 46, 95, 181; *see also
following* trade *entries*; international
trade; West African participatory
trade politics
trade barrier 14, 62, 155, 157
trade economism 19, 60–68, 76, 77,
124–25, 159, 184, 188, 190;
confrontation between different
actors 185; historical trade
economism 60, 66–68; informal
economy 163, 165, 166; logical trade
economism 60, 64–66, 67;
neoclassical economics 62, 64–65,
67, 74–76, 77, 80, 177; shortcomings
61, 64, 65, 67, 159, 163, 176–77,
184, 190; utility maximization 6, 61,
62, 63, 65, 70, 184; variable trade
economism 60, 61–64, 67; *see also*
economics; neoclassical economics;
trade policy formation theory
trade law 22, 52, 180, 181, 187–88;
world politics/international law link
187
trade liberalization 21–22, 163;
definition 22; EPA 43–44, 46, 49, 53;
GATT 22, 154; NANTS 44; poverty
reduction 43; sensitive products 52,
58; Uruguay Round 22; West
African region 154, 157, 163; *see
also* free trade
trade policy formation theory 60, 68–
76, 177, 184, 189–91; adjusting
trade policy formation theory 184–
88 (conceptualization 185, 186, 188;

230 Index

trade policy formation as process of continuous learning 187; trade political interests 185, 187); classical school 68–70, 73; depolitization 65, 75; desocialization/dehistoricization 6, 63, 67, 72, 74–75, 176–77, 184; economic theory 62–63, 75; efficiency/legitimacy deadlock 6, 60–61, 76, 77–78, 177, 189–90; historical/socio-economic interaction 143–44, 184–85; interests/ideas interaction in trade politics 184; marginalist school 70–74, 188, 189; methodological controversy 68; neoclassical economics 62, 64–65, 67, 74–76, 77 (economistic trade policy formation theories 75–76); realigning trade policy formation theory with real life 55, 67, 72, 75, 186, 189; 'trade as special politics' 188, 189; West African participatory trade politics 60, 76, 78, 176, 178, 184–86 (theoretical generalizations 25–28); *see also* social embeddedness; trade economism

trade policy-making: clear-cut trade policy positions 181–82; contestation 3, 5, 19, 176, 177, 185, 190; consultative mechanism 3, 15; democratization 5, 36, 76, 117, 119, 140, 159, 179, 188, 191; informal economy 163, 165, 166; legitimacy 3, 5, 184; participatory policy-making 4, 15, 41–54, 184; politicization of 32, 35, 43, 103–4, 182; representation 5; 'trade as special politics' 188, 189; transparency 5; *see also* West African participatory trade politics

trade politics 6, 67, 187; interests/ideas interaction in trade politics 6–7, 15, 63, 64, 78, 178, 184; politicization of trade 32, 35, 43, 103–4, 182; social embeddedness 6, 178, 184; *see also* trade policy formation theory; West African participatory trade politics

trade reform: development 21; EPA 35, 45–46, 176; European Commission 45–46; socio-economic impact 35, 43; trade liberalization/free trade 21; Uruguay Round 75; WAEMU 157; West African region 157

(socio-economic hardship as consequence of 161, 163)

trading diaspora 146, 147, 148–49, 151, 166, 190–91; Dioula/Hausa 146, 149, 163, 167; *see also* West Africa, history and trade

transparency 5, 103, 114; Platform 41, 120–21, 132, 176, 178, 183; West African participatory trade politics 120–21, 132, 176, 178, 183

Trefler, Daniel 75

Trentmann, Frank 19, 22, 63, 65, 166, 178, 185

Tullock, Gordon 75

TWN (Third World Network) 33, 35, 96; EPA 43, 44; TWN Ghana 35, 50 (Hormeku, Tetteh 50); *see also* ATN

UN (United Nations): Millennium Development Goals 158; UN Human Development Index 19, 20, 21; UNCTAD 155, 158; UNECA 160–61

United States 74; Great Depression 70; tariff 69, 71, 73; Truman, Harry S. 21

Uruguay Round 22, 75, 89, 109, 141, 155

utility 72, 73; individual utility 70, 72, 74; marginal utility 71; utility maximization 6, 61, 62, 63, 65, 70, 184

Van Tuijl, Peter 131

Viner, Jacob 74, 78

Von Bülow, Marisa 6, 87, 98, 99, 138, 178, 186–87; *Building Transnational Networks* 17; relational approach 17–18, 138, 178, 186–87

WAEMU (West African Economic and Monetary Union) 16, 119, 121, 123, 157, 160; Common External Tariff 8; EPA 8; membership 9; RNC 12–13; trade reform 157

Walker, Michael 159

Walras, Léon 73

war and conflict 147, 151, 158; World War I 73; World War II 74

West Africa, history and trade 35, 144–52, 165; arrival of Europeans 35, 146, 147–52, 165 (colonial

Index 231

system 149, 150, 151, 152, 165; competition 149, 150, 151–52; dependence on European trade 148; marginalization and regression 148, 149, 151, 165; negative impact 149–52, 165; regional trade 148; war and conflict 151); arrival of Islam 145–47, 152 (Islamization 145, 167; Muslim trade 145–47; war and conflict 147); capitalism 145, 147; independence 153, 154, 157; intra-community trade 144, 145; kola trade 146, 167; maritime trade 148; pre-colonial West African trade 145–47, 152, 162; trading diaspora 146, 147, 148–49, 151, 166, 190–91 (Dioula/Hausa 146, 149, 163, 167); transatlantic slave trade 51, 52, 144, 148, 150–52; *see also* West African participatory trade politics

West Africa, state/society relations and trade 144–45, 152–65; colonial system 121, 122, 153, 155, 162; democratization 158; GATT 153–56; growth problems and poverty 157–58; influence of international institutions 153–59; informal economy 159–65; political struggle 158; regional integration 145–46, 154, 157, 161–62, 164; socio-economic hardship 152, 157, 158, 159, 161, 163, 165; state 152, 153, 154, 158, 159, 161, 162, 163, 166; trade liberalization 154, 157, 163; trade reform 157, 161, 163; World Bank/IMF SAPs 157; WTO 153; *see also* civil society/public officials interaction; informal economy; West African participatory trade politics

West African participatory trade politics 4–5, 11–14, 15, 14–28, 41; civil society 11, 12, 13–14, 17, 25, 28, 42, 96–101; contestation 18, 87, 110, 114, 115, 179; democratization 119–20, 179, 191; development 21; EPA 7, 11, 41–42; informal economy 165–66; interests/ideas/institutions interplay 78; negotiating structure 11, 12; political tensions 54; private sector 11, 12, 14, 124–25; state/market/civil society triangle 25–26, 37, 110, 119, 124–25, 153, 166; theoretical framework 17–28

(theoretical generalizations 25–28); West African Regional Negotiation Committee 11; world politics/international law link 187; *see also other* West African participatory trade politics *entries*; ECOWAS; EPA; Platform; social embeddedness

West African participatory trade politics, assessment 114–42, 176; achievements 114, 115–25, 139, 179 (balance of power 115, 121–25, 139; capacity 115, 116–18, 139; inclusiveness 115, 118–21, 125, 127, 130, 139, 178); challenges 115, 121, 125–39 (civil society, definition 115, 119, 125–28, 139; legitimacy 115, 119, 125, 133–39, 179; representativity 115, 119, 125, 127, 128–33, 139, 179); political authority 115, 120, 125, 126, 130, 135, 139, 183; political autonomy and freedom of speech 122, 123–25; sustainability of the model 117, 137; transparency 120–21, 132, 176, 178, 183; *see also* civil society; West African participatory trade politics

West African participatory trade politics, historical evolution 7, 11, 14–28, 87–113, 178; advocacy 88, 89, 90, 96–101, 110, 178; attitudinal change 87, 88, 105, 106, 179; civil society participation 11, 13, 90–93, 95–96, 108, 109; consolidation of participatory policy-making practices 87–88, 106, 109; Cotonou Agreement 15, 88, 90–93, 95, 96, 108, 109, 178, 186; emergence 87, 107, 165–66; from exclusive to inclusive policy-making mechanism 7, 15; individual activism 88, 96, 107–9, 110; informal economy 165–66; Marrakesh Agreements 88–90; sense of unity and solidarity 94–95, 106, 110; state 14, 106, 159; technical knowledge provided by the Platform 88, 96, 101–7, 110, 113, 179, 180; West African socio-economic context 88, 93–96, 110; *see also* West African participatory trade politics

West African participatory trade politics, lessons to learn 179–91; adjusting trade policy formation theory 184–88;

232 *Index*

attitudinal change 182; capacity 179, 180–81; coordination 179, 181; institutional relations 179–80; legitimacy 183–84; networking 180; politicization of trade policy debates 182; representativity 183; right to participation 179; trade and democracy 188–91; transparency 183

Wilkinson, Rorden 23, 178

Williams, Marc 103

Wolfe, Robert 188

World Bank 19, 20, 35; SAP 157, 161

WTO (World Trade Organization) 22, 74; 1996 Singapore Ministerial Conference 58; 1999 Seattle Ministerial Conference 89, 97; development 89, 99; dispute settlement procedure 180–81; DSB 8; EPA 35, 52; establishment of 22, 89; legitimacy crisis 3; market opening 53; West African region 153; WTO+ 35, 47; WTO-based campaigns 97; *see also* Cotton Initiative; Doha Round; Uruguay Round

Young, Allyn 73

Zeleza, Paul 145, 148, 150, 151, 152, 167